'Away From the Numbers'

Tony Beesley

Printed by ACM Retro - www.acmretro.com
(2013)

Cover designed by David Spencer

For my best pal, John Harrison – through the craziness and trials of life our friendship has endured and continues to grow to this day

In Memory of my Auntie Amy

"To have a dream and to not chase it... must be one of life's greatest regrets."

ISBN 978-0-9565727-3-8

First Published 2013 by 'Days like Tomorrow books'

Contents

Tony Beesley is the author of the 'Our Generation' trilogy of books and 'Kid on a Red Chopper Bike: a Ride through the 1970's' – the first instalment to this title.
He is also a freelance writer for 'Vive Le Rock' and 'My Kind of Town' magazines and various websites

Introduction

There he was, Paul Weller: chatting with Style Council drummer, Steve White and looking as smart as ever. Dressed in white Levi jeans (just like the pair I had) and a casual European-style shirt, shiny tasselled loafers topped off with a short Mod hair style, his blond streaks now grown out, he truly looked the biz! Wow! Wish I could be like Paul Weller!

I went over and introduced myself, shook his hand and started to nervously chat away like nobody's business. Paul was responsive and friendly and listened intently to my speed-limit shattering stream of non-stop questions and compliments. Trying to cram in my whole Jam-obsessive life so far into an unabridged verbal attack of Yorkshire mixture slang-saturated conversation... perhaps convincing Paul that I was his true number one fan, I squeezed in as much time as I could before the security would decide that it was high time for me and my mates to move on. Paul twitched, half-grinned and gave a few looks of 'Please slow down and speak the Queen's English'... but remained attentive and interested throughout. Cool... I have his attention!

I was wearing my 3-buttoned two-tone suit, candy-striped Ben Sherman shirt and a pair of Gibson shoes. For 20 minutes or so, rattling away, as if I had known Paul all of my life, I felt like I was within an unattainable far away world: one that existed with my musical heroes on first name terms with me, maybe best of mates, even? This was the second time I had met Paul face to face and maybe one day, I could well be on the Christmas card list of the coolest guy on the planet, our 80's face and the Top Mod of them all! Then I bloody woke up as the security brutes came over and started to politely shove us away out of the Sheffield City Hall's unforgiving doors and off into the cool autumn night... back within my own world and its tormenting dreams of really being someone!

Yes, I was gonna be someone in the 80's. That was my aim. Or something like that anyway. More like "In yer bloody dreams, kid!!!" To be honest I didn't really wanna be a Rock star, cos I hated what all of those over-paid pompous tax exiles like Bono, Sting and the like stood for. I just wanted to be someone in a band; someone who had something worthy to say and project it through great songs. Punk had encouraged me to continue to disobey the rules and that anyone could have a go at being a musician, if they tried hard enough... and at least had some decent talent to offer. So why not me I wondered? Well no-one was gonna do it for me were they? I wasn't going to let all of the confidence knockers around me put me off having a real good crack at being a musician... and a songwriter either. No matter what, I was going to give it my best shot; I had decided that right from the very start.

As the 1970's drew its final curtains and we welcomed a new decade that evoked images of futuristic technology, brand new possibilities and a new designer-infatuated world, in truth no one really knew what to expect. How could they? Personally I had high hopes, that's for sure, but then I was still naïve and living in my own rebel (with an interchangeable cause) world. The kid on the red chopper bike was already a thing of the past by 1978. It was no longer cool, or fun, to knock about on what was once the greatest bike I had ever set my eyes on. The bike I had once loved, along with the whole bag full of 1970's culture- toys, comics and whatever else I had been so obsessed with, was all laid to rest and filed away as a distant memory. So much can change in so little time when you're a young lad. Music, namely punk, had taken over my life and was all that mattered, instilling in me a new purpose for living and a new identity: absorbing the ever-present anger and restless energy I had within me. The new young idea was now firmly in my life and the feeling as the 70's were coming to a close was that something truly great was going to happen!

No one can deny that the 80's were a decade of political turmoil... and class war. Of a crumbling society split into disparate factions... suburbs of shattered communities broken forever by the relentless onslaught of 80's Thatcherism.

'Loadsa money' gurned Harry Enfield tongue firmly in cheek... while Stock, aching and Waterman attempted to keep us in place (and well away from the barricades) with their piss-weak soundtrack box of cheap lucky bag crap! It is true, the 80's were selfish as hell and without a doubt helped set the scene for a future that back then seemed so far away... a future that, for us, would eventually become tagged as Broken Britain.

We started the decade with records, cinemas and Top of the Pops and ended it with CD's, rental videos, MTV and Sky television! The Space Race ended and the football hooligan was held in check. The Berlin Wall came crushing down ending years of Communist-stifled paranoia for many, Nelson Mandela was set free and we met Del Boy and Rodney and co for the first time; whilst The Young Ones changed comedy forever and Cagney and Lacey shoved Starsky and Hutch out of their Saturday night slot. From the early decade peacock foppery of the new romantics, through the updated crooning's of mullet-clad rock dreamers to terrace scrapping Casuals and baggy jeans-wearing Acid House ravers... the 80's were a decade of change and apparent progress and the world just could not stop moving.

The 1980's also consisted of constant changes in my life. I started the decade a punk-obsessed angry young lad free of his two-wheeled wonder and accompanying long hair and Barry Sheene worship, yearning for a future of self-expression through the Punk-Poet-musician medium or similar: lazy school day afternoons spent trying to appear as if keeping up the work at hand, but in fact, scribbling away at poetic rants of undiluted anger and incredibly naïve notions of changing the world - or at least my world. From a time of post-bereavement and confusion and self-discovery to a decade's closing chapters that were as far removed from its starting grid than could have been imagined in 1980, a whole journey was to begin.

Through the 80's, I gained and lost great friendships, fell out with my family more times than ever, floated between meaningless jobs, the dole queue and periods of frustration and apathy, but still managed to laugh at the world and myself throughout, often with a pint and a song in hand! Besides we didn't want to grow up and knuckle down and be bloody normal did we? While the country (and the world) tore itself apart out there, amidst strikes, war in the Falklands, disasters and the IRA.... none of it ever stopped us having a good time- always holding onto my ambitions and dreams along the way!

Away from the Numbers - Tony Beesley

Lying awake at night, whilst the kling klang and bangs of the steel works not so far away in the distance brought me back down to earth, racing through my non-stop hyperactive young mind were the constant dreams of making things happen in my life; enlightening my over-active imagination with notions of what could quite possibly come true!

Even though, my 1980's was a decade of laughs, confusion, character demolishing and false journeys, it was always full of new and varied experiences ultimately bringing forth a rush of new-found optimism with each chapter. The world of responsibility and adult seriousness had no appeal and I tried every possible option to take an alternative route to the one mapped out for me. Sometimes going around in circles and returning to base, tired out, pissed off, pissed up and ready for another go.... But I never gave in. The punk spirit in me just wouldn't die... and the restless and unruly junior school kid was also still (thankfully) alive and active within me, constantly endeavouring to question the general scheme of things and the world around me.

Throughout all of those times, I kicked at the system, aspired to creative fulfilment, spouted ill-informed politics, never took adults seriously and defied all notions of settling down to a future of a pipe, slippers and a rotten mortgage lifestyle. That was for proper grownups, surely? Yet would the decade and all of that was happening in my life eventually snare me and force me to conform? Would I become just like everybody else? Would I discover life's meaning and purpose beyond its teenage euphoria? Just maybe I would escape across the tracks... to where my dreams awaited me away from the numbers.

Join me on my journey. I promise plenty of laughs, nostalgia, naivety and irrational mistakes. If you have even the slightest of a rebellious streak within you... a tendency to say no to those in charge, question the status quo and are inclined to look out for a different path than the one people would like you to take. If you vote for the individual; the joker with a cause and the eternal misfit. If you have ever truly wished for your dreams to come true: then I am confident that you will be my mate along the way... 'ducking and diving' and pogoing all the way back to the 1980's!

Chapter one

Last of the Punk Rockers!

"DEAR SIR - I am truly sorry for misbehaving and not succumbing to your righteous authority: for challenging the mundane rules and rituals of school and laughing (often) at your threats of punishment. I promise to attempt to bring my homework in complete, with no scribbled logos of punk bands scrawled across... and I also promise to turn up to school in the required uniform instead of my own alternative version of what I think it should be!

Away from the Numbers - Tony Beesley

Forget all of that... I just can't conform; it's simply not in my nature. I am a restless and free-spirited, questioning, mischievous, anti-authoritarian individual. I am an endless prankster and I cannot help taking the piss out of your serious and stifling world of acceptable human behaviour that thrives upon the subjugation of self-identity and freedom of the mind. Sir... it's not that I hate or even dislike you or even consider your world of rules to be bad; it's just that I am a 15-year old punk rocker with issues and want to question everything around me before I accept it all... finally, I dislike being controlled and monitored and.... I find that your adult ideals are relentlessly BORING!!!!!!

That was my manifesto as the brand new decade arrived! The fast-moving 70's were history and the future of the 1980's was here. The world had changed so much and who knows what this exciting new decade was going to bring our way? Maybe an alien invasion or a real planet of the apes.... Or, even more realistically (it seemed at the time) the eventual outbreak of World War Three: the way the Ruskies and the Yanks were carrying on that really would not have been a surprise. But... never mind the bigger picture out there. Enough had changed in my life too, so I really didn't have time to spend worrying about a mushroom cloud landing on the Sheffield fly-over obliterating everything and everyone in its path. There were far more important things going off for a fifteen year old ex-Chopper bike-riding kid who couldn't yet quite figure out what life was truly about. I was leaving behind a world of wonder, pubescent fun and mischievous innocence to move forward and experience a new world of wonder (or blunder?) flavoured with teenage kicks and further mischief and rebellious defiance! Umm... sounds great to me!!! No teacher, alien, Dalek or greased-up Elvis lover was going to stand in my way- no matter what!

As 1980 began, the mood was optimistic and it seemed like anything was possible. Music was fantastic and everything seemed to be in place. The age of self-expression and creativity was upon me and I aimed to continue my crazy, but passionate, obsession with new ideas alongside a deep-rooted desire to not conform or fit in; feeding the inner rebellion along the way. My heroes were now no longer Barry Sheene, Bruce Lee, Tony Curtis or Alf Tupper but Joe Strummer of The Clash and my greatest influence, The Jam's Paul Weller. My punk heroes were street-wise, young, anti-establishment, self-educated and even tougher than Tupper and were right up my street... so there!!!

Away from the Numbers - Tony Beesley

I was far too young to be seriously involved in the very first waves of early punk but already having the punk attitude firmly at hand - sharing my anti-authoritarian ideals and attitude with teacher and parent alike - I was itching to catch up during those final few years of the 70's. I now couldn't wait for what the 80's had to offer too. Would it be as much fun, inspiring, colourful and exciting as the 70's had been, I wondered?

I was still only 15 years old in 1980. Teenage acne, which never hit me that hard, was thankfully almost behind me and sex was still something to work up to when there was time between music, mates and finding a lass that would be willing! 1978 and my Dad's death and the confusion and frustration of that period seemed like a life-time away: so much had happened. Our home had gone from being a lively bustling family-crammed one to just being myself and my Mum. It was strange to watch my Mum start to show her age too: her once auburn hair now being replaced with sporadic hints of grey; whilst her breathing got so bad that, one day in 1980, she finally packed the fags in. No more sending me for a pack of Park Drives or 2 or 3 single ones to put her on till the bingo; nor struggling to carry the shopping up Walsh's hill because of her smoking-inflicted smokers cough. To her credit she never touched a fag ever again. But nothing ever put our Paul off fagging it! He continued his impression of a human chimney oblivious. Why break the habit of a lifetime?

Our house at number 10 Warren Avenue - built not long after the end of WW2 - had a hell of a lot of our history invested into it. In 1980 if you closed your eyes when it was deathly quiet, you could almost hear the sounds of family life reawakening. My Dad moaning at my Mum, our Glen getting face on cos Rotherham Utd had lost yet again and us daft and long-haired kids running around laughing and tormenting each other. We were the only family to have lived in that house and the once noisy, busy family home was now gone. It did seem strange for a while, just us living there, but family life had already been replaced by one of mates, music and laughs and there was plenty of all of those to get well excited about. And of course, the legacy of punk in my life!

Punk was (and is) the centre of my life. It all began as a bit of a joke really with my long-haired excitable-self colliding into my first real punk rocker on my good old dependable chopper bike. I had missed the opening scenes but before long it became so important in my life that I eventually (both) questioned its integrity and depended, quite foolishly, on the major figureheads of the scene to show me the path to adulthood and help pave the way for my future!!! How insane does that sound now? Of course, seeing as my Dad had died I had no fatherly figure to steer me away from the apparently corrupt influence of punk rock: I was there for Johnny Rotten's taking, so to speak!

The years 1978 to 1981 were my core punk years and, along with a small gang of like-minded punk-loving accomplices, I made it my intention to be a real part of it all (from a young teenage git's perspective anyhow). Not even a full-blown beating from two over-grown rock 'n' roll apes called Brutus and  Urko in the middle of Rotherham town centre in broad daylight put me off my love of punk! To start with, we didn't look that much like your typical punks either: it being enough to wear straight leg jeans and a tight-fitting t-shirt and have fairly short hair. As I gained confidence the lure of experimenting with the more visual attraction of punk came into being. Self-created shirts with zips, painted slogans, PVC trousers and torn blazers... yellow-sprayed DM boots (I attained my very first pair of Cherry Red Doc Martens in 1977... finally throwing away my old segs-infested 70's Brogues). The punk look changed by the week as our small punk gang embraced the rebellion, living it out at the youth club disco and buying as many records as we could lay our huge pound note spending money and paper round earnings on, first in Rotherham and then on many vinyl-hunting crusades to record shop Mecca... Sheffield! In our old-fashioned pit village of Rawmarsh, people would stare at us as if we were aliens as we stepped out of our school clothes like some real life version of Mr Benn into our torn, sprayed, zip-plastered punk rock clothes of many garish colours! Invasion of the punk Airfix model snatchers - Part one!

Sheffield was far more punk-orientated for us and it did have far more record shops. Us new wave intoxicated school kids with our look of 'Punk straight from the Orphanage Oxfam' style trekking on the classic number 69 bus route to vinyl heaven; laughing, joking and creating names for people we passed on our journey, rudely mimicking and pointing at passers-by who couldn't retaliate with anything more than an angry shaking fist in the air.

Heading straight for the Castle Market area and strutting along with the arrogance of a poor kid's Sid Vicious... sneering and glaring at shoppers and straight-laced kids in their flares and cheesecloth shirts, trying our best to disguise the fact that not that long since we had also been wearing Brutus jeans flares and the like. Those very jeans were still being worn except me Mum had sewn 'em in to look like a pair of zip-covered drainpipes. Our chopped and dishevelled haircuts and Dennis the Menace sweaters were worn with cheap plastic jackets or donkey jackets (mine emblazoned with 'Ignore Alien Orders' in lime green Humbrol model paint across the back) and tennis shoes or Dockers. When we walked past some real (older) proper punk rockers, we felt like crawling under the fruit and veg stall at the bottom of the market, realising that we were in truth mere punk pups. Venturing out of the top Castle Market exit of Woollies and along the Gallery to the Mecca of punk record buying we would arrive at Revolution Records.

Revolution Records was unbelievably small and poorly lit and it could well be a perilous excursion when dodging the assembled gangs of local skinheads knocking about on the Gallery. Sometime, later on, when future Sheffield musician and virtuoso, Julian Jones, who we had taken under our wing due to his exuberant passion for punk, was hanging out with us, we would send him scouting around the corner saying "If there's any skinheads knocking about, then quietly let us know." Julian would shout "Hey up lads... there's a reet gang of skin 'eads round 'ere." Gangs of fully braced, booted up and shaved bovver boys would turn around, spot us and keenly chase us off. The shop, which was run by two proper punk kids who played in bands and who we saw support The Clash a few years later, was a gathering place for local punk and alternative types and it was amazing how many kids could actually fit in there. No fire regulations in place at all up there on the Gallery, that's for sure.

A momentous punk event over at Revolution Records had occurred while I was only just catching up on The Jam on the Marc Bolan show during the summer of 1977. Paul Weller and The Jam arrived at Revolution Records chatting to fans and signing Jam record sleeves the day after their first Sheffield gig. I later met and knew lads who were there that day and I would be a damned liar if I said I wasn't downright envious of them. Christ, I was bombing around on my red Chopper bike yet to experience my Marc Bolan show Jam epiphany (sparking a life-long obsession) while these guys were chatting away to one of the new wave's most iconic and idealistic musicians.

My mate, Pete Roddis (along with my other best mate, Andy Goulty) was also crackers on punk and we spent hours listening to and experiencing it... be it gigs, the punk spot at our youth club disco, reading the NME and Sounds or endless hours in our front room. Pete lived around the corner from me: we had known each other since the Infants school; he was a tough, no nonsense type of lad, dependable and a great laugh. We shared fantastic times together and would do anything for each other. We smoked banana skins together, got caught nicking Chipsticks from Marks and Splinters, wrote angry anti-establishment punk poetry together. We dyed and cut each other's hair-punk style: we were inseparable and you'd be hard pressed to find a better mate, to be fair! We even conjured up our very own invisible punk dog called Halifax. Going down the Moor or 'Little Carnaby Street' (Chappel Walk), we would pretend to be walking Halifax on his lead... "C'mon, Halifax, c'mon now lad," we would command and the look on people's faces was better than any disqualified Crufts' dog owners. Heads spinning around like Clement Freud after swallowing a dog's holiday-sized tin of Chum... looking all over for our good old Halifax. Bob Carolgees had 'Spit the Dog'. We had 'Halifax the punk dog'.

Sheffield was our second home and vinyl was our plunder in endless ventures of expeditions. We ventured to Doncaster's Tracks Records meeting up with hard-core Donny punk kids. We sometimes did Donny, Sheff and Rotherham in one day. And then there was the old stalwart and greatest record shop to ever exist in Rotherham... the amazing and iconic Sound of Music!

The subject of countless previous visits during the poptastic era of pre-Punk 70's, the Sound of Music record shop was vinyl utopia. I went to the shop that much that I knew almost all of their stock and where it was located. It was a record shop legend and will always bring back many happy memories for me. When The Jam announced that a new single was due, I was there before school even began, pestering the staff to save me their new record on the very first minute of availability. For weeks I was living a daily existence of barely containable excitement at the prospect of the release of 'Down in the Tube Station at Midnight', 'Strange Town' and 'Going Underground' with its FREE Live single. Likewise with each and every new Clash release!

This is the Modern World

**Paul Weller outside Revolution Records, Sheffield, summer 1977
(Photo copyright of www.davidmuscroft.com)**

When their 'Going Underground' went straight to number one the week after its release, me and Pete Roddis leapt into the air with joy!!! We had helped The Jam to get to the top of the charts and our reward was the thrill of hearing, and having within our collection, one of the greatest records of the whole era.

Typically, laughs soon entered the equation. Whilst browsing through records in the Sound of Music, me and my mate, Clarkey, spotted a lad who we had been taking the mickey out of right at the door, stood swaying and gazing straight over at us. We had nicknamed him Thomas Rotherham after a school assembly lark around and as we stood trying desperately not to laugh, he saw us and shouted "Tossers, you bloody tossers" which made us split our sides at the spectacle. We loved taking the piss; it was our sole purpose in getting out of bed some days. Clearly the 80's were to be a decade of taking the piss and having as much fun and laughs as the last one: only this time the stakes had been upped as our victims' locations spread out further afield! Around the region taking the piss in 80 different ways!

The Sound of Music was a social gathering place (it was far too tight to do much more than price sticker swap or rummage quickly through the records in Circles down the road), especially at the weekends. If you saw some kid buying something dodgy you would be sniggering. Then, when some older kid saw what we were buying he would often do likewise. All sorts of characters could be spotted in there, even celebrity look-alikes. I was convinced for some time that I had seen Mick Jones of my heroes The Clash stood buying records there on the release of 'Clash City Rockers'... what an impressionable plonker I must have been. Another look-alike knocking about was Phil Lynott of cool rockers Thin Lizzy. Now he was the spitting image of him. Every now and again a scuffle between Mods and skinheads would break out in the shop, usually spilling out into the adjoining market but - generally speaking - music came first and each tribe mostly kept to themselves and out of bother.

The Rotherham town centre of 1980 was a different world to what it is now. It was bustling with activity, people, music and shops. Coopers toys, Britain's, Sexy Rexy's, Pecks, Omnibus café, Wigfalls, Muntus and didn't March the tailor suit you up bloody well, sir! From the aroma of Brooks' fresh exotic coffee to the smell of brand new record plastic in the Sound of Music, the whole town was booming with plenty to offer and enthral. So much would change during the coming decade and beyond for our Rotherham town centre.

The legendary 'Sound of Music' record shop

Speaking of shops, my friend Clarkey got to the stage of being so daft that he couldn't walk into a shop without laughing. He always got himself into daft situations, from being stood at the side of a George Peppard look-alike asking for a bag of horse chestnuts to being stared at by the ghost of Macbeth on a poster behind our English teacher. One day we stood outside the Chuck wagon shop (our name that one) and I said to him "I bet you can't walk into that shop

and ask for something, say a bag of Ringos or a Marathon, without laughing."
"Course I can, don't be silly," was his response. I mean surely it couldn't be
that hard? Rest assured he wanders in past the cream bun woman (a local
woman who couldn't go in the local shops without managing to exit without a
fresh cream bun) and up to the glass counter where a woman with an out-of-
date sixties beehive hair-do was waiting to serve him. Clarkey made the
mistake of glancing straight out of the window at me. I simply grinned with a
sure confidence that he (in no way possible) could complete his task. Call it
telepathy but seconds later... and that was it. He came belting out of the shop
laughing his head off, tears running down his face. "I told yer, didn't I; you
really can't walk into the Chuck Wagon shop without laughing." And it's a fact
that he couldn't resist the infectious disease of not being able to hold off
laughing whilst in a serious normal situation. The ailment continued to haunt
him like a prison sentence.

There was not just Revolution Records and Rotherham's iconic Sound of
Music to visit for plastic (often of multi-coloured shades), though. The city
centre of Sheffield was littered with record shops. Bradleys, Impulse Records
(across from Cole Brothers, which had its cave like walls plastered with punk
7" single record sleeves), the legendary Violet Mays, Curtis records and Phillip
Canns on Chapel Walk which resembled a reminder of a bygone era with its
old-fashioned dept. store set-up where you almost expected to hear 'I am
Free!' to be announced across its shop floor. Then there was Richard
Branson's empire trading post, Virgin Records at the bottom of the Moor
where we would be served by older blokes who, to us, represented the old
school of seventies Rock... the Bob Harris brigade, prog-loving Mike Oldfield
relations and obsessive viewers of the Old Grey Whistle Test: the real genuine
and authentic old guard!. I am not saying all were as such, but as a rule, we
were treat with total dislike and sometimes they would threaten us to get out of
their shop. When I picked up 'Johnny Thunders and the Heartbreakers'
'L.A.M.F' LP the long-haired neck-bearded Mormon-looking music expert
almost threw it at me with disgust! When they caught us trying to half inch a
massive promotional poster for 'Cool For Cats' LP by Squeeze out of their
backyard skip, they chased us halfway up the Moor! Maybe that's why they
hated us... but this was the new revolution for us kids and back then it really
was us against them! We were young with teenage hang-ups to match any

generation and unaware of life's demands. For us to, begin with, there were no rules, no expectations and everything was new and ours for the taking within our Grange Hill certificate teenage punk revolution!

As the end of the 70's approached our journey would take a new route. Christmas 1979 was the time of 'London Calling' by The Clash and via that influential double record set, me and Pete were heading towards a transitional period in our musical outlook that would spread throughout the new decade. Reggae, Ska (Laurel Aitken's 'Rudie Got Married' was a fave), Rockabilly and the synthesiser (stand up Bill Nelson and your red noise!) alongside much more varied sounds all began to infiltrate their way onto our record decks. Of course, the 10p singles and £1 LP's section at Revolution Records did help some.

On the very last day of the decade me and Pete went out wishing the new year in at the stroke of midnight. In our donkey jackets, with collars turned up just like Strummer and Jones and co, we cajoled our way into grown up parties and drank lager, wine, cider, lemonade and whatever else the pissed up insanely grinning adults were throwing our way. We got pecks on the cheek from 99 per cent proof-breath ladies who we might well have fantasised about before or thereafter... amidst hand-shakes and back pats from red-faced, George Best lookalikes in 'March the Tailors' waistcoats and flares. House after house, party after party we gate-crashed with our nice, resident-friendly door knocks: somewhat less aggressive than the ones we would have dished out a few years previously while partaking our knock-a-door run ventures. In fact that bloke who used to chase us right up to the point of Old Bryner's tree and shake his pathetic feeble fist at us... well he only went and shook our hands wishing us 'Happy New Year Kids', this time around. Maybe all was forgiven? Blimey it must have truly been the death of the 70's as we knew it!

By 1980, my school years were winding down and most kids were knuckling down and getting as much schoolwork done in preparation for leaving school. I should have been looking forward to a career down the pit or over at Sheffield

Away from the Numbers - Tony Beesley

Steel, chasing the postman around asking for 'Any jobs mate?' or writing endless letters for jobs that probably may not have existed... but I just wasn't interested. That was for proper grownups and squares. I wanted to be a musician, a poet, a writer for the NME, a New Wave artist... anything of genuine heartfelt and artistic interest that would also match up to my aspirations of avoiding the adult doldrums! Before all the pressure of that crap got thrown my way, there was a hell of a lot of fun to be had and I was determined to avoid growing up. In 1980, there was plenty of time left, if I managed to dodge those boring, sleep-inducing careers lessons with that teacher with the big rubber mouth who never shut up. I didn't so much as brush the prospects of having a future at British Steel with Nigel under the carpet as I consciously drowned all notions of a boring working future into oblivion: sod that crap, let me be 15 bloody year old for a while instead!!!

I was still angry at 15 and blessed with bucket loads of frustrated teenage energy to burn off. When we joined in with the mass sea of sweat-drenched bodies at the Sheffield Top Rank punk nights we were lost in the event... miles away from the humdrum of school, of the approaching onset of adulthood and unwanted responsibilities. When I went to the youth club for a dive about I truly meant it... it was literally a massive wave of nervous pent-up energy being released in the act of the punk rock pogo! As we created new dances to the new sounds of Joy Division and Killing Joke, while 2-tone kids and pork pie hat-wearing Mods looked on with a mixture of confusion and interest, we were outside of ourselves. I felt as though the future was here now and nothing could take it away from me... I was loving life and in transitional Transmission!

1980 was the year of the SAS Iranian embassy siege, which hordes of us watched the culmination of after six days live on TV one evening in May. As grenades were thrown into the building from the arms of balaclava-wearing elite soldiers and the smoke billowed out, a film script was quite conceivably being written to star Lewis Collins of the Professionals while a certain Mrs Thatcher was plucking her plumes in celebration of gaining some British Bulldog support! The Falklands were a mere two years away!

Back in February, Aussie rockers AC/DC lost their singer Bon Scott to alcoholic poisoning. The year saw yet more celebrity losses with the death of Led Zeppelin drummer John Bonham and the final great escape of film idol

22

and one of my childhood heroes Steve McQueen. But it would be the end of the year that saw the most profound loss to the world of music and significantly laid the final nail into the coffin of the sixties dream. John Winston Lennon at the age of 40 was shot dead in New York by Beatles fanatic gone mad, Mark Chapman and the world wept for its loss. Meanwhile an ex Hollywood b-movie film star sneakily crept into the Whitehouse and pushed the world further to the right! Yet still that fella on 'Hawaii Five O' was still looking through the bloody window every week, without fail, on a Friday night!

On the home front and away from my punk-loving pastimes, there was still another year to get through at the Stalag. Yawn, bloody yawn! But, hold on... here's the paradox. I wasn't over-keen to actually leave school and become a boring adult but neither was I relishing school (sometimes opting to go to the Park and read the NME instead). I suppose I had almost given up on school work as such, with the exception of my European Studies lessons and the occasional History lesson. Throughout the rest of the tried and tested curriculum I opted to mess about and have a laugh. Actually I only liked European Studies because our teacher was clued in and would spend time talking with me about my ideas and read my punk poetry. She was a Stranglers fan too and waved at us from the balcony of the Sheffield Top Rank when we were diving about at the front of the pogoing mass of punk rockers! Unlike most other teachers, she related to me and I respected her a lot for that. When she accepted my suggestion for my studies project, I was well chuffed. My project's theme was how punk and the new wave had influenced popular culture within Europe since 1976. No surprises there then, except that I was given the go-ahead to actually do it. Good on yer Miss Taylor, wherever you are now, you were a real star!! History was two years of endless and meaningless drabble in which our teacher was far more interested in discussing the weekend's football scores than actually inflicting any grand visions of historical importance upon us: lessons often comprised of us being left to our own devices. My last year at school rapidly descended into classroom chaos.

The most exciting part of those schooldays was our one hour lunch-break. Within that hour, I would zoom home, grab something quick to eat and back to the dinner-disco armed with a handful of singles for the DJ to play. In-between the Buggles and the Nolans, I would exert all the morning's classroom boredom into a 15 minute pogo session to Lurkers, Damned and 999 records!

The Styles of 1980

School was Rawmarsh
Comprehensive, which was still
transforming itself from a Kes-styled schooling affair to something half-modern (including the mid-day school disco Roxy club re-enactments). My years there starting from 1976 had been colourful, to say the least, and had been a unique learning experience. It was a time of mates, music and anti-teacher rebellion. Episodes of boredom and mind-numbing repetition being off-set with the kind of belly-laughs and naïve fun that you really only get at that age and within those surroundings. I was the joker, the expressionist unassuming rebel, occasionally quiet when craftily plotting a campaign for school room anarchy! Unrestrained laughter, raw and vicious rock 'n' roll and intermediate chaos was my emotional release and I hated serious well-meaning school doctrines that inconveniently stood in the way of any of this!

Away from the Numbers - Tony Beesley

A week's schooling would begin with Monday morning Assembly! What a bore that was. Welcome back to school and all that crap. Here I was; a weekend of mates, trips to Sheffield and maybe a gig at Steely's the night before behind me; enjoying the freedom of being young and care-free, not a care in the world, taking the piss out of people and life and now we are all jammed into a fusty room with a boring old crusty teacher telling us how it's going to be such a fantastic week with all that they have planned for us... oh no!!! As soon as I sat down for Assembly I would look around to see if any of my daft mates were around. My heart would sink if they had sent a sick note in. On spotting Clarkey or any of the others, I would straight away start conjuring up some stupid names to make 'em laugh and disrupt the droning sleep-inducing text-book-like adult meanderings of Sir! "Beesley, belt up, is it you again," the addressing teacher would shout my way after spotting me nudging Clarkey and whispering "Kenikorax on a tandem riding down the school banking," to him enticing him to giggle uncontrollably at the absurdity of the crazy Python-esque image in his head. Clarkey would say "Don't look at me, don't say owt, you always get me done, geer oer nah." But it never made a blind bit of difference. The urge to laugh and deny the lecture being given by Sir was too much to ignore. "Hey up, Clarkey, can you imagine if Macbeth came charging through the room and belted that pillock," I would reply. "Beesley, one more disturbance from your corner and you will be paying me a visit after your last lesson," Sir declared to my under-the breath-Mutley styled mumblings.

At quarter to four, I would be stood outside the head teacher's office, not for the first or last time. I didn't care. They could belt the hell out of me, slipper, cane, blackboard rubber, intimidation, and threats... the whole lot. I was used to it and it never stood in the way of having a laugh. The thing is, no matter how many times I got caught, I accepted that the teacher would dish out his punishment. It was fair game and I never dodged it or complained. 'Just get on with it Sir.' It was all part of the experience of going to school for me. If I got caught I got done, simple as that. It was the way of things. I never held any grudges towards the teachers for it. In my mind it was worth it, cos to have a laugh was my great escape! It was everything... it was my release: along with music, it was a damned good teenage hormone checking device. It also eased the anger within me at losing my Dad and being robbed of his presence and maybe saved more potentially smashed windows than the school ever knew.

Away from the Numbers - Tony Beesley

When I arrived in school wearing my bus conductor trousers, Clash t-shirt, the legendary banned denim jacket (with The Adverts painted across the back in red model paint) and white tennis shoes, my form teacher had had enough. He had been impatiently shouting the odds at us for weeks now about school uniform requirements and me and my mate Shaun Angell had been wearing our donkey jackets in defiance. On this day, the little patience that the teacher had left was exhausted and he literally picked me up by the backside and carried me out of sight into the lockers area, where no-one could see. I called him some pretty crude names and he proceeded to give me a damn good hiding. When I escaped and re-entered the classroom, he followed. I sent the best look of defiance his way and called him something even worse than I had done already... and that was that! No grudges or hard feelings. We both got what we deserved. He was the teacher and I was the rebellious little git!

It's true that the teachers were the enemy back then, but they were human too. Looking back, I kind of feel sorry for them having to deal with our generation of kids: there was a fair share of nutters and delinquents around amongst the respectable good hard-working scholars. Still, as much as we were sods, we were hardly ever malicious and generally knew right from wrong. You certainly wouldn't catch us going around mugging old people or setting about someone at more than one on one. Drugs to us was something on an episode of Kojak or Starsky and Hutch... we just didn't really come across 'em in school or down at the school gates back then. Though, that ruling did have one exception when some lads I knew took it upon themselves to start wagging school and go boozing up Mexborough, resulting in two of these particular kids getting hold of some marijuana and bringing it into school to smoke at the back of the school yard. When we piled into our Physics lesson they were stoned out of their heads and couldn't stop laughing at the teacher who was trying to figure out what could be wrong with them. I started laughing at their laughter and the teacher's impossible face and before you knew it the whole class room was in stitches to his dismay: maybe we all got high on their breath? I mean it was a Physics room so anything was possible? No matter it was one of those strange and surreal school days that you always remember.

On another occasion, yet again during a Physics lesson, but with a different teacher (the Sir, this time, being a fatherly relative to a certain Arctic Monkey member)... well we got out of hand again and turned all the water taps on while Sir was down the corridor chasing some kid off who had banged on the window. Pretty soon, the classroom was nearly half a foot deep in water that was still gushing out of the taps. Kids were up on the tables and all the lasses were screaming with the giggles. When Sir returned he was greeted with a surge of council pop flowing straight down the corridor. "What in the name of heaven has gone off here... you imbeciles!!!" he declared. When the main culprits were all rounded up, after the lasses spragged yet again, they (including yours truly) were all sent along to the head teacher's office and given a damn good whacking from the big boss!!! It did hurt but we were used to it by now: anyway not long left to go for school now so make the most of its occasionally anarchic freedom. The poor teachers must have been counting the days down for us all leaving and most likely having nightmares at the thought of any of us stopping on for sixth form, which was about as likely as England winning the World Cup again! As I said, the teachers were only human after all!

One of these (very human) teachers would set us up with some work and leave us to get on with it whilst he sat at his desk pretending to be reading up on some relevant paper work in relation to our lesson, while in reality he had a mucky book stuck between his work book. It didn't take long for a couple of the lads to cotton on to what he was up to and as kids started to snigger, they would be constantly going up to his desk to ask for something while trying to peer over the top of his open-page book. "What's that yer reading Sir," we would bravely enquire. The book would then be firmly shut tight and a command of "Get back to your desk and get your work completed," would be the agitated reply. Urges must be met, I suppose!

Other human traits of the enemy were the typical (and obvious) over-interest in the more, shall we say, developed lasses in our final year. Some teachers had reputations for just about drooling over big-breasted Susie Woo. They must have thought we were simple to not notice. Of course we could tell what they were looking at. I mean, they would turn around almost cross-eyed after a feast of knockers galore in their faces. Times were different then and nobody ever really thought anything of it: nowadays they would get locked up with tabloid headlines of outrage and disgust at the mere thought of it. Luckily for them, punk kids were considered far more dangerous than pervy teachers by the media/tabloids in those days, for some strange unfathomable reason.

Amazingly these teachers actually had real interests too... footie, cricket and even music... God forbid. Embarrassingly one teacher attempted to copy our new dance to 'Xerox' by Adam and the Ants at one late-period school disco... The horror!!! When I bumped into the U-Boat Captain (a teacher) one Saturday afternoon on the Moor in Sheffield, it was as though I was looking at an alien. Our begrudged gathering and reluctant politeness being similar to the famous meeting in no-man's land between WWI British and German soldiers that Christmas on the Western Front all those years ago. As I say, they were the enemy, but I suppose they had their own precious lives too. We never did get to borrow those Hustler and Escort mags of theirs' though!

During one tiresome Sports lesson, whilst playing fielder for a game of cricket up on the top Sports field, I managed to save the day... but in the meantime busting the red-hot throbbing boil I had acquired on my finger. It was an aptly boiling day and I had been stood there for ages, most likely representing a dead ringer for Billy Casper's enthusiastic sporting display in 'Kes'. This was a sequel boil to the one I had been granted with on my arse back in 1978 and certainly no low-budget follow up. The usual sports addicts were doing their stuff and I was away in the clouds day-dreaming of going to see the Undertones at the Top Rank at the end of the month and what sessions John Peel would be playing that night. The distant sounds of corky whacking cricket bat and shouts and curses of the game were a million miles away from my mind as the damned ruby-red corky ball came flying my way amidst a sudden flurry of excitable voices all shouting "Beesley, get it man... go on Beesley catch the bleeder." As I cast my gaze away from the blur of the mid-May sun and realised they were all shouting me and tryna get my attention, my extra-large fingered hand, courtesy of my fresh 1980's boil... well it stretched out, arm aloft and caught the whizzing projectile headed my way. An explosion of blood and green infection splattered into the air on impact as I grabbed the ball. A loud epic hurrah swept through the balmy early summer air as my side all cheered and shouted "Well done, Tone, well done Beesley lad." My finger, and whole hand, throbbed like a bastard, but the Boycott-like adulation I was receiving almost numbed all signals of pain to my brain. Who invented boils anyway? Why do they always seem to develop in places that you either sit on or... catch a corky ball with? That was my last great contribution to the great schoolboy tradition of the Sports lesson and typically it was tainted with a shadow of human infallibility and my trademark unpredictability. The next lesson was back to the classroom of teacher mediocrity and predictability.

I suppose, being (apparently) human, teachers had to have their nicknames too. Bentneck Balford, Jobey Egghead, The Penguin, Hamster Hamstead, Ernie Wise special, the Tartan Terror, Batman and Little Werewolf (the truly meek teacher who lost his rag and punished a tough pal of mine by making him bend over and have a smack on the arse with a piece of A4 paper... the sheer agony of it eh... we laughed our way from A to B block at the sheer magnitude and severity of said punishment). Then there was Sweet Lips (who looked like a Peter Ustinov as Nero in 'Quo Vadis' reject), Mr Giblet, Terry Scott and more. Some of the teachers hated each other too and under persistent interrogation, if you caught them in the right mood, some would expose what went off in that cigar-smoke and pipe-stinking mysterious staff room and who they couldn't stand... "ha ha ha", we would laugh... "So and so hates Mrs blah blah!, that's right funny, that." Mind you there was a few of those teachers, the ones who had been there the longest and had dealt with the very toughest and unruliest of generations of kids, who we well and truly respected and feared.

This small creed of BIG fellas who smoked sailor's pipes, listened to Trad Jazz and bet on the horses in their dinner breaks were to be feared and respected. I made it my business to steer clear of those guys, I can tell you. One of these teachers caught sight of one of my mates - a lad called Ricky who was off school sick - on our local TV news programme 'Calendar' on the telly on the same night. The next day at school, Ricky was confronted by the teacher who asked if he was feeling any better and how ill had he been the previous day, to which he replied "I am feeling quite a bit better, Sir, but yesterday I was in a terrible state." "Oh that's funny then, lad: you looked very well when you went strolling by laughing and waving at the camera in Sheffield city centre yesterday afternoon." Me and the rest of the lads pissed ourselves laughing when we found out. His cheek did wangle him out of that one, though.

Away from the Numbers - Tony Beesley

Fun stuff like this helped destroy the monotony of the latter-day school years and kept the boredom at bay for a while. By the end of a school week, though, I was desperate to get out and buy some new records and just have some fun with my mates. Proper laughs with my best pals, hanging out, taking the piss... watching kids scrapping with each other in the park cos one was a shaven-head, braces, Dockers and Harrington-wearing skinhead and the other was a mini-rockabilly lad with a lacquered quiff and grass-stained blue suede shoes. That's how youth tribalism was back in those days. Lads would knock the hell out of each other for the slightest insult thrown at their Specials LP or a wrong step on their blue suede shoes, but no-one ever went and mugged old ladies or broke into people's houses. Oh there were bad 'uns for sure, but no matter what there was still an unwritten code of ethics to adhere to.

Fun too, when dodging the big 'uns at Rotherham Statis fair, who would clip us round the ear for cheeking their birds and saying "I wun't half gi your lass one, pal... she looks just like Sally James with bigger tits 'n all!" Well, I didn't have the bottle to shout that at 'em... but I knew a very good pal (or two) who did. We were teenagers and needed our kicks. 'Teenage Kicks' could be quite literal when we went to the wrong night at the wrong disco and attempted to do our crazy dances in view of a horde of over-aged, out-of-date lads in check-patterned demob looking suits who couldn't wait to boot us off the dance floor for them to shake their big tough legs to 'Heartbreak Hotel' and Matchbox! And they had the bloody cheek to spit at us as we passed by the stairs below them! That was really... not fun at all!

No, the true ethics of fun largely comprised taking the mickey and if you gave it, then you had to bloody well take it back when it was your turn. After dishing out names to kids such as Smokey Bacon Face and The Omega Man who strangely never accepted their monikers, it was only polite to get laughed at too, once in a while. One day, I realised the reason that a couple of my mates were saying "Hey up Bandido." and "Hey Amigo" was due to the little growth of fluff resting under my nose. It had appeared almost out of nowhere and was an unwanted sign of impending adulthood, which was not welcome and being held firmly at bay. One day I was sporting a smooth upper lip area and the next I was a potential Mexican bandit being followed by the soundtrack of The High Chaparral... eh, Manolito! It had to go... for sure!

So one day after school I had had enough of the bloody thing. The punk look just did not look cool with the addition of a junior Magnum PI sat there waiting for a piece of French Fries shrapnel or Anglo bubbly to get tangled up in it. I was going to see the Undertones at the Top Rank that night and wasn't gonna risk being pointed at by the bondage-trouser wearing punks at the ramp leading the way up to the doors. What can I do? I went and asked the next door neighbour if I could borrow his Victor Kyham razor, not realising both the unhygienic element of doing so and the result it would have on my previously unshaved chops. I got tucked into my first proper shave and felt the relief of saying goodbye to the fluffy bristles, laughing at all of the flaky hairs disappearing into dust and drifting into the sink. "Got you, you bastard, you fluffy pathetic waste of a moustache," I remarked in celebration to myself. Half an hour later I was suffering the wrath of that now fully fledged haunting ghost of a moustache as my upper lip turned from soft, smooth and freshly shaved to something resembling a leper's outbreak of irreversible acne! Umm, lesson one of bloody adulthood's many mysteries... don't cohabit with a fellow shaver. I went to see the Undertones that May night of 1980 looking like the child of Fu Man Chu after a session with a set of tweezers. By the time they played 'Teenage Kicks' and 'You've Got My Number' and - following a fantastic support set by an unknown Irish band called the Moondogs - all was forgotten and the stinging of sweat oozing around my ex-moustache area was all part of the experience and euphoria of seeing the Undertones in concert!

School and being introduced to the world of beard and moustache erasing were still very much far down the chart of interests, as my passion for music went from strength to strength in 1980; quite possibly one of the best years in music for me as the world of punk collided with all that came afterwards, from the John Peel show-obscure post-punk to 2-tone, ska, the new electronic sounds to power pop and the last bastions of punk itself.

Of course, 1980 was not all punk related music. The usual trash and chart fodder was still around. The girls at our Youth club disco and the Miners youthy were still dancing and giggling to records by the Gibson Brothers, Earth Wind and Fire and the Dooley's: and they were amongst some of the less embarrassing ones. The lasses truly met their mentor when Sheena Easton arrived on the scene around this time. By now my attitude to non-punk music had slightly altered and the previous year's exclusively new wave-embracing agenda had now given way to the liking of such less dangerous records as Split Enz 'I Got You' and the Korgis 'Everybody's got to Learn Sometime' along with The Specials and Dexy's Midnight Runners and a revival of sessions listening to my brother's old Bowie and Bolan records, my 1970's first musical loves.

Whilst Dexy's were searching for their young soul rebels, Bowie returned with 'Ashes to Ashes' and its accompanying Steve-Strange and co supporting cast music video. A new elite music and fashion magazine had also been launched earlier in the year called The Face: starting off well with Paul Simenon of The Clash on the front cover, the monthly mag soon retreated into a self-conscious, art-house inverted snob mag. I stuck to my Sounds weekly and NME's instead.

I bought my music mags from the old fashioned local newsagent, which had recently been converted into GT News. I got a paper round there in early 1979, thanks to my mate, Andy Goulty whose Mum worked there. Unbelievably The Angelic Upstarts walked in there after stopping off, mid-tour at Bryan Bell's gaff. My mate, Pete Roddis also had a paper round and we would join up our two individual rounds together and lark around. One morning we turned up with our dog, Sheena in the news bag, much to the disbelief of the newsagent boss. He was a bit of a fuddy duddy and was always getting fed up with us, constantly warning us to simply do our rounds and behave. No tearing pictures out of the music magazines and posters of The Jam off the back of Jackie magazine before posting and also stop waking people up with stupid noises while doing our rounds. Those days of delivering papers were great, though. 6am starts with us meeting up in our parkas with bed-fluff matted eyes: braving the elements in winter and dreading Friday mornings when we had to deliver 100's of broad sheet-sized Rotherham Advertisers. But, we had loads of laughs taking those papers out and it became me and Pete's pre-school social meeting time, when we would talk about music, chocolate and girls, general daft stuff and what records we were going to buy at the weekend.

Away from the Numbers - Tony Beesley

One morning I even caught a glimpse of a Mrs Robinson protégée who stood full-frontal naked at her open curtain window for me to obviously see. Like, my screen nemesis Dustin Hoffman in The Graduate, I fumbled around, felt daft and red-faced and didn't do so much as to blow her a kiss, merely just deliver her paper. What an idiot: imagine that, me being able to recite my first true sexual encounter with a thirty-something fully-grown mature woman before I had even started my first school lesson of the day. Oh well, life's full of ifs! No rest for the 15 year old virgin... off to deliver Mrs Pickles' Daily Express I went!

Something called the Cold War, which had been going on between the West and the Ruskies since the last days of WW2, was still, unbelievably, going on in 1980: in fact it kind of reached a peak around the time. The Russians - requiring their very own personal Vietnam - had invaded Afghanistan the year before as tensions between the Yanks (and as usual us in-between) and the Molotov cocktail guys became more tense. The threat of Nuclear War was once more knocking at our doors. A KJB leak indicated plans that the Tinsley Viaduct was on the Russians list of prospective targets whilst David Blunkett declared Sheffield City Hall a nuclear-free zone... like that would help!

Ignoring the prospects of the apocalypse during the summer of 1980 my mate, Pete Roddis and I were hanging around with Beanz (Dean Stables) and a lovely lass called Tracy- having some great times to a fantastic soundtrack. Strolling around without a care in the word, long hot summer evenings down the woods - laughing and larking around - these were the last few days of our youthful innocence. It may have rained on our youth parade once or twice, but we barely noticed, apart from one dumb blind date me and Beanz embarked upon, meeting 2 girls with lovely telephone voices under the shelter of the Park Golf Hut. It was pissing it down and completely wet-through, we ran off to get even more soaked upon sight of our dates with mugs like broken old clocks with no alarm calls to warn us off. Time to run to snog another day, lads!

Meanwhile, away from the outdoor courtship elements, lasses indoors were having parties almost every week: rooms packed-full of punks, Mods, 2-tone kids and in-betweeners - all high on the exuberance of youth and aiming to get off with someone and get sozzled on cider to the sounds of The Jam, The Specials, Squeeze and endless renditions of 'Echo Beach' by Martha and the Muffins. The lads wearing 2-tone trousers, army fatigue strides, Jam shoes and Doc Marten boots (not all at once you understand), topped off with button down shirts, Clash t-shirts, Fred Perry polo shirts and leopard print t-shirts. The lasses in black and white short skirts, pointy shoes, ski-pants and check jackets with make-up experiments copied from the self-help guide in My Guy. Teenage chocolate bar acne spread evenly amongst the lads and pink lip gloss spread like Dulux paint across the lasses pretty faces. What more could you want at that age? As soon as the lights went out and the Sex Pistols 'Never Mind the Bollocks' had been replaced by the Bee Gees 'How Deep is Your Love' and other girly songs, all bets were on. It was all innocent fun (and groping), the journey to exploring the opposite sex... hands like octopus tentacles, explorations of the unknown... Party Party was the order of the day!

By late summer and the beginning of our last term of Stalag 16 we were almost within touching distance of being bitter-sour sixteen and the old gang began to disperse. Pete and Tracy were now an item, Beanz had gone more hard-core punk than ever and had hooked up with a suitably hard-core Punk bird who couldn't stop compulsively phoning Johnny Rotten up and getting told to "F**k off!!!" and I was hanging out with the last remnants of a post-punk gang of kids... Posh Punk, Clarkey, the Cooper, Daz Twynham, Richey Cousins, the Artful Dodger and a few other like-minded curious music fans who floated in and out, some of whom would sometimes go to a couple of gigs with me and then never to be seen again. Often we would tag along with four years older punk veteran, spikey-haired bleached blond, Bryan Bell and on the way we would wait outside the King's Arms pub in town (where WH Smith now stands) while he knocked back a couple of pre-gig pints before emerging out of the Victorian-like establishment flagging off punk-despising regulars... much to our innocent amusement and rounds of applause.

As well as John Lennon's passing 1980 was the year the music world lost two much respected figureheads of the punk generation. 23 year old Joy Division singer Ian Curtis was found hung on May 18th at his parent's house. He had committed suicide, leaving behind a short but massively influential musical legacy to last decades. This was followed on July 14th by the heroin overdose of Ruts singer Malcolm Owen, aged 26. On both occasions of these tragic premature deaths, punk-despising kids at school laughed and took the piss out of us for our musical losses. Cruel sods!

While the music world had its losses, so did our family. My Grandma had never recovered from losing my Dad at the age of 53. Her heart was truly broken and barely a visit to her passed when she didn't speak, without a tear-filled eye, of Dad. She idolised my Dad and worshipped the ground he walked on, as did his brother, my Uncle Nip, and likewise the rest of us. The last time I saw Grandma was during that very summer when Uncle George and Aunty Betty brought up to our house in a wheelchair to visit us. Something seemed sad and final about the occasion. I took a curious note of the solemnity in the air and buggered off to listen to 'Messages' by Orchestral Manoeuvres in the Dark. Grandma sadly passed away that summer and I am truly convinced that her cause of death was of a broken heart at the loss of my Dad.

Since Dad had gone, the family unit had splintered. We still held a fairly close relationship in some ways, but it was never the same afterwards and, a few laughs aside, we were like a constantly conflicting political party. The heart of the family had passed with Dad and we were all spread out into our little family groups. In context, I was out there on my own completely: my 'weird' punk leanings were never ever accepted by much of the family, except via a short influence on my good old nephews, Dave and Steve who went through their own small and short-lived punk period, gracing their school discos in their punk gear and constantly picking my brains for what punk sound was in and was not. Mum just let me get on with it throughout. She displayed the patience of a Saint with all the many visiting punks of all sizes, ages, hair colour and varying degrees of familiarity. She put up with a Comprehensive school spurned punk generation frequenting our nuclear fall-out shelter for punk mates and strays for a good 2 or 3 years, never once complaining or losing her temper... only occasionally shouting through from the living room... "Turn yer stereogram down, Tony, you'll wake up the dead, or if not you'll shake the next door neighbour on nights out of his bed with that racket. We don't want reporting to the council again do we?"

That summer saw me cast away a hefty proportion of my past. My childhood loves... comics and toy soldiers were bagged up and given away to anyone who wanted them. Bulging bags of Britain's and Timpo figures were sold for a pound a bag to kids down the street, others given to young relatives I had never seen before who turned up for the available plunder, whilst bundles of comics- Valiant, Tiger, Hotspur, Wizard, the seven penny nightmare Action, and the first full year of 2000 AD went in bags to the comic stall in

Rotherham market. Every so often, I would sneak a look in the newsagents and check out what Alf Tupper and Billy and his Boots were up to while I was away. Meanwhile, a full suitcase of Victor comics managed to remain untouched by Stalinist punk era-purging hands lying undiscovered for years at the bottom of my bedroom cupboard awaiting re-evaluation within the coming decades!

Summer 1980 ended with a series of punk concerts at the Top Rank, most notably one by The Damned which I managed to get on a cassette from the back pages of 'Sounds' and on which I could hear myself shouting for 'New Rose', one of my favourite Damned songs. That late summer, The Clash finally caught their 'Bank Robber' and released him on vinyl and Paul Weller took his Beatles fixations to number one with 'Start', the first Jam single I didn't fully embrace and love avidly, as good as it was. The 79 Mod Revival was almost dead and 2-Tone's shine was fading, whilst a new record instigated by home taping piracy, 'C-30, C-90 Go!' by a Malcolm McLaren-endorsed act called Bow Wow Wow hit the shops, encouraging me to stock up on even more 15p tapes from Pennywise in town. I created my own punk vinyl and tape archive of records and John Peel sessions; the tapes were then treat to my own self-drawn covers too, as I tried to express my artistic side through punk art and creativity. The final school term was also looming for me almost as quick as a C-90 played out and the summer of my punk youth was rapidly coming to an unwanted close.

Throughout the punk era, visits to the cinema were few, everything other than music taking a firm back seat. Three films appeared in 1980 that warranted my interest and unsurprisingly all had their roots in punk! The first one was The Clash on the road semi-documentary styled 'Rude Boy', the soundtrack of Clash songs (home-taped off the John Peel show) had been constantly blaring out from my Alba music centre for weeks already.

One day after school me and Beanz (who was about to leave school) ran home, got changed and caught the 109 bus to town and straight to the Classic cinema where 'Rude Boy' was showing. Expecting a crowd of Clash fans and punk rockers blocking the path outside we were met by a total crowd of NONE!!! On entering the cinema we were stopped by the box office staff who asked us if we were 18 years old. "Course we are," we cheekily answered, being used to fibbing our way into gigs anyway so that convincing these Irene-

Copyright: Colin Sutton

-Handl protégées was a synch. But, they weren't budging! OK, time to get that rotten old Sex Pistols badge out of my pocket. I turned around saying "We are old enough... we go and see bands all over... we would be still at school doing our homework (bare-faced cheek of a lie) if we weren't old enough wouldn't we?" On spotting the rusty old Sex Pistols badge that I had pinned on at the side of my Clash badge, one of them said "Look they must be old enough... he's wearing a Sex Pistols badge, his Mum wouldn't let him out wearing that if he wasn't old enough, would he?" So off we ventured, laughing to ourselves up the stairs to the screening of 'Rude Boy' my very first X-rated film!

Expecting to see the missing hordes of Punks and Clash fans all inside the darkened cinema whose screen was playing the Westler's hot dogs ad, we were amazed to be amongst all of five viewers... one of which was an old man in a raincoat sat there with his hands down his trousers sweating and getting excited at the showing of an X rated film called 'Rude Boy'! It's true, the old pervert was sat waiting for a good niff film to come on (er umm). Imagine his surprise when the sounds of 'Revolution Rock' came from the crackly old screen! Following the sounds of 'Garageland', 'White Riot', 'Complete Control' and others, the mucky old git finally got his wrist-jerking dessert when the star of the film, Ray Gange - Clash roadie, got a mouth gobbler from a Joan Jett/Gaye Advert look-alike in a toilet cubicle! Rude Boy indeed! The Clash... truly reaching the parts (and climaxes) other bands simply could not reach!!!

The next 1980 cinema visit was for the premiere of the much-anticipated Sex Pistols film 'The Great Rock 'n Roll Swindle' down at the town's other cinema, the Scala. The Scala on Corporation Street was originally the Regal and then the Odeon and was a frequent cinematic haunt of mine as a young kid when I would queue for light years to get in to see Charlton Heston get chased around by a planet of monkeys and Herbie go bananas for some reason. Opened way back in 1934 it became known as the Scala in 1975. Many a now classic film was first seen by crowds of Rotherham cinema goers there over the years and what fun they would have all had. This time, unlike our 'Rude Boy' experience, the place was actually full of punk rockers and Sid Vicious look-alikes and when Sid did his famous 'My Way' sequence the whole place erupted into a mass of pogoing kids with flaying bondage straps and flapping leopard skin bum flaps. Deciding it wasn't cool enough to participate, I sat laughing and soaking up the joy of watching the usherettes getting knocked all over with ice-cream and pop being spilled all over the emporium by a horde of Sex Pistols addicts. One Pistols fan I knew called Paul (who was the boyfriend of my ex-girlfriend, Denise), was ecstatic and totally immersed in the whole experience. That day's spectacle could be termed 'Anarchy in Rotherham' and a scene never to be seen and heard of ever again in a Rotherham picture house!!!

The final cinema visit of that year saw me and a pal go and see the Hazel O' Connor-starring film 'Breaking Glass'. Her single 'Eighth Day' had been a late summer hit single and had seen her grace the stage of Top of the Pops endearing herself to many a young punk kid that summer. 'Breaking Glass' also starred 'Quadrophenia' star and Mod hero, Phil Daniels and proved to be a worthy and exciting film to end the punk film trilogy of 1980. The Scala cinema lasted until 1983; its final screening being 'Porky's 2 on Friday September 23rd, whilst the Classic bowed out early in the 90's heralding the end of the era of the Cinema in Rotherham town centre!

Autumn saw new 13-part series 'Hammer House of Horror' creep up onto our tellies. By this time, I only very rarely watched the telly due to the continuing mass invasion of music in my life (though me and the Cooper would sit and chuckle at 'It'll Be Alright on the Night' as it was all about people getting things wrong which was right up our street), but this new series, which began its first ITV screenings on Saturday evenings, did the business for me. With its perfectly Gothic (opening credits) visuals (the Peter Cushing Castle itself, it seemed) its peering figure at the window and haunting music this meant some creepy Saturday nights in. I even turned down our Paul when he called for me to go for a couple of sneaky under-age pints at the club.

1980 was also the year that our much-cherished soon-to-be comedy classic 'Only Fools and Horses' was unleashed on the public. Amazingly, series one suffered from poor ratings and very nearly didn't continue any further, but luckily by series two the British public had managed to warm to the hilarious ducking and diving of Del Boy, Rodney and Granddad and the crew, eventually earning the show the distinction of becoming quite possibly the most loved and most fondly remembered UK comedy show ever! I first came across the show one day whilst paying a visit to our Paul's. He was sat laughing at Del Boy and pretty soon, I was laughing along as well and asking our Paul how long it had been on the telly. I was soon well and truly hooked on the knocked-off hooky gear and dodgy antics that writer John Sullivan and his characters brought so truly to life on the small screen. Somehow Del and Rodney and the gang seemed like family members and the 1980's comedy angle was set in motion.

Autumn/Winter 1980 also saw a new busy season of gigging in the local capital of post-punk activity - Sheffield. Me and my punk mates saw a pre-fame Adam and the Ants (Me, Pete and Tracy being chased for the last bus by a gang of skinheads again), Buzzcocks, UK Subs, Cockney Rejects (where the skinheads ambushed unsuspecting rockers making their way to a City Hall Scorpions gig), Siouxsie and the Banshees supported by Altered Images, Cabaret Voltaire, The Fall, proto-Goth from The ('Black Album)

Damned, Bow Wow Wow at the Limit and a clutch of intoxicating pub gigs from one of Sheffield's finest acts, Artery! I also felt a real sense of achievement on seeing The Jam live with their new 'Sound Affects' and meeting the band afterwards, though the flock of fans surrounding Weller prevented me from actually speaking to him face to face on this occasion. One other truly stand out gig was from The Skids who played an amazing set at the Polytechnic: my mates, Shaun Angel, Ian Hillman and his brother, Ivor (cousins of singer, Richard Jobson) saw them the night before at Doncaster at Rotters nightclub.

Setting off for the Skids Sheffield gig, a young Punk fan called Jonathan (even younger than us) came running and pleading with us to take him along, trying to get on with the bus with us as his worried Mum shouted him back. We set off waving our tickets from the bus window, but secretly feeling sorry for the lad. The final days of a never-to-be-repeated era were being played out and this lad was missing out on it completely. Life can be cruel sometimes!

Support that night was from a band called On the Air, who were led by Pete Townshend's younger brother, Simon, and included Stuart Adamson's future Big Country members... but it was the Skids we were here for. The Sheffield Polytechnic was packed out and was its usual red hot and claustrophobic self. My mate, Richie was so hot when The Skids were halfway through their set that he almost passed out in the over-heated and exhaustive pogoing foray. Skids guitarist, Stuart Adamson shouted angrily at excitable punk kids to stop spitting at them: unbelievably there were still kids out there who had not got past that pathetic 'Punk by Tabloids' stage. I had huge respect for Stuart.

Throughout this epic gig we were treat to all of our Skids faves; everything from 'The Saints are Coming', 'Of One Skin' and 'Into the Valley' to 'Charade', 'Working For the Yankee Dollar', 'Masquerade' and 'Arena'. Singer, Richard Jobson even did his famous dance (the one we all copied at the youth club disco). Running home for the ritual last bus it started to piss it down yet again. Why did it always piss it down for each and every Sunday night gig we went to in Sheffield? As we boarded the no.69 bus, yet again, I saw a gang of mean-looking Pond Street skinheads pacing up and down searching for some likely prey such as us. I was seriously glad when we were safe on the bus on our journey home. Now, should I go to school in the morning? Or should I fake some rare form of sudden illness instead of going to the Stalag? No, sod school, I concluded: a day of Skids records and 'The Absolute Game' instead.

The Skids 'Absolute Game' tour 1980

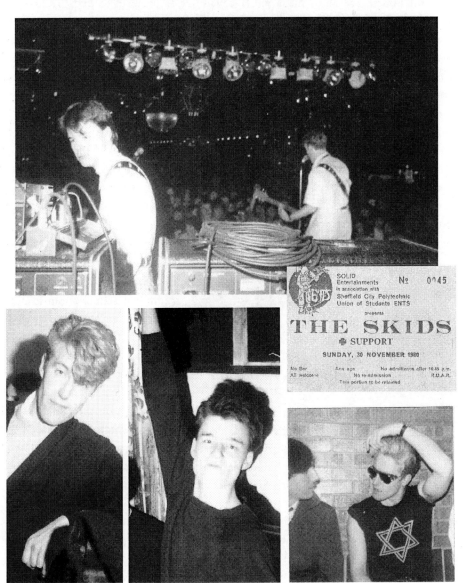

Skids photos courtesy of Gary Penkith and Ivor Hillman (bottom right)

41

Those days were the very best of my gigging days. I was still a kid, naïve and excitable and to see all of these much-loved bands perform records we loved; ones we had read so much about in the music papers was awe-inspiring. Seeing my favourites, The Clash on their iconic 'London Calling' tour and The Jam were both amazing life-defining musical experiences as was sharing my 'True Confessions' with the Undertones and screaming 'Homicide' at 999, along with smashing it up with The Damned and 'Hanging Around' in black with The Stranglers and other bands. I truly felt part of something and the influence and energy of that period would never leave me. The gigs aside, it was also the do-it-yourself creativity – from clothes to art and the sense of identity that totally enthralled and captivated me. I just can't imagine doing anything else at that time that would have captured my intoxicated interest so much and continue to influence my life forever. It truly was a fantastic time to be alive!

Joe Strummer of The Clash at the Sheffield Top Rank, 1978

Still, there was the annual traditional school photo to be endured. My last one ever and amazingly the first one that my Mum cared not to partake in purchasing. The previous two years of punk rebel sneer with a spiky tuft on the bonce were seemingly nothing compared to 1980's portrait of me scowling at the camera. A freckled, lip-twisted sod off attitude graced by a mop of Keith Richards's styled unkempt hair truly persuaded my Mum to decide to keep her pound notes and ten bobs for the delights of the good old bingo hall instead!

My school reports of the period spoke of a confused, non-conformist anti-authoritarian under-achiever who really needed to buck up quick. I had reached the peak of my school rebellion that's for sure. I can still see the teacher's puzzled faces now after seeing me stand up midway through a lesson and shout out their full Sunday best names and spontaneous rants of 'Being bored, being bored and being bored'. I ran off from detention;

once right under the teacher's door-blocking arms and when one of them gave me a pencil to write out my punishment seminar, well I just snapped it in half and buggered off. The only resemblance of a uniform I wore at school was my 'Zulu War' red jumper (with a Clash t-shirt underneath) that shared a get up of teacher-defying black straight legged jeans and my beloved tennis shoes!

One old pal of mine from the very earliest days of being a kid was Gary Mitchell. We had been mates since before going to the infants' school and shared slippy banana skins, three-wheeled bikes, mini soldier brothers, getting chased all over the estate and searching for the presence of the real Rolf Harris together and that was only a small part of it. We had grown apart some since starting at the Comp, but that didn't stop him from sending me Christmas cards with swear words and daft names in and also providing us with some on-going laughs throughout the remaining school years. We all had P.E together still, which could be a good laugh with towel scraps in the showers and general rowdiness and mayhem being the on-going theme, usually driving our P.E teacher round the bend with our boisterous antics. That, along with Metalwork, during which lesson, good old Gary gave a bunch of us a right belly-busting laughing session at the end of one particular school day.

He had his eyes on a lovely 'good as new' self-created and school kid-designed golf club that one of the other more-technically-minded clever kids had made. Gary sized it up, measured it and gave it a few swings, nearly knocking some kids over that were passing the class room's entrance. Then with a decisive statement of "Well, it's a bloody lovely piece of work... I am having this bugger," his expression as serious as Monday morning's assembly teacher's face, he shoved it straight down his school trouser leg and hobbled off with it down the corridor looking like Long John Silver meets the Ministry of Funny Walks. Me, Clarkey, Benji and a couple of other lads were rolling about on the floor, crying with laughter at his cheek and insane walk as the head teacher marched around the corner just missing him. The kid who had made that golf club never found out who had claimed it... but it did really go to a right good home and the incident passed into a schooldays legend for me!

One day, not long before Christmas, me and a gang of lads went on a off-licence bootlegging session to daft old Ernie's: he still didn't care how old we were and it was like taking dandelions from little Miss Burdock, getting alcohol from him. We came out with brown paper bags - with no handles - full of plonk (just like in those American films with Robert Redford in) and made our way around Kilnhurst... bombing around laughing, singing 'I Fought the Law and the Law Won' fuelled by bottles of Newcastle Brown and Bulmer's cider from Ernie's, just for the sheer teenage hell of it. Like I say, it was a fantastic time and for once, we had the empty bottles to prove it.

My punk years had not quite ended yet, but the golden period had now passed. Those times of naïvely getting it wrong (big door-knocker Adverts, Jam and Boys badges included)... from the Adidas sports top hugging kid of late summer 1977 without a clue to Bowie trouser and mohair sweater-wearing youth club Clash-loving teenage maniac... the core of that time had almost passed. We had laughed, shocked, snogged and pogoed our way through our teens; been chased by Heavy Metal Saxons, booted in the face by brick head Teddy boys, spat on by disco Travoltas' and moonstomped upon by Nazi skinheads... but it was a journey I would not change. I could sense a new era approaching now, though, and before long those days would seem like they never even happened! You never have times like you do when you're at school again, that is sure; little do you realise it at the time. The mates you have and the experiences that you share can never be the same once the school years have gone. In 1980 the big-boring world of the giants was fast approaching and they just won't leave you alone once you decide to answer the bloody door. Life was still fine, though, as the first year of the decade began to fade away. Yet, in the thinking corner of this 15 year olds' confused mind, I was seeking just that little bit more! I felt a great conscious desire to make one massive great leap into the future!

Chapter two

School's out forever!

Local New Romantics at Rotherham Art Centre to see My Pierrot Dolls: my mate, Pete at far right.

Lads with long and floppy wonky fringes and pencil-thin moustaches topped off with frilly shirts... and even a dash of makeup smeared across their chops! All of this in a tough Yorkshire pit village... Blimey, whatever next? But... this was a spin off from punk... a Roxy Music and Bowie-influenced scene boasting a musical heritage of synth legends such as Kraftwerk. Emerging from punk, how could any of us get narrow-minded about it all anyway? Punk had kicked down the barriers; allowing the so-inclined the relative freedom to express themselves via music and clothes and a much-needed release of energy. The safety in numbers Joe Normals never even tuned into that one bit: the straights, the bores, the thick-skulled morons who felt threatened by anything (and anyone) different. OK, I wasn't gonna pay a visit to Boots for some perfumed concrete and join in with the Cabaret party, but the Futurist scene was new, inspirational and, most importantly consisted of some great music.

Sheffield's Human League giving it some 'Love Action' at Doncaster Rotters. Photo copyright of Gary Penkith

It really was like a sudden invasion! One minute our generation's gang was made up of predominantly punks, avant-garde post-punkers and 2-Tone-loving Mod-inclined kids. The next thing, and this would be around October 1980, the youth club was full of this new fashion... the Bowies we termed them first, after the new 'Ashes to Ashes' video. These daring lads and lasses – many of whom were my punk friends – were now turning up minus their strikingly-coloured tight-fitting jeans of reds, yellows and lime greens and stripped of all leather jackets, zips and punk pin-on badges. In their place they wore long rain macs, winkle picker shoes, frilly white shirts (very Bohemian) and suddenly newly-grown Soul Boy styled fringes. My old punk mates Andy and Pete even wore Spandau Ballet endorsed knickerbocker leggings... ahhhh!!!!

The Futurists/Blitz Kids/New Romantics had been there just about all the way through punk or a prototype relative anyway if you had taken the time to look for them. They were a mix of working class Art school kids and middle class-leaning intellectually minded kids. Inspired by their musical heroes David Bowie and Roxy Music along with a love of German electronic pioneers

Kraftwerk, topped off with a diet of John Foxx era Ultravox!, Visage and our very own local heroes The Human League and other electro wizards (with a sprinkling of Gary Numan for some)... the guitar and punk was pushed into the background in favour of the synthesiser. New bands emerged in this wake, most famously Spandau Ballet, who to begin with presented a far less glossy pop-led vision, along with OMD, Japan and ultimately Duran Duran who brought with them the germs of the new pop glam years.

The new flock of new romantic dandies that I saw emerge at the Youth club disco were not middle class, however. These were kids I had known all of my life, just about. They were simply bored by what they saw as the decline of punk and excited with the prospect of something new to replace it. They also had their own local band to complement the new scene. Spiral Vision (later simply Vision who, with a revamped line up, managed to be a big hit in Italy with their Disco hit crossover 'Lucifer's Friend') were led by local punk and Futurist face and anti-stereotype embracing vocalist, Ivor Hillman: a right character 'n all.

I already had a fair sized selection of these new sounds, which interesting, fresh and often alternative. Singles by B-Movie, Japan, Ultravox!, Human League, Visage, Spandau Ballet and OMD amongst others and they were soaked up into my record boxes, sitting beside Bill Nelson and The Skids. As for the clothes? Well, I never felt any real urge to go that way. As with a lot of what came and went after punk, I stole portions of what I liked and added them to my own individual style. Wearing a fireman's double-breasted shirt with my bus conductor trousers and unkempt hair and shades of punk and Mod influences may have confused some onlookers I suppose (well it confused me too), but the era was all about creating self-identity after all was it not?

If 'Fade to Grey' by Visage had signalled the end of punk for many, by mid to late-1981, the whole New Romantic phenomenon itself had peaked and (locally at least) had mostly been dropped by much of the class of 1980's legions, especially the lads. I could probably make a calculated good guess that the garish foppery of the new emperor's clothes would not have gone down too well for some of the lads who went down the pit or got recruited by British Steel to join the rat race of adulthood? Our New Romantics always did struggle to get around from one place to the other anyway. We did live in a tough Northern pit village that was (mostly) intolerant and often aggressive to anyone different after all. I can personally vouch for that from first-hand experience.

Away from the Numbers - Tony Beesley

**Gregory's New Romantic Girls: some of the lovely lasses from my
year at the Comp – and other local schools**

As 1981 arrived, I was counting down the days until I left school but unsure
what I was going to do. The know-all teachers had taken me out of my Art
lessons on the first day of the new term as the class was too large and they
felt I would be better suited to Technical Drawing instead, thereby totally
ruining my plans for Art school on leaving the Stalag. The last year at school
didn't start too well either. Now there's a change. I got choked by the Invisible
Man during a Physics lesson: it's true. I was sat there, concentrating on my
school work (for once) and I felt a tightening grip around my neck and
windpipe. I turned around, fully expecting my pal, Shaun Angell to be messing
about again and leaning over tryna choke me to get my attention, and there was
no one there. I stood up going "Arrrgh", trying to remove the invisible hand
away from its cruel grasp and the teacher looked over at me with a perplexed
face and said "Beesley, what are you doing now to disrupt my lesson?" The
rest of the kids were laughing and as the strangulation started to recede I
replied "Nowt, sir, am just trying to get shut of the Man from Uncle's hand

48

from around my neck, he's just tried choking me, the sod." The class was in uproar with laughter as the teacher just shook his head in disbelief.

Some of the lads from school, including (from 3rd left across) punk fan Rob Cheetham, Stranglers fanatic Nicky Booth, and junior school pal Benji

The Yorkshire Ripper was caught on 2nd of January on Melbourne Avenue, Sheffield. Unbelievably I had unwittingly predicted that his next move would be in Sheffield and that was where he would be caught. I told mates this over six months beforehand, an eerie coincidence or some inner psychic talent? I could have also predicted the loss of my paper round in January which was not a good start as it meant the loss of £3.75 out of my pocket which helped subsidise a good proportion of my record buying and gigs. The newsagent had had enough of me. I simply showed little zest for my job anymore and he was fed up of me and Pete messing about and hearing reports of us waking people up on our rounds. One morning he asked me to hand the news bag in and not bother coming in again, to which I threw it straight at him over the counter hitting him in his Quality Street tin styled chops accompanied with a few choice words. 'Some people take their jobs far too seriously,' I thought as I walked out of GT News venturing home to prepare for another day of potential school chaos and the prospect of my final exams on the horizon.

Music was still my salvation but the revolution was almost at an end. Adam and the Ants had turned into flamboyant pop stars overnight, The Jam had seemingly disappeared after a superb 1980 tour and The Clash were being ridiculed for their much maligned but highly adventurous and ahead of its time triple LP, 'Sandinista', which annoyed punks and pleased me no end. Those dark days of the dwindling winter of 80/81 were spent going to see bands such as Cabaret Voltaire, TV21, Gang of Four, The Cure, Spizz Energi (now the Spizzles) and more... all the time waiting for something refreshing and new to occur! Something was sure to happen, soon. I was even leaving school in a few weeks in nervous anticipation and preparation for a new adventure in life!

I attended all but two of my exams, tried my best at the exam sheets put in front of me and made the most of it being non-uniform turning up wearing my Clash-styled zip jacket, Clash fatigue trousers and green food colouring in my hair, much to the disgust of the attending teachers. The day I left school, we were invited to meet our teachers for the very last time. Likely! There was a mandatory early morning meeting that you had to attend in order to officially sign out of school for good, which, understandably, I was compelled and more than willing to attend... and then there was an invite for coffee and sandwiches with the righteous flock later on... sod that! I can clearly remember walking down the school drive for the very last time as a pupil and feeling the joys of freedom. My whole life minus school had begun! What was I going to do? The new decade ahead had only just really started and this was my future and life was there for the taking. I ran home and charged into the house shouting in celebration at having completed my 12 year sentence. My Mum was just dragging the twin tub out of the pantry singing along to her Mario Lanza LP as I ran into the house excitedly... her nearly jumping out of her skin, being so alarmed at my entrance. "Where you off to now that you've left school then, Tony," she enquired. "What about that job at British Steel our Paul and yer Uncle Nip have been telling you about?" "Umm, let me get back to that later," I thought, and took one look at the puzzled face of my Mum and went and got changed into a t-shirt and black jeans, throwing the red fifth year school jumper away forever. "I am off up Sheffield, Mum... see thee later on sometime, have a lovely washing day and don't start smoking again while yer at it." I ran up the path to the sounds of my Mum singing one of her old war-time fave tunes 'We'll meet again, don't know where, don't know when.' I got some money and buggered off to meet my girlfriend, Sarah and we went up Sheffield for the day. We visited record shops, lazed around in the Peace Gardens, gorged on French Fries and fizzy pop at the Wimpy and snogged endlessly and passionately down a back street near the Crucible Theatre. It was one of those perfect days that you just don't get very often. Everything seemed just right and in place. I had left school, had a gorgeous girlfriend and my whole future ahead of me, sore lips 'n all. Wow!!!

When I got home, it was all over the telly about the Yorkshire Ripper being charged in court. I met up with my mates that evening and hung around the park; swapping our collections of school stories and figuring out what each of us were going to do now that we had left school. That was my last day at school. No fanfare for the liberated or a wave of sudden adult confidence. No exactly mapped-out plans: just the certainty in the fact that it was all over. No more being told what to do by conceited superiors, either...or so you think is the case at that idealistic age.

I had met my girlfriend Sarah at a Stiff Little Fingers gig and was besotted with her. When I had approached her and her mate, along with my old pal Ian Cooper (a big SLF fan), she had tried to give me the brush off. I had already been given the cold shoulder once at that same gig by another lass who I had arranged to meet there after getting off with her at a gig at the Top Rank, so I decided to see this one through. Rejection was not an option, this time.

Sarah caught my eye, after the gig had finished, this northern new wave beauty, sat lounging around the bar area as we were passing by. She had gorgeous eyes with long eyelashes. Short wavy hair and a body to kill for, she looked like a cross between Clare Grogan and my favourite fantasy, Kim Wilde – to my teenage lustful eyes at least, and I just had to have her. "Hey up what's your name then," I asked her in my typically uncouth undisguisable Yorkshire dialect. "C'mon, tell us yer name, then... can I see you and take you out," I followed up. "How long you been into the Fingers, then." I went on and on, my confidence in unusually top gear. She said she had had enough of lads and it was nice to speak to me, but no thanks! Making me even more determined, I continued my chat up, offering (off the top of my head) to take her to see a band called Spiral Vision at our youth club disco, and to my astonishment she made a complete U-turn – probably in an effort to get shut of me – and said "OK, here's my telephone number, give me a ring and I will see you." I felt elated and on top of the world... YES!!! I was in business. Me and the Cooper ran like mad for the last bus to Rotherham, him in disbelief at my stroke of luck, me feeling like all my dreams had come true. My heart was beating like mad, as we ran for the last no.69 bus, with the pulsating exuberance of being young, free and potentially hitched up with a lass who was real good looking and... really something else!

When I rang Sarah up the next day from the battered and graffiti-rendered red telephone box on the hill around the corner from our house she was surprised to hear from me. She said something like "I thought you was just on the pull and wasn't really that serious." Was I serious? You better bet I was! We arranged to meet in Rotherham bus station and I would take her to the Spiral Vision gig at the Youthy that I had promised to take her to. When the day came, I stuck another jet-black dye on my newly-cut spiky hair and gave the old leather jacket a once over. I made sure that I had a SLF badge on and that I looked as clean as a young punk kid could. I wanted to make a proper impression this time. Listening to the traditional record session before going out, I was a bit nervous, but proper excited. The sounds of 'Pretty in Pink' by the Psychedelic Furs, 'Is Vic There' by Dept. S and Teardrop Explodes 'Reward' gave me a boost... would I get this right, though. I had buggered up far too many chances with potential girlfriends so far, so maybe this was the big one? Or maybe it would be yet another disastrous non-sexual encounter?

I had started throwing a little bit of extra attention to the opposite sex from my early days at the youthy when we started the comp back in September 1976. The trouble was that I was a bit shy with the lasses and would usually bugger it all up by saying the wrong uncouth words by trying too hard to appear confident with typical lad's stuff. The lasses with their Farah Fawcett flick hair styles that received my attention mostly good-humoured or merely cuddled me as a rule. 'Giz a snog, then', ended one courtship that had showed good potential: me and my runaway gob buggering things up again. Teenage love life was clumsy, daft and fun, but that was how it was back then. We were all innocent, naïve, exuberant and untrained; with much to learn about life, relationships and growing up... hopefully sometime in the very distant future that would be.

One girl that I stupidly encouraged to go out with me during those formative days would embarrass me with her shouts of "Follow me behind the schoolyard wall and I will give you a big kiss." Aaaahhhh" the shame of it. I then ended up dodging her each day at school, but when we went to the youthy, all was forgiven. We sat with our arms around each other, snuggled up on the seats surrounding the dance floor watching the Northern Soul kids dance like mad, creating moves I had never seen before in my life. Those kids must have all had Twister for Christmas surely! To the sounds of Chuck Wood's '7 Days Too Long' me and my daytime-stalking girlfriend would watch the world of the Rawmarsh youth club disco go by whilst smiling at each other like soppy little soft buggers. This was all ok at the Youthy, but not so cool during school hours whilst dodging lessons and getting chased by teachers with yer mates who just loved to see you get shown up by amorous Cindy! When that 1976 prototype courtship fizzled out and my admirer got fed up with chasing me all over the place, it was back to square one.

Another courtship was the Northern Soul lass. I was 14 and she was almost 18. We met at the youth club Disco (where else?) and I got a bit serious in the way only daft young kids with an older girlfriend could. We spent all of our time at Discos and probably looked slightly out of place... me looking like a Sid Vicious does Grange Hill on Spangles kid and her smothering me under her long black 'Soulie' leather. We kissed to the sound of Chairmen of the Board singing 'Just a Little More Time' and then I would halt snog practice to jump up and race to the dance floor to dive about to 'Sound of the Suburbs' by The Members. Me and my Soulie girl/almost woman lasted about 3 months, our time spent doing the nightly rounds at the local youth clubs and discos, until Valentine's Day, when I received a gigantic sized card from her and forgot to even send her an home-made playing card sized one back. As a consequence of this misdemeanour I gave her the elbow to make up for it. We parted on fairly good terms: well I walked home with my mates and turned around to see her crying like mad... and that was that! We never met eye to eye ever again.

Things continued in much the same vein during those last couple of years at school. No matter if I did give my 77-78 Boomtown Rats scrapbook to one lass I had the teenage kicks for, or if I smiled like a lunatic every time I saw others of the first division lasses... it never came to owt in the end. Besides, music was far more important in the scheme of things back then, after all.

Back to 1981 and my love of music had been kind enough to present me with what was looking like a real good chance of getting somewhere with a Division one girl and a step up the coolness chart and envy of some of the lads. I was now ready for the date and hopefully all would turn out just fine. What could go wrong? I was nervous but confident as I caught the 107 bus to town and as I got off the bus in the station there she was. Looking as gorgeous as when I had seen her at the gig, she didn't look as new wave looking, but that impressed me all the more... she wasn't a punk rocker in the hardcore style at all and she was as feminine as anyone I had ever clapped my eyes on. Stunningly thin and perfectly shaped, all my teenage dreams had come true. Best not bugger this up then eh!! Let's get her in the mood with some new romanticism, courtesy of Ivor and the lads at the youth club, then!

My Pierrot Dolls (Ivor – 3rd from the left)

The singer of Spiral Vision was the afore-mentioned Ivor Hillman. Ivor was more than a bit of a legend around our end and he had bags of talent and charisma. Decades before the X Factor and Britain's Got Talent, young Ivor was challenging genres, performance expectations and the status quo. Not long after this gig Ivor created a new Futurist band called My Pierrot Dolls!

At the Youth club disco that night, it was full of the New Romantics and Futurists: Bowie fans that I mentioned just earlier; all turned out to see Spiral Vision. I knew most of this frilly-shirt wearing, floppy-fringed new posse in town. My old mates who I had grown up with, Pete Roddis and Andy Goulty, along with other ex-punk rockers such as Stranglers obsessive, Nicky Booth, the new wave luvvies and good female mates of mine, Lynne, Tracy and Julie amongst others – and a few new faces too; there they all were... lapping up the 'Sounds of the Crowd' and waiting for some 'Love Action'. Strolling in early on with my new gorgeous girlfriend Sarah proudly attached on my arm – for a while – I felt like the only punk rocker in the building!

Away from the Numbers - Tony Beesley

Our school Youth club Disco DJ, Kev would frequently introduce his set with 'Exodus' by Biddu Orchestra before spinning his usual set of chart hits, Heavy Rock, Northern Soul and Disco. This time it was a new set of the sounds from Visage, Kraftwerk and Human League. I parked myself down with Sarah and kept my attentions firmly upon her for the duration... I couldn't tell you a single thing about Spiral Vision that night, I am sorry to say. I was so besotted and had entered a completely different parallel world. In around two and half hours of new romantic mania, while the futurists danced away, I gazed like a plonker into Sarah's eyes and talked her head off, trying to make the very best impression humanly possible in-between our sloppy snogs.

For the next few months, my time was split between Sarah and my mates. She would come over to my house and we would fling and contort ourselves all over our front room settee for hours on end. We would laugh together and listen to records, chat away for hours me ribbing her for her love and open admiration for Stiff Little Fingers drummer, Jim Reilly. We listened to the sounds of Devo, The Undertones, Moondogs, The Jam and the Specials. One night, we got completely carried away with ourselves and didn't hear my Mother banging away at the front room window to be let in on her return from her job at the club. We held our heads down as we sheepily exited out of the house and I walked her to the bus stop. A few weeks later, I bettered that one, when I buggered off to the Limit club on West Street in Sheffield and returned home in the early morning hours to the sight of my Mother sat on our front wall. I had taken her key and left her locked out from 11pm to 2am. Whoops!

The summer of 81 was in full flow and me and Sarah spent all of our time together. Front room canoodles, trips to Sheffield, the disco and walks in the woods- one of which we were brought back from lovers' land by a dog licking the side of my face. It could have been worse, I suppose? We were sprawled on the sliding grass banks being watched by an old pervert with binoculars, the dog's owner so told us. Such is life. Nature is not always so innocent... Lesson learnt. When Sarah went on her holidays, I was like a little lost puppy. The David Cassidy of punk rock! She sent me a right soppy letter to keep me going and on her return we made up for a week of being apart, snogging that much it's a wonder that we didn't stick together. Everything was perfect: Sid and Nancy had nowt on us two. One day the love bubble burst when Sarah called for me with tears in her eyes. I was wondering what was wrong and awaiting an explanation. She said that she had to do a babysitting job for a month. 'Big deal', I thought. After endless hugs and the reassurance that we weren't all through with, we parted with me promising that I would phone her every day and after this job was done with, we would carry on as normal. It took me four months to get around to phoning her!!! What a stupid and selfish fool I was!

1981 was the year my brother, Glen's first son Darren was born. It was also the year of Lady Diana and her image will forever be linked with the conservatism and glamour of the said New Romantics, even though her big-eared Charlie was a huge fan of Status Quo! It was also the famous Royal wedding, that very event that appears to re-mould the country into a Royalist-loving over-sentimental nation and thus inspiring working class street parties and Union Jack bunting. It happens every few decades and bores the hell out of me. None more so than during the summer of 81 and all of its tedious overkill!

When the right Royal day arrived, after watching Bob Hope in 'Son of Pale Face', I went and called for my punk pal, Barney Rubble who was quite keen on the idea of creating our very own anti-Royalist travelling party. Calling down for Barney, he appeared leering out of his loft window with a fag and a Sid snarl, shouting "Oi! are tha up to some pissing about and ruining some Wedding celebrations of that twat Charles and his bird?" Laughing I went in and waited while Barney got himself ready, dragging on his bondage trousers and tartan kilt, all ready to walk the streets and engage upon our very own Royal Wedding celebrations of a slightly alternative (and naughty) nature.

Looking like Sid Vicious punk personified, Barney, in his tartan kilt, leather jacket, and studded wristband topped off by jet-black hair in car paint-sprayed spikes was a King's Road punk pose walking special. No Japanese tourists to take snaps around our end, though. Barney was punk through and through, in the style of Anarchy and Chaos anyway and was up for anything all of the time. We had some amazing laughs and chaotic fun together.

That Royalist holiday day saw us pulling wedding bunting down, getting chased off by fat-bellied beer-guzzling blokes with hairy sideburns for swearing and poking fun at 'em and Barney throwing dog shit (with his hands) at the windows of a family sat watching the wedding. It was wrong, unkind, immature and extremely childish... but it was equally funny and a healthy antidote to joining in with the mindless drone-like obsession with what was

56

going off in another place inhabited by rich people who couldn't give a monkeys about us or any of the nation's working class. Before any readers out there declare me as being an anti-royalist yob, please let me set the record straight. I am not overtly anti-royalist or a revolutionary anarchist; being no huge fan of our dear Royals nor a badge-wearing anti-aristocracy crusty. I really couldn't care less either way: but when it comes to adulating them I am not gonna join in either and - as always - if something is setting itself up as being over-serious and breaking the boundaries of conformism, well I am by nature, certainly up for disrupting the nice and cosy little party!

Barney Rubble - the Royal Wedding disrupting anarchist was Mark Barnet. We had been mates right from the infants' school: we were even put into a class of kids a year younger than us for messing about. He had been in a local paper for having Rolling Stones styled long hair way back at the tail end of the swinging sixties... and he was only four years old. He was bound to grow up a rebel at some point. In contrast, by the Comp, Mark had settled down and had become a bit of a swot, getting all of his school work done on time and keeping his head down. By 1980 he had developed a bit of a fascination with the music of Gary Numan and Tubeway Army and started wearing Combat trousers. I spotted the change in Mark and managed to talk him out of that Numanoid Dummy nonsense. Inviting him to hang out with me and my mates, he soon changed his persona and before you knew it he was a proper hard-core Punk Rocker and never looked back at his school work again.

Mark went and had his hair cut spiky, and then dyed it jet-black. He acquired a tartan kilt, bondage trousers, Doc Marten boots, a real leather jacket and an assortment of punk t-shirts. He listened to my Clash LP's, Damned, Eater, Slaughter and the Dogs records and went to see the Angelic Upstarts with us. Me and my older punk mate, Bryan Bell dyed his hair first bleached blond and then crimson red and to rinse his hair we threw buckets of water over him on Bry's garden as locals passed by in disbelief. Bry was taken by Barney's increasingly zany sense of humour and we all went to see The Damned in Sheffield together, after also bleaching my hair blond in return for me painting Penetration on the back of Bryan's leather jacket. On leaving school, Barney left a calling card in massive white paint letters on the slope of the school's tennis court stating that the (named) PE teacher was a bastard. Unbelievably the crackpot signed it with his own name too! Another time, I set

the record player up right on top of our bay window outside and climbed out of
the window, followed by Barney. Listening to the sounds of The Adverts
'Crossing the Red Sea' we were having a laugh and taking the piss out of
people as they passed by. When I saw one of our regular piss-take receiving
clients, the Monty Python man, I had an idea up my sleeve.

The Monty Python man was a small fella who looked the spitting image of
one of the Michael Palin Gumby-styled characters on the show: he had the
same sort of tight-fitting Gumby jacket on, identical spectacles and thin
moustache. He really was a dead ringer and yet another addition to our daft
list. Well this fella was fed up of us laughing at him every time we saw him and
had lost his patience. What a great time to spring a trick on Barney! As the
Gumby got closer up the street, nap-sack in hand for an afters shift at the
factory, we were giving him some lip and pointing at him, laughing our heads
off: Barney was in hysterics and doing his hilarious laugh, tears running down
his face. At that moment my trick was sprung. Making sure, all along that I was
the closest to the window, I grappled back in as quick as a ferret down a rabbit
hole and shut the window behind me, leaving poor old Barney on his own to
deal with the full blown wrath of the greatest Gumby of the village going
crackers at him and shaking his fist, threatening to climb up and see to him.
Barney was still laughing his head off and banging on the window. Inside I too
was laughing my head off at him and the situation. It was a true classic comedy
moment like so many incidents that summer.

By a few months into his punk apprenticeship Mark had totally merged into
the legendary Barney Rubble and, heavily influenced by our encouraging dares
and confidence building, was up for anything for a laugh: so began Barney's
almost mythical urban legend!

Royal Wedding aside, the long fun-filled summer of 81 was our very own
never-ending party too. Me and my mates were living in a twilight zone of no
man's land between school and the working week. It was a time of insane fun
and friendship only being disturbed by the need for sleep each day, or the
sight of a daft lad called Jonesy stood at our gate throwing house bricks at me
and Barney for taking the mickey out of him a bit too far. A time of gigs at the
Marples, West Street venues, the Polytechnic, the Hallamshire Hotel and many
other venues. Each day was one long exciting episode of discovery, laughs and
music. I really couldn't wait to wake up each morning and get out there with my

mates and cram as much as I could into the long hot days. Maybe that's the reason why I had shoved poor old Sarah to the back of my mind?

By now, Andy Goulty had ditched his New Romantic fad and opted for a new earthier and revived punk outlook. He was back into the three chord world of punk rock and was soon championing the new street sounds (and fashion styles) of Oi!, reverting back to his 1978, Sham 69-inspired skinhead crop. Along with Deano, Clarkey, Barney Rubble, Podder, Daz Twynam and a whole gang of ever-changing punk and associated punk spin off fans, we went hell for leather on getting to as many places as we could, hearing as many records as possible and reaching that perfect buzz level that is only possible at that age and with the knowledge that we can never be sixteen again!!!

Me and Andy ventured over the Pennines to the second city of Punk, Manchester; the home of Buzzcocks, Magazine and Joy Division! Excited about sampling the hardcore punk venue, the Mayflower, which was on the rough (to say the least) outskirts of the city in Moss side, we would dodge the fare and sneak onto the National Express coach in Sheffield's Pond Street station on Saturday lunchtimes and spend the day in Manchester city centre until the gig was due to start.

We were nervous but excited to be spreading our punk wings so far and lapped up the experience. Supping cups of tea in back street cafes, O.A.P.'s, Coronation Street extras and greasy bacon sarnie gulping builders would stare at us as we sat nervously counting our pound notes and ten pence pieces. Eating our very own home-made sarnies in the Piccadilly gardens and reading 'Grinding Halt' fanzine, we would then catch a bus out to the venue, which sat right in the middle of what appeared to be a war zone. One night at the Mayflower, fighting kicked off and we saw bald skinheads get bottled right in front of us falling down on to the beer and piss-soaked floor as blood seeped into the river of anarchy while The Damned sped along playing 'Born to Kill'. We dodged local proto-casual Perry boys under the bridge down the road at daft 'o clock after gigs, got accosted and partially mugged by a guy with a flick knife on one occasion and then would usually kip for an hour or so on the deserted train station waiting for the early morning post train to arrive to take us home to our mates and a brand new fresh, sleep-lacking Sunday morning! Sneaking in to the house around 5am, my Mum would shout down "Tony, is that you? You were a long time going to the shop, where have you been?"

Our summer of 81 belonged to our pal Barney Rubble as he provided our gang with a hefty percentage of laughs and never refused a dare, even partaking in a Saturday afternoon public-invited bath with a bar of soap in Rotherham town centre's fountain. As we were hanging around the local park, one balmy evening, one of our girl mates had got her Collie dog with her as she was chatting to us. She always had a thing for my mate, Andy and would hang around with us a lot that year. Anyway, out of sheer boredom and to inject the evening with a bit of Barney craziness, one of us got Barney to chase the lass's Collie dog all over. "Come here little doggy," laughed Barney. You have never seen a lass and her dog move as quick in your life. Following some further antics she scarpered up to the top of the park to a police car that was parked up there outside the café, the police officer talking to around 30 or more kids. Barney was rolling around the floor and we were all pissing ourselves laughing, tears running down our faces. As we were calming down we saw that the lass and her dog were talking to the copper. Well, no sooner had we noticed this, when all of those kids who had been talking to the cop, suddenly made one massive dash down the park. The cop had told them to Go forth and catch Barney. It didn't take much, with Barney's reputation to get a policeman's attention. As we looked up, it was like a cattle stampede as kids charged down the hill towards us. It was hilarious to see. Barney noticed and on a comment of "Oh shit, I think they are coming for me," he scarpered. It was like a scene from a comedy film. Something that couldn't be repeated, it was so funny. We all watched as Barney shot off like a madman on the run being chased by the hordes of vigilante kids and car 54 behind them. We took off too. We didn't want to get done either. The chase went on for a few hours, but the Sheriff and his Deputy Dawg sponsors never caught Crazy Barney. He hid out in someone's back yard that night, like a proper fugitive afraid to go home. A notice went out as something like 'Wanted, Barney Rubble and gang...

for attempted Dog assault.' You never got that sort of fun while watching repeats of 'Lassie' did you...?

While we are on the subject of animals let me tell you about the punk cat I acquired around this time. Following in the family tradition of adopting unique pets such as our Paul's dog, Micky (aka Scooby Doo), we gave a home to Tommy the punk cat. We had been to the RSPCA and were told "We don't have any cats, but we do have this." This being the 'not so pretty and far from cute'

meowing and scraggy black kitten that we named Tommy. He was as nasty a cat you could ever meet and beat up dogs, chewed up any animal smaller than him, assassinated rats, gave you a nasty bite if he felt that way inclined and like some 19th century Comanche Indian he went out on days-long raiding and mating sprees. He would come back, each time, with a new injury, but nothing could stop him on his paw-lined tracks. Tommy lived life to the full, was mates and boss with our dog, Sheena and had a few admirers for his hedonistic partying and hell raising approach to a cat's life. One day, he had been missing for a good week or so, which had us worried even for him. Maybe someone had gone for the reward offered on the wanted posters? A friend called on us saying they had spotted Tommy dead at the side of the road near at side of the Monkwood pub. I wasn't surprised. He had probably been for a pint there and got thrown out and then been hit by a lorry. Off I went and there he was, all mangled up and stiff as a board. I bagged him up and took him home, the end of an era. I dug up a spot in the back garden and set about burying him and as I shovelled the last bit of soil over his grave and said a few words for him, I heard a meowing. "Crap I've buried him alive," I thought. But he can't be alive; he was in a right state, stiff, bloody and motionless. As I looked up the garden path I caught sight of where the meowing was coming from. It was Tommy strolling down the path arriving back to base after a long faraway vacation. Tommy was alive and well and had a good few more years left in him. I had buried a look-alike cat, maybe one of his offspring, who knows?

Away from the Numbers - Tony Beesley

If Tommy, whilst on his pioneering travels throughout the Wild West of cat-land had passed any saloons and bars, I am quite confident that he would have partaken of a few large whiskeys from time to time, in-between his many bar room brawls and law-breaking incidents. As for us pesky punk generation lads, well we weren't really that avid beer drinkers yet as we certainly didn't aspire to join up with the boring white shirt beer-swilling brigade so the regular habit of drinking, especially in non-gig hosting boozers was quite rare and didn't match up to the fun we could have without any alcoholic intervention. True, we did get pissed when we felt like it (often on Barney's Dad's rather potent home brew wine up in Barney's attic) and we also had a few pints if we could manage to get served at a gig. Back in the Top Rank days, we were so pleased to get in the place and see our new wave heroes that we daren't risk too often the chance of being thrown out for asking for a pint at the bar: me and Pete Roddis usually more than satisfied as we stood supping two pints (of Cola) each at the bar at Jam and Clash gigs after returning from the throng of pogoing mass, exhausted and totally dehydrated. Beer and cider was for parties and piss ups. Even so, around this time a few of us felt the need to enhance our excitement by trying our best to infiltrate a grown man's watering hole. A kind of unspoken and potentially dangerous challenge, I suppose.

First we tried the Marquis Hotel drinking den at the other end of Manor Farm. Me, Deano and Barney went up there hoping for a pint and a listen to the Eric Bristow fans and laughing beer bellies. Dressed in our most typically punk clobber, not one of us sporting a natural hair colour, we walked in through the main doors of the establishment. It was exactly like one of those scenes in all those countless afternoon Westerns when the lone stranger walks into the saloon to the scene of a sudden total silence as everyone turns around. Well, we three 'Punk Rock amigos' re-lived that scene in absolute perfection as the gang of pint-hugging waist expanders with grins, the epitome of disdained sarcasm and hate mingled with pure amazement at our front for even thinking of gracing their domain... all swivelled around on their creaking bar stools to view the proposed local freak show! The bar man peered past these breathing fossils and gave us one simple assertive motion and one simple word; pointing his finger aggressively behind us towards the door we had just entered, he proudly proclaimed the expected word... "OUT"!!!

Laughing as we turned around and vacated the joint, we thought about the next watering hole we could invade. We succeeded, this time, in digging out a corner in another local boozer not too far away for us, called The Queens. In there, we got ourselves a table and made it our own, just like all those legions of pub regulars and working class men always did. Each week, for around two or three months, we went in regularly for a few pints and we were left alone. Not one person said anything hostile to us once. In fact one lad who was about two years older than us started to come and chat with us. Years later the lad lost his mind and I wonder if we confused his fragile self with our tales of there being an alternative to the dreary 9-5 existence of life. Whatever, before long, we soon tired of last Orders at the last saloon and moved on. The place we moved on to was the earthy and enigmatic Marples pub in Sheffield.

Sheffield's Marples pub had been putting on punk and plenty of Alternative gigs for quite some time. We had seen local faves Artery there, along with other Sheffield scenesters I'm So Hollow, the Stunt Kites and a promising up and coming band called Pulp who featured a quirky and enigmatic singer with a cutting wit and attitude called Jarvis Cocker. Jarvis

Gaz Stables, Neil Cresswell, Dave Frost and Nigel 'Nobby' Noble at Sheffield Top Rank

and Pulp had also played their very first gig in Rotherham at the library's Arts Centre the year before. I was at the John Peel road show when Jarvis handed Peel a cassette of Pulp which earned the band airplay on his show. That night, I stopped John Peel as he walked past us and asked him to play some Clash and he gave me a strange, annoyed look as if to say "Get lost". He said he would try, but he never did play any Clash for me: all those hours that I had put in listening to his show too. Never mind he was a legend all the same!

Punks and Beki Bondage of Vice Squad at the Marples by Kristan James Melik

In 1981 over at the Marple's the gig scene turned its attention very keenly to the new breed of punk bands emerging at the time. Along with old wave faves such as Chelsea, Angelic Upstarts, the Outcasts, and others, the venue, under the leadership of legendary music promoter Marcus Featherby, booked just about every street level punk band of the time. Anti-Pasti, Vice Squad, Chron-Gen, Charge (featuring the late Stu-p-didiot guitarist fella in a black leather skirt and fishnets), Flux of Pink Indians, Discharge, Crass, UK Subs, The Exploited and many more. When Gary Bushell and Oi! came to town a little later on, it was the Marples who gave them the stage to perform upon.

The summer through till the end of the year saw me and my mates pay a visit there around twice a week on average, often more. We had some fantastic nights and it was the real grass roots punk place to be for a while. Gravity-defying spikes, heavy duty punk leathers, chains, studs and glue galore... my punk-duties were taken up with rescuing a girl called Ann from flying pints of beer and piss, hanging out with Anti-Pasti and snogging Clare Grogan punk look-alikes in the dark and seedy corner. Hardcore punk mates such as Barney Rubble and many others had truly found their home. I had begun to tire of the whole scene, and soon it would be time for me to finally leave the uniformity and nihilism of modern day punk behind forever, dragging the original ideology and influence along with me to a brand new musical soundtrack and future adventures. As the new 'Punk's not Dead' magazine came onto newsagent's shelves along with new punk saturation in Sounds music weekly and a visit to a Killing Joke gig at the Polytechnic in July, I came to realise that this mass tribalism was no longer for me. I wrote a song called 'Fashion Parade' on my cheap Woolworths guitar when I got home that night.

Me and my good punk pal, Beanz (Dean Stables); mid 1981

That summer saw the youth of this country stand up and say 'enough is enough' as riots kicked off all over the UK in protest at high unemployment, urban deprivation and the S.U.S laws of the Police, amongst other issues. Unlike the riots of recent times, the ones of 1981 - though not an ideal way of expression - did have at least some form of genuine discontent. Toxteth, Brixton and Manchester's Moss side were battlegrounds as black and white united to hurl bricks at the system in protest at their social conditions and bleak prospects.

Away from the Numbers - Tony Beesley

The Clash's Mick Jones (whom I met briefly a few months later) disowned the partially White Riot's declaring that he was no good at rioting, to which an element of the punk elite reacted with predictable scorn: I was glad to hear him say that as (despite my rebel inclination's) I wasn't fooled nor taken in with any romantic rebellious notions attached to the act of rioting either and felt it a total waste of energy and a pitiful waste of property and as for rendering actual physical harm to anyone in the process, well forget it... the cause is then lost. No... I was (and am) for creating not destroying. Though sometimes (in fits of unrestrained anger) I struggled with that ideology!

At the same time, in Southall, the image of the controversial, and largely misunderstood, OI! street Punk movement was sealed forever when race riots sparked off between Asians and infiltrated Right Wing groups. The incident hit the front pages of the Tabloids and the skinhead image was forever firmly (often unjustly) associated with Racist politics and the Right Wing. Around the same time, the legendary Specials played an open-air gig at Herringthorpe playing fields, a gig that saw gangs of Sheffield and Rotherham skinheads battle against each other, fighting and chasing each other all over the town and its vicinity. Me and Andy (on the way back from Manchester) caught a no.69 bus home from Sheffield that day which was invaded with a whole war party of skins who thankfully saved their knuckles for the Battle of Herringthorpe Playing fields. The Specials wrote the iconic youth anthem of that summer, 'Ghost Town' and promptly split up not long afterwards.

Me and my mate, Andy Goulty (on our visits to Manchester earlier that summer) witnessed first-hand the after-effects of the Moss Side Riots; shops and buildings were boarded up, the occasional fires still burnt and debris spread across the hostile landscape while an air of un-focused aggression still pervaded the air. Our home-turf exploits of dodging ageing Teddy Boys and shaved head thugs couldn't compare to Manchester's apocalyptic air of tense violence and bruised headache-inducing anxiety. Arriving back to Sheffield felt like a return from the Front line and the sense of relief to be back in relatively friendly territory was actually quite nice and occasionally welcoming!

Another summer was almost over and the real world beckoned after our blood. "C'mon lads, you've had your fun and games, run the race long enough now. It's time to bloody grow up, get yourselves a job and act like grown-ups,"... the voice of reason and that swear word called responsibility was screaming our way. Personally, I wasn't the slightest bit interested or remotely attentive. My first summer out of school went speeding by and it now seemed like a lifetime away since I had left school that May; so much fun had been experienced. The most important thing in my life had been my mates and having a laugh, along with (and it goes without saying) music and gigs. Lasses had been a poor 3rd or 4th down the chain. Snogs, courtships, rejections, complications, and a few fleeting scenes of sexual euphoria that summer simply did not compare with the crazy and care-free times of hanging out with my ever dependable mates.

Mum and a hillbilly admirer, Blackpool, September 1981 with our Steve

In September, whilst my Mum was at the seaside with our Paul's wife, Megan and our Dave and Steve and chatting up motionless California gold miners whilst wearing a slightly over-sized cowboy hat, me and Andy signed on the dole: he drew a few giros before signing on for a job down the pit. I went around searching for employment in the most unlikely of places, supermarkets, pubs, amateur acting school (full of negative angry ranting thespians) and obscure factories, turning up in my leather jacket, torn at the knee jeans and hair spread around my head in all directions and shades of growing out past colours. One manager of a factory in Masborough actually showed me around the workplace, describing what the position would entail and then introduced me to the workforce who stood staring at me mouths open-wide with shock, amazement and disgust at the thought that they may be working alongside a real in the flesh punk rocker. Naively I never understood their indifference and even more naively why I never managed to get the job. Ok, what about that British Steel job me Mum had mentioned a few months back?

I decided, under duress, to have a wander down to the British Steel offices and enquire about the job I had been told about. Dressed quite normal and only my freshly dyed jet-black hair giving away any hint of being not quite Joe Average, I found myself in a maze of corridors and offices that looked like something out of The Prisoner TV series. When I banged on a door for some attention, I was met with an over-weight white shirt-wearing (oh no!!!) pig-ignorant steel works gaffer! He looked me up and down and didn't even attempt to disguise his complete disdain and hatred of youth. "What do you want," the real Tetley Bitterman award winner bellowed. "I heard there was a job going," I replied, starting to feel just a little bit like Billy Casper going for his visit to the careers officer in Kes. "What job? There are no jobs, who has told you that nonsense, boyo," he barked. "ME BROTHER, OUR PAUL," I barked back, getting pissed off at the attitude he was throwing my way. Something clicked... he somehow knew that I meant our Paul, without even asking for our surname. He disappeared behind the door and after rifling through a stack of drawers, pulled out an application form and popped back round handing me one and concluded our meeting with "Here tha goes, get this filled in and leave it on that desk over there... and then get thi sen off and out of here." The door slammed shut hard and when I sat down with the form to have a crack at filling it in, hoping that the Steelworks monster from outer chin face wouldn't be my boss, I saw that the bloody form was already damned filled in by someone else! And to make matters worse, I even knew the bloke who had filled it in. He had gone to school with our Glen and used to come round to our house on Friday nights for a mess around back when I was a little un. I was furious. The bastard must have known. I wrote allsorts in the remaining spaces of that 4 page British Steel application form. Swear words, general idiocy and a special message to swollen chops himself... "UP YOURS!" I couldn't believe it when I didn't get the job and I bet the poor bloke who had originally filled it in felt the same too! Years later, I returned back to that very same work place to do some contract work painting girders blue for an extension they were having set up. I never saw the nasty twat up there in the offices and it's a good thing he didn't spot me too. Maybe he would have wrapped one of those paint-splattered girders round my neck on sight of me... or just maybe he would have received the full physical demonstration of said girders in the exact manner that I had left scribbled on that old application form!!!

I drew my giros for a while and then took a job on a year-long (non YTS) training scheme for Painting and decorating that paid me a whole £33 a week. My work buddies on this journey of paint and paste, spent doing up old folk's centres, bungalows and Council-rented joints up and down the region, were a mix of ex-Borstal boys, average delinquents, directionless school leavers like me and my mate and even a couple of fellow ex-punk kids. Under the guidance of a lovely old fella called Walt- who was old school, ex-National service and as old fashioned as Bobby Charlton's comb-over, we set out in vans each day to do a contracted job or spent the time playing football in the yard or endlessly varnishing tables at our Kilnhurst base. There was one poor kid who was a bit slow and a couple of the older lads would hang him by the arms from the top of the stairs. They weren't bothered about owt those lads and wouldn't bat an eye lid at doing a stretch inside for any of their misdemeanours, but I hated what they did with that lad and to my shame, I uncharacteristically never said anything. One day we hung out of the windows right at the top of a building in Rotherham town centre where we were doing a fortnight's painting contract and painted our names on the outside. For years afterwards I would pass and see my name up there right at the top for all to see.

Throughout that apprentice-styled experience I encountered my first sighting of a new fast food thing called a Pot Noodle, I learnt how to paint and decorate for a lifetime, to be thick-skinned and how to spend my wages in the pub like proper Yorkshire lads. Ultimately, though, in those days of Thatcherist wasteland, it didn't manage to get me a full-time job. The day I finished I decided to pick up my guitar and try and form a band again.

The musical project this time (following my school-years failed attempts at forming bands) was Voxx in which I wrote countless poorly-structured songs displaying my naïve poetic visions and Marylyn Monroe obsessions all performed via my frenetic and uncompromising style on my cheap punk rock guitar alongside my pal, Barney Rubble on Flintstones bass and Rick the Mod on Chad Valley drums. We performed to curious mates and then after that screwed up it was back to plan B! Form another bloody band... what else?

Away from the Numbers - Tony Beesley

Barney Rubble gave up his bass playing duties and when he wasn't on the run from the police or some irate Dad after his blood for corrupting their daughters he had now acquired a love nest of his own: a garage at the bottom of someone's back garden where he would take lasses for a quickie. One Dad was chasing him all over the show that year, if only he had gone and rented a garage he might have caught him. Other lads such as good pal Gaz Stables and numerous others also joined us from time to time. The meeting place was still my Mum's front room and no one can calculate exactly how many punk and associated cults passed through our meeting place, it was always bustling with activity to say the least. We would take lasses back there too and if we thought we were in with a chance, would couple up with one we fancied, cuddle up to 'em and hope for the best. It sometimes worked, often not!

Whilst trying it on with various members of the Gregory's Girls gang and associates, we also made a few returns to our much-loved Youth club disco. To a brand new soundtrack of Pigbag, Duran Duran, Altered Images and Modern Romance of the Smash Hits-buying pop kids, we sat around trying to look cool. There had been no follow up live bands (to my knowledge anyway) perform there since Ivor and the lads' futurist evening back in May, which was a pity. But, there was still a regular Monday to Friday 6.30pm till 9pm disco keeping kids out of trouble and a chance to grab some after-school socialising. Years before the net and chat room sites, never mind heroin and coke for sale on the streets, that's how kids got together and communicated.

The Disco had moved to the smaller Rosla room since our days and wasn't anywhere near as atmospheric seeming to have lost its vibe or maybe it was us who had changed? One night, we got the DJ to put on my 'Radio Clash' single and the lasses carried on dancing to its prototype Hip Hop sound. We joined in with a weird jerky Punk/Funk dance and they looked at us gob-smacked wondering why we were showing enthusiasm for something sounding so un-punk like. They didn't believe us when we showed them the cover of the Clash record. We invited some of them back to my house to listen to some more interesting sounds and to our surprise they agreed. Get ready to dim the lights when the times right then!

Our front room: the sounds of punk, Futurist, Bowie and Bolan, Mod and Ska could be heard on my Alba music centre, which was still remarkably in one piece. We sat around laughing; making names up for people, banging on the window at gullible passers-by and every now and again, the subject of forming a band would arise yet again. One day, just you wait... one day... I was gonna play in a proper band. In the meantime, I continued writing words for prospective songs and taking lasses back there when they were willing. If not, then I would have to resort back to my Kim Wilde fantasies instead! Well I did manage to partially live out my Kim fantasy when I saw her at the City Hall.

As punk evolved faster, harder and even more back to basics, I began to drift even further away from it all. By the end of the year, it was pretty clear that - on the whole - this new revised punk offering was tired, revisionist, uniform-like and musically apathetic, nothing like the creativity and imagination of early punk: the only positive aspects being the energy and political realism offered by such figureheads as Beki Bondage! In late 81, this whole package of new punk power arrived in Rotherham town centre at the Clifton Hall! A mixture of curiosity and loyalty to the dying cause led me there.

Rotherham Clifton Hall

Rotherham Clifton Hall had seen some commendable acts perform there. Locals such as Rotherham's first punk band The Prams, Sheffield Mods The Negatives and steel city post-punk faves, Artery performed on a stage that also welcomed the Angelic Upstarts (who popped into the nearby Charters pub for a pre-gig pint), The Lambrettas (around the time of their 'Poison Ivy' hit), Soul fave Johnny Johnson, 60's popsters Dave Dee, Dozy, Beaky Mick and Tich and a certain now famous Rock n' Roller called Shakin' Stevens and his

Sunsets. There were also regular (and very popular) fondly- remembered Northern Soul nights held there. Oxford bags-wearing Northern Soul fanatics would travel from all over the country to attend those nights of Soul euphoria; dancing and spinning on the talc-laden wooden dance floor to the sounds of the latest underground rarely-heard vinyl discoveries. Locals such as Jonny Parkinson, Snowy and Steve Downing amongst legions of other devoted Soul followers spent their hard-earned cash on records, clothes and nights out on the Northern Soul circuit. Further afield at legendary places such as Wigan Casino and Stoke's The Torch, but also on their faithful home turf here at the Clifton Hall, where for a block of highly anticipated and excitable hours of exuberance and non-stop dancing the outside world was forgotten amidst a hot, sweat-inducing, floor-swivelling Soul revue!

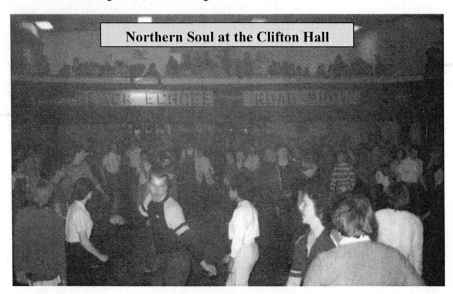

Northern Soul at the Clifton Hall

From 1979, the venue also became a popular Mod attraction... many of the same Northern Soul sounds finding a new audience; even a young pre-Stone Roses Ian Brown would attend Mod and Soul nights there and down the road at the equally Mod-friendly Assembly Rooms.

A few years later I too would perform at the Clifton Hall to the local Mod crowd! On this late 1981 occasion, though, it was a hall full of the region's punk rockers that had turned out to see new punk hopes Chron Gen, Vice Squad and Anti-Pasti play and I was there too. As we arrived to the soundtrack of The Clash 'Give 'Em Enough Rope' album much to my approval (a depiction of which I had painted on the back of my leather jacket), the place soon filled up: punks I had never even seen before amidst all styles on display, from six inch high-lacquered spikes and Mohawks to leopard spot close-crops to a uniform of tartan kilts, bondage trousers, zips, bum flaps, arm bands, studs and leather, all united in the common punk cause. Our pal Barney Rubble was there too: he had truly arrived at his nirvana!!!

Also with me was my good mate, Gaz Stables (above) an enthusiastic punk who I had known right from my red chopper days. His dad was a classic true northerner and treat me like an old mate, inviting me down to their parties and always having us in stitches with his earthy humour. Earlier that year during Gaz's first days at work after leaving school, he had an accident ending up on crutches for quite some time. His leg gave him physical grief for many years, but didn't stop him turning out for heaps of punk gigs and playing drums in a punk band down at the Dusty Miller pub in town, where I would pop down to support and watch them practice now and again.

Gaz was always good for a laugh and shared a very similar sense of humour to me, often encouraging me to go one step dafter than I already was. One day, Gaz called for me and took us both for a few pints at notorious town rough house saloon, Crestas on a mid-afternoon. Me and him, two 16 year-old punk kids with a proper bloke's pint each sat in-between grisly outlaws, bikers, Rotherham wide-boys and Ivy Tilsley look-alike women... and we were welcomed by all of 'em. We shared some great laughs for a while, me and Gaz. We never fell out once and even though we went down separate musical paths, we remained good friends. He never even got the face on once when we would leave him struggling behind us on his crutches and we would run off and leave him. He would just laugh and shout 'Wait for me, you sods'!

Following the punk tribal gathering at the Clifton Hall where in true punk style we met and chatted with the bands afterwards and which wound down with a bomb alert, for some insane reason, we made our way back to the bus station for the last bus. It was quite late and a gang of older toughs were congregated there. It was nothing new to us in being berated and threatened so we took no notice of the usual traditional anti-punk repertoire. This time, though the gang meant real trouble and were just about to lay into us when an old school pal of mine, who was good mates with the gang, appeared and instructed them to leave us alone. "Leave 'em, these lads are alright, I went to school with some of them," he said. Good enough for me, now where's the 108 bus? It was my old school mate who had shared a special treat of getting slippered for falling asleep in Assembly one morning back in our early days at the Comp. He was a tough un, but also a good un and always on my side, thank God.

After that tribal punk gathering I never avidly went out in my punk gear ever again and my tastes in music veered totally away from typical punk. I had a ticket to go to the Christmas on Earth Punk festival in Leeds but as the day approached, partly influenced by the atrocious snow we were having and partly due to disinterest, I decided to give it a miss. I really couldn't stand the thought of all those apocalyptic punk bands churning out all of their punk-by-numbers sets out all day and night drooled over by cider-swilling Mohawks and 'Punks not Dead' fanatics. That Clifton Hall gig had been well enough for me anyway. It was all becoming far too static, nihilistic and ultimately boring!!

By this time, my look was evolving too. Through the influence of Theatre of Hate, who we had seen supporting The Clash after blagging our way onto the guest list and also at the Limit club, me and my mate, Beanz went for a makeshift quiff style. This suited him no end, but I looked a bit of a pillock so ended up combing mine down into a more Mod style after a week or so. I was wearing tartan-lined black Harrington jackets, Chelsea boots, red braces and Sta-Prest trousers too. My look was a kind of hybrid of punk, Mod, and slight hints of original skinhead in unequal measures. Beanz began to look increasingly cooler: a clear emulation of his hero Paul Simenon of The Clash. He had his look sorted good 'n proper. I was more confused and not quite sure how I wanted to appear. I experimented with Bowie-styled Fireman's shirts, blazers and a long fringe but none of it ever felt right. Eventually, I paid my farewells to the punk look for good when I gave away my treasured leather jacket (Clash signatures inside too) and threw most of my punk gear either in the bin or the back of the wardrobe and opted for a razor cut Mod hairstyle and a selection of Fred Perry polo shirts, Ben Sherman button downs and the return of my old Jam shoes. I had reached my destination and had jumped off the tired circus of the latter-day punk rock express forever!!!

That Christmas eve of 1981, I went out on my first proper pub crawl: well I ended up crawling home anyway at least. Me and my pal, Paul Clarke did a few pints in every pub round Rawmarsh, quickly getting proper sozzled and laughing like proper daft pillocks. This wasn't like the stuff in cans. It was real bloke's draught stuff and was the first time I had really gone for it large style. When we got up to the other end of Rawmarsh and ventured into the Trades and Labour working men's club, we were well and truly pissed. Our Paul, Glen and the wives were in there: their faces a bloody picture when they saw their arrogant little punk brother walk into the place. I wasn't zipped up and was wearing straight leg black trousers, a button-down shirt and a black thin-lapelled blazer and my hair was short and neat. I suppose this was still enough to embarrass my elder relatives, especially when you took a look around and saw all of the out of control sideburns and Kev Keegan poodle hair do's matched with flares and drooping shirt collars. "Oh, bleedin' hell, look what's come in, Glen... the punk!!!" I lip read our Paul say. Before long, me and Clarkey were beaming with immature drunken pride as bloke after bloke bought us pints; obviously thinking it was worth it to see how many we could down. Like an idiot, I necked down every single one of them and even managed some shots of Rum and Whiskey to chase 'em down. The last thing I saw was a bloke I couldn't stand stood at the other end of the bar laughing at me, while the sounds echoing all around the smoke-infested function room almost made me throw up there and then. A waistcoat-adorned crooner who looked like a throwback from a Carry on Abroad club act who had failed the audition for

'New Faces' was screeching out 'ooh ooh ooh Delilah der der der dum.'

Following a night puking up into a bucket, I got up that Christmas morning feeling like an alien from a long forgotten dying planet: nothing like I had ever felt like so far on every other Christmas day past. Gone was the kid's excitement or even the dull anticipation of wondering what colour of socks I had been bought. I was dead, but breathing... only just, though!!!

Our Glen came to our house just before mid-day and took me back to my previous night's entertainment hole for a few Christmas day beers. Cheers!!! I stood at the bar, in my lime-green ever-growing Mohair jumper that my Mother had made me a couple of years before... the contrast of its garish colour to my pasty white-faced ghost chops standing out to all and sundry. A zombie-looking kid surrounded by working class proper drinking men. As our Glen got the beers in, my head dropped to the bar and I fell asleep for over five minutes, eventually raising my head to take a sip of the Tuborg lager I had in front of me. Hair of the dog, they say? Bloody hell... it would take the whole fur of Crufts Dog show to reinvigorate me, feeling as I did. That night, Clarkey came around and we tried to revive ourselves to the sound of Kim Wilde's first LP. It would have taken my pop fantasy Kim herself in the room in person to revive me. Even the sounds of The Clash failed on that occasion. By Boxing Day I was beginning to feel almost human: my 2-day beer belly dissipating and I was feeling almost human enough to think about going to a few Christmas parties and indulging in a few more liquid lunches and suppers! Oh go on then!

I celebrated end of the year of 1981 by phoning my girlfriend Sarah up: it had only taken me around four months to make the journey to the phone box at the bottom of Walsh's hill. I had been living a life of mates and never-ending laughs to an obsessive and alternative soundtrack of music and, shamefully, had not reserved even 10 minutes to even bother ringing her up.

Sarah had been my dream come true and I had been infatuated by her. We had experienced some great times together earlier in the year, but foolishly I had cast her into the back of my mind as I opted for spending time with my mates. The ideology being to make the most of what time we had before we all went our separate ways onto the humdrum path of adulthood's signed and sealed future; I could always pick up with Sarah where we had left off in a few weeks was the foolish and selfish reasoning. Those weeks kept flying by and it was late 81 by the time I decided to make a put and ring her up. When she answered the phone, after only a few rings, to hear her voice again was as if it had only been yesterday since we were together. The buzz came flooding back. I had decided, foolishly expecting no obstacles in my way, to renew our relationship and take up where we had left off. I can't recall our exact words, but suffice to say, this was not going to happen. She had given up on me, believing I didn't care, and who could blame her. The fact is, I did care, but I was sixteen years old, daft, irresponsible and inconsiderate and had failed to stop for a moment and think about it all. We had a bit of a catch up and we were still nice with each other, but soon the call ended and we said our goodbyes. I saw Sarah a few times in and around town during the next year or so. We would always say hello and I still detected a distinct spark between us. As we saw each other everything seemed just right. I could sense her joy at seeing me too and I felt the nervous flutter in my stomach as I caught sight of her and when she looked at me and spoke with her soft and sultry voice. We always spent five or ten minutes talking and then said our goodbyes. I rang her up one final time in some last ditch desperate hope of us getting back together. She answered the phone again and it was great to hear her speak once more. This time, though, she was truly wondering why I had phoned her and before I had any chance of saying anything worthwhile she announced that she was engaged to be married. I acted the brave soul and surprised her by saying that I was really glad to hear that (blatantly lying through my teeth) and wished her all the best... I truly hoped that she would be really happy. I said a goodbye to Sarah for the very last time that bleak and wet winter night in that freezing cold traditional red telephone box. We never saw or spoke to each other again!

Christmas 81 was the season of the aptly-titled 'Don't You Want Me' by Sheffield's very own Human League. Everywhere you went, you were met by the song: from the number one spot on Top of the Pops to the crappy little transistor radio in the Chuck Wagon shop came the words, "You were working as a waiter in a cocktail bar when I met you." With their huge selling album 'Dare', the Human League seemed to take on the whole world and helped, in no small way, to put the steel city firmly on the musical map of the world. ABC with their 'Lexicon of Love', gold suits and new 80's glitz were soon to follow. A brother of a mate of mine played trumpet (or was it saxophone) on some early ABC songs. He was doing fine and having a good old party for himself –

getting the odd session work here and there - until the day he decided to hold up a post office and got himself thrown out of Dodge and into jail! A really nice hombre, he was too!

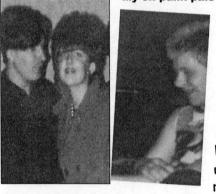

My ex punk pals Pete and Tracy and hard-core punk Barney Rubble

When I had recovered from my Christmas Eve bender it was then a time of new parties, including some that we weren't even invited to. One party saw Barney banging at the window and when a girl came to the window with her tough boyfriend at her side, Barney said "Let us in, I want to shag your girlfriend." Needless to say, we didn't get into that one. We had to run as fast as we could, slipping all over on the glass ice that had settled from the (almost) white Christmas we had just had. We went to all night stop over parties, drunk ourselves sober and listened to heaps of punk, Soul, Electro, Ska and Mod records, me getting involved in long conversation with some of the local Mods we knew and trying to convince them that Mod and punk had much in common - I was even wearing proper skinhead red braces and tartan-lined Harrington and Jam shoes to prove it. At another all-nighter (New Year's Eve this time), a good mate of mine went psychotic and pulled a knife on me for some unknown reason. Cider must not have agreed with him. On the way home in the early hours, he couldn't apologise enough, but I found it hard to take in and accept. At another party, not long afterwards I got another knife pulled on me (again by a so-called mate and this time the weapon being a huge kitchen knife) merely for me bringing a girl back to his house who he objected to. What was it with my mates and wanting to stick a blade in me? Had they been watching too many 1981 video nasty slasher films or what? As the end credits to Sundays' traditional late-night showing of the Phil Silvers show came to a finale, signalling the end of the weekend, then one other thing was clear, as 1981 also shut down, my circle of friends and associates certainly needed a healthy and immediate refresh!

Chapter three

Do You Believe in 1982?

Who you looking at? Spring1982

1982... out with the old, in with the new! Well, you would have thought it was still the blinking 1970's in our house. Our living room walls were still decked out with classic 70's wall panelling, adorned with plenty of left over brass intact: but not quite as brassified as days gone by it has to be said. Could they ever be? There were no signs yet of 1980's modern gimmickry such as a remote controlled telly or a Hi/Fi stack set up nor a modern freezer or contemporary washer either. We had a settee that defied fire regulations and amazingly didn't ignite a towering inferno with its numerous fag burns from mates who had missed the ash tray. We still had no house phone or central heating and the good old dependable old-fashioned coal fire was our main source of heat. In short, the 80's had arrived but times were still tough for us and many others. No sign of affluence and Thatcherite-inverted snobbery in our house I can tell thee!!! Did I believe in 1982? Well I wasn't quite sure yet!

We used to sneer at those few that started to buy their houses, but in hindsight who could have blamed them. In 1982 round our neck of the woods it was still quite relatively unheard of to actually own your own house. Soon that would all change when the Iron Battle-axe took it upon herself to encourage a nation of working class council tenants to start buying their homes. Nothing to lose was the train of thought. Me..? I still had no idea what a mortgage actually was. Wasn't it summat to do with getting divorced? Mortgages and insurance policies go together in a package for grownups with responsibilities, surely! Certainly of no interest whatsoever to yours truly in any case!

Sometimes blokes in dodgy 'Shine on Harvey Moon' throwback suits and spouting persuasive policies would knock at our door on Friday evenings while I was trying to watch The Munster's, to ask us if we wanted to sign up for a new insurance policy! Fools!!! Umm or was that us? Mum fell for 'em every time. My only connection to the tweed suit pipe-smoking world of official Insurance salesmen and all those confusing words they accumulated like endowment (something to do with treating dead bodies?), was when I also fell for the con and signed my name up to be insured. Insured? I was only bloody seventeen! It was a standing joke with my Mum. She would say to the insurance man, one of whom I had nicknamed Elijah, "Listen luv, I wouldn't bother setting our Tony on with any of your policies, he will be asking to draw it out in less than a month." Rest assured a few months would pass and I would be skint and asking how much I could draw out. Not even the prospect of being told that I would only get £7 out of the £33 I had paid into the policy would deter me. OK, what time is Elijah due round then?

When the unscrupulous insurance-man eventually turned up it wouldn't be the dog he had to worry about. It was our Tommy he had to be wary of. "He's a lovely cat, isn't he?" ('Lying sod... he's the ugliest cat on this planet and you know it', I would be thinking). If the man in tweed was foolish enough to invite that lovely little cat onto his knee while he counted my cash out and sorted the form out for me to sign... then he was in for trouble! Our Tommy loved to be fussed (when only he decided that is) and would relish a nice cosy lay on your lap session: the only trouble is you were NOT allowed to pick him up and put him back down. He was there to stay, purring like mad with drooling puffed-out chops, contentment and giant explosive whiskers protruding with Top Cat authenticity. The victims Tommy has claimed when they decided to stand up and gently lift him down are immeasurable. The noise and actions would be so quick that the victim would hardly know what had hit them. In slow motion you would see a smiling gentle-natured potential cat lover being slaughtered by paws and claws scratching a new six-way motorway up their arms with sabre-teeth plunging firmly into the designated area chosen fit for a nasty flesh wound. The victim's smile and relaxed composure now being replaced with a distraught, traumatised nervous wreck of a disposition and a feline distrusting defence nature is born! "That's for ripping me off, Elijah... you bugger," I would quietly think with revengeful glee! Poor old Sheena would be sat trembling in the corner, teeth clattering together with fear, her days of havoc and anarchy long dissipated and belonging to her past.

While Sheena the punk rocker dog was mellowing, Tommy the crazy punk cat was well in his stride: taking on any animal that came his way. My mates would laugh in disbelief when I told them how he looked after our dog; that is until they saw it with their own eyes. A vagrant dog passing through the town, paws and nashers unchecked at the Sheriffs office, would have a pop at our Sheena sat minding her own business at the front gate. In no time at all, Tommy would appear and chase the canine enemy all the way down the street. God help any brave (and unwise) dog that ever turned around to confront 'the black panther from beneath the hedgerow'. There were rumours in Dog circles that some did try but never lived to yap (or wag) the tale or tail any further!

As our serial killing cat, Tommy strolled cockily up our ever-changing street - the Warren Avenue of my childhood - he would have passed scenes of changing life in motion. Old fellas nearing retirement coming home from their long shifts at factories, pits or the steel works, empty snap tins hanging by worn out straps over their shoulders and flat caps still proudly worn following decades of wind, sleet, snow, war, nagging wives and fag ash... the classic working class street man earning the bread to put on the table! It was almost coming to an end, though, now: this generation of men and women; the ones who had either served through or at least experienced the war years. Watching the dwindling exodus of traditional working men slowly ebbing away, it reminded me of those old John Ford Westerns and the symbolism of the American Indian's final pages of history. Our last bastions of Post-War year veterans were being prepared to be put out to graze on their pitiful pensions dished out from the despised Tory government's grinning political vultures. Those conceited card sharp-cheating outlaws nursing a hatred for the working class whilst sat in cigar smoke-filled board rooms and MP Chambers right down there past the red river and across the border in Thatcher land!

In early 82, as the old world began to make way for a new one and shadows of the 1970's began to very slowly fade away, I was still getting over demolishing my relationship with the first lass I had truly cared about yet carelessly discarded. I had to face facts; Sarah was history and so the search for a replacement began. A Futurist lass around the corner fancied me so we would meet up and go for snogging sessions in the park and nights of lust in our front room to a soundtrack of The Jam, Ultravox!, Kraftwerk and Soft Cell. She eventually gave up on me, complaining that I was too passionate for her: I suppose there were just far too many teenage hormones bursting out of my bleached Levi jeans to keep under complete control! It was fun while it lasted though and every now and again we would rekindle those days for one-offs.

Then there was the gang of lasses me and the lads hung out with, who still freaked out when we turned out the lights for a nice and cosy groping session. What was it about us lads back then? As soon as we thought we were in with a lass, we would lean over and turn out the lights, scaring the hell out of lasses who imagined that they had hitched up with a creature of the night vampire. One lovely lass got so fed up of coming round and me turning out the light that she once brought a blinkin' torch around! I was having a bloody lovely time with one little beauty I was snogging during one of these 'Lights out, grope the nearest' sessions until it all went fruit cocktail shaped as a pal of mine laid unrepeatable insults in the direction of one of the lasses within our love nest. My final attempt at some proper dating during those late days of 81 and early 82 was with yet another futurist girl in a mac and a lovely wonky fringe. The enticing sounds of Ultravox!'s 'Systems of Romance' LP and a promise to pay to take her to see The Mobiles - then in the charts with 'Drowning in Berlin' - for no financial fee, wasn't enough to swoon her... so it was back to that other great love of my life... (Music) for the time being!

Musically, 1982 had started well with some great gigs including a superb Theatre of Hate date at Sheffield Polytechnic jam-packed with a frantic crowd of Harrow Punkabillys and a scattering of curious students and local punk kids. This was the future for music for a few brief and exciting weeks!!!

In March I went along to see my faves The Jam at the Top Rank for two nights running, and as a double treat, support was by Irish punks, Rudi. It had been two years since I had last seen The Jam and they had reached their musical peak and height of popularity. Weller was all over the music papers almost every week, spouting his ever-more prevalent political views and love of Soul music. This was a different Jam to the punk-energised young 3-piece that had set me on my new wave journey a few years ago, but they still had that on-going fire and power and meant a lot more to me than all of those 1982 pop stars or the moaning and groaning punk rock bands that still remained wallowing in their rejection and pleading for 10p tips and attention.

The Jam for their 4th visit to the Top Rank signed autographs outside the venue that afternoon and, as was to be expected, was amazing on both nights. My Mod mate, Ricky (who had a Moped instead of a scooter, and often fell off it when he wasn't getting chased by the local skinheads) joined up with me and Barney Rubble. When The Jam came on with 'Strange Town' the whole place erupted into one massive pogoing mass. From 'Down in the Tube Station at Midnight' to 'Town Called Malice' and every other Jam classic spread across two nights, along with their new LP 'The Gift' (Soul ballad 'Ghosts' and 'Carnation' with its crafty lyrics and Foxton's heart-wrenching bass line being 2 highlights of the gig), this was pure Jam heaven, proving that music was still exciting and subsequently life felt just great. Little did we know, at the time, that one of our favourite band's days was becoming increasingly numbered?

By this time, I was expanding my musical horizons like nobody's business yet again. post-punk, Reggae, Ska and 70's glam were now joined with the sounds of Soul - helped along when my mate's lovely auburn-haired Mod girl left her 'Supremes a Go-Go' LP behind when she went off to the fair in the park. Uncharacteristically, the year before had seen me stretch my ears to tune into a set of Bob Dylan LP's that I had borrowed off our new next-door neighbour, Graham, a festival goer who aspired to learn to play the guitar. Now the Dylan LP's were being replaced by scores of classic sixties Soul as I began collecting as much of the back catalogue of the Tamla, Stax and Atlantic labels as I could and nurtured a fondness for Soul icons such as Curtis Mayfield, Wilson Pickett and Bobby Bland. I became intoxicated with the true sounds of Mod along with 60's bands like The Who, Small Faces, The Kinks Creation, Spencer Davis Group, Yardbirds and of course The Beatles (especially 'Revolver') and these would lead me deeper into the world of obscure Soul and early R&B and the world of being a Mod!

Now what was being a Mod all about to me... the punk kid? Well, Mod means lots of different things to lots of different people, and that's maybe part of its appeal, but for me (to begin with) it was all a reaction against punk, or more to the point, what punk had become! It was about looking smart, adding detail to clothes and creating a new identity: a natural extension of my inner punk self. The side of Mod I was interested in wasn't the 79 Mod revival that I had briefly and half-heartedly embraced during the spring of 1979, though some of that was good.

No... it was all about Soul and the influence of Soul and the original 60's bands that had utilised it in their sound. Also, quite importantly, like punk, Mod was a celebration of being young and was anti-adult. Suits me fine then!

Mod's sensibilities celebrate consumerism and I was now spending all of my cash on clothes and records. The existing Chelsea boots, 3 button blazers, Harrington jackets joined a new selection of button down shirts, polo shirts, leather box jackets and paisley cravats and scarves from the charity shop! My days of dying my hair were now done and dusted forever too as I went for a short Mod crop courtesy of Vic the barber which finally got rid of any previous colour left-overs. My previous Joe Strummer epileptic-fit guitar playing-copying stance was now replaced by Pete Townshend windmills, knocking my Airfix HMS Hood and Bismarck models off their shelves and all over the bedroom in the process. I did paint my guitar black with Humbrol model paint to make up for it, though!

Maybe it was the frustrating schizophrenia of trying to appease myself with the dual loves of punk's ideals with the ever-increasing love of a music that had supposedly had its great hey-day before I was even born and been confusingly revived only quite recently... maybe that's what led to me awaken one night to the sight of my wardrobe shaking like mad and the sounds of an enormous roar omitting from it? I really don't know. Had I imagined it? I was wide awake, though, as I saw and experienced it and I could not move, or even twitch a muscle. The phenomena engulfed me and scared the hell out of me! Umm... was this the first signs of mental disturbance due to an unhealthy (in adult eyes) obsession with music and its meaning? My Mum always said "Those Sounds mags will drive you bonkers, Tony". Was it the side effects of those poppers that a local lass I knew had persuaded me to take that served only to inflict a banging headache upon me? Or maybe it was purely and simply some kind of nasty poltergeist that loved 1950's antique home furnishing and scaring young punk kids with over-active imaginations? Maybe I will never know? The question is... do you think I am mad? OK, forget that question!

Talking of unknown activity, one evening after me and Clarkey had just wound down a night of playing records in my front room, a video nasty maniac tried to break our door down, scaring the hell out of us both. We never found out who it was either. We had heard of stories of loony's with knives attacking kids out on their own after dark. Maybe this was the very same loony's? No way did we dare to wander the streets at midnight to find out while the shadow of Jason Voorhees was knocking about. Video Nasty's were all the rage back then and we didn't want to star in one of them! Creepy goings on continued occasionally into the decade, the most notable being when my guitar (placed carefully on its stand) in our very cold little bedroom, began to pluck its strings all by itself. It gave a performance every so often, and a number of people can testify to its guitar solo renditions of the theme from Psycho.

Clarkey (Left) was Paul Clarke (my old school-days punk pal) and we were proper good mates. I had first met him on going up to the Comp back in 1976, but it wasn't until the summer of 1978 when I saw him pass me by in the school corridor with a copy of The Jam's latest single 'David Watts' in his hand that I showed any real interest in being proper mates with him.

Paul was the same age as me. He lived not too far away and we would meet up almost on a daily basis. He was a great laugh and maybe I was a bit of a bad influence on him at times whilst dragging him away from his first musical love of Heavy Rock. He studied fairly well at school and was lucky enough to get himself a job on leaving school. By 82, as well as having a crush on one half of the original Cagney and Lacey, he was working on a building site up Sheffield for some firm and also hoping to learn to play bass guitar (he was briefly a member of one of my crap punk bands, maybe that ruined his dreams?). Clarkey may have been working and joining in with the big blokes' world, but he was still up for a laugh. On one occasion I arranged to meet him round at the local Thorogate shops. As I waited for him across the road from the bus stop, the bus I was expecting him to get off sailed straight past. On searching for a glimpse of him getting off, I saw that he was sat at the back of the bus with a paper bag over his head with the eyes and nose cut out, just like The Damned had on their 'Neat, Neat, Neat' single. As the bus sped by, he was sat upright, bag on head and stretching his neck out as far as he could whilst shaking his head from side to side. I was laughing my head off but God only knows what the bingo-heading blue rinse pensioners on the bus were thinking, let alone the bus driver?

Another time, back in our school days, I had gotten bored (as usual) during a Metalwork lesson and on popping a strawberry bon bon in my mouth I stood next to Clarkey. The sucked and shrunken bon bon was nestled neatly inside the top of my lip resting just below the right of my nose. Clarkey looked around and said "What's tha up to now, hey up what's that in yer mouth?" I decided to have him on and said "It's a bunion." "Gi oer wi yer, its nowt like that," he replied. "I am telling thee it's a bunion kid, it's what they call a chunnion... a cross between a bunion and a chapped lip," I managed to explain without laughing. Clarkey's face changed from disbelief to belief, much to my own disbelief. "He's fallen for it," I was thinking. The next minute a daft kid with steamed up glasses (who we called the steamy bar kid) walked past and says "Give us another one of them spogs, Beesley." My cover blown, I could now laugh and as I did I spat the saliva-coated bon bon over into the red hot furnace where it sizzled like mad and caught (the teacher) Bentneck Balford's attention. Clarkey was in stitches laughing at my daft story and that he had believed it too. Then, a serious lad we laughed at for being serious says "Sir, look what Beesley and Clarkey are doing, they are eating sweets in class again Sir." Oh yeah nice one, can't have a bunion in yer gob in peace nowadays.

Clarkey was always getting belted back in the punk days. He got smacked all over the place, usually by some drunken straight who took offence at him laughing at something I had said. He got knocked over the bus shelter in Rotherham bus-station by a drunken nutter, punched in the nose by Pond Street thugs after coming out of a Damned concert, shoved into Our Price record shop window on the Moor by wannabee skinheads and knocked the hell out of at the summer 1982 fair in Rosehill Park by local toughs. It was all part of how things went, Clarkey got belted now and again and that was that. It never deterred him one bit, in fact he grew to expect it and often saw it coming... "Oh heck, I am gonna get belted again here," he would whisper and rest assured someone would appear and deliver the goods!

By around this period, Clarkey had started to gradually retreat back into his Rock roots. We went to see the new super group Lords of the New Church at the Limit club and the following year (with pal, John Harrison) at the Leadmill- where me and John tried, but failed, to impress two sober lasses with our un-sober chat up lines. Later on, we went to see Hanoi Rocks at Sheffield Dingwalls. Clarkey went full on and it wasn't long before he was going to see new Glam merchants such as Motley Crue and later developing a taste for a new band called Guns and Roses. He also grew his hair to his longer pre-punk style. We soon became polar opposites in musical tastes and fickle as teenagers are, we simply could not share each other's musical landscapes and slowly grew apart. Except for bumping into each other in the local drinking dens and catching up on things, laughing at life and ourselves, we rarely saw each other afterwards but we shared some memorable times together.

1982 was the year of the Falklands War and all of that conflict's flag waving
and Thatcherist Imperialistic rhetoric. Personally I was never quite sure what I
felt about the politics of that war, one that saw a brave local lad from Eastwood
- Sgt McKay - lead a fatal charge against an Argie machine gun post and
subsequently awarded a posthumous VC. I know it was trendy at the time to be
anti-war and opposed to what was going off over on that small little heard of
island. Me and the lads I worked with at the time were just glad that we didn't
get called up to go. What bloody use would we have been, anyway? Stood
pointing and laughing at the Argies and making names up for 'em while shot
and shell went whizzing by. 'Arrest those privates, Brigadier!' There was
another on-going war continuing too: with the IRA. A lad I had gone to school
with in the juniors tragically lost his brother, Keith John Powell, in the Regents
Park IRA bombings in London. I really cannot stand terrorism! In July, an
intruder called Michael Fagan sat on the Queen's bed: the year before I had
stated to a few of my mates that someone was going to break into Buckingham
Palace in the near future. The wonders of teenage intuition!

Back on the home-front, the summer of 82 saw me and my mates as daft as
ever and trying to avoid having to grow up and give in to the pressure to get
out and get a proper life-long job, not that there was many to chase. I would
arrive at the careers office to see the careers officer, I mean c'mon... an
officer? What was that all about? Did they think we were bloody squaddies or
something? Anyway they knew me well and my objections to YTS schemes were
written in bold black pen straight across my file. She also knew that I was, in
her eyes (her being a little Miss Moffatt crumply cardigan bore) an awkward
sod with a different shade of hair colour (and often style) on every visit. The
nearest these kind of stuffed up know-alls had seen to a rebel was the kids on
'Murphy's Mob' on the bloody Telly. It must have confused 'em no end (as my
image evolved) to see me arrive in a button down shirt and skinny black tie.
Most importantly, they knew damn well that most prospective employers
wouldn't even give me a look in as regards to full time employment within their
respectable establishments; such were the prejudices of the era!

As a result, my early years of post-school employment consisted of a series of dead-end jobs (some not lasting longer than a day or two), jobs on the side, temporary casual ones and non-YTS training schemes interspersed with chunks of signing on at the rock n' roll office up at the top of San Francisco hill as my mate, John called it: most people would know it simply as Ship Hill! To use the name of a Talking Heads song, I was on a road to nowhere. But, I did not care; I had youth on my CV and that must count for something?

New Pop cast its sickly seed all over 1982: Howard Jones, Yazoo (actually not so bad), Culture Club (decent singles but as conservative as Thatcher herself), the despicable Royal family of Duran Duran, Spandau Ballet, the sickly sweet synth/pop of the Midge Ure-led and John Foxx-vacated Ultravox and a whole plush carpet of giggling new pop stars and sickly egotists snorting cocaine and playing the part of a new pop aristocracy. How could the musical climate have gone downhill so quickly? But none of that was as annoyingly brain magnetic as Tight Fight's 'The Lion Sleeps Tonight' or the laughable 'Eye of the Tiger' by Survivor, which inadvertently gave club land a drunken crowd pleaser for decades to come. Even Soul-Rebel, Kevin Rowland and his Dexy's gang embraced the Top of the Pops club with their 1982 anthem 'Come on Eileen' - a future wedding do anthem for my Mum. Kevin was so popular that year that he dropped in to Sheffield (with Dollar for company) to open the brand new HMV store on the Moor, the city's first HMV. The main consolation prizes of 1982 were The Clash who presented us their new troubled and flawed 'Combat Rock', The Damned coming up trumps and smelling of 'Strawberries' and The Jam giving us Paul Weller's new 'Gift' of punk-infused Soul music. Is this the bloody lot? How could so much change in two years? Blame the Blitz kids, they started it all! Is this going to be the way forward for the 1980's?

As a nation of telly addicts tuned into earthy drama Alan Bleasdale's 'The Boys from the Black stuff' which brought the social politics of the un-working man of the Thatcher years to the TV for the first time and we said farewell to our 70's faves, 'The Goodies' and 'It's a Knockout', I was preparing for my next musical venture, if only within my head. While Mum laughed along with 'Just Good Friends' and our Paul chuckled to Del Boy's TV antics even the emergence of The Young Ones and Tim Roth's mesmerising out of control right-wing skinhead performance in 'Made in Britain' could do nothing to lure me back into the square box in the corner land. Music was still my life and hopefully soon, I would be able to project my passion for it via performing in a band.

There were no good old fashioned family get-together bonfires in our back garden that year. I had forgotten to pay my subs into family affairs during recent years and was effectively an outcast, being invited only to the most trivial family occasions. Plus, me and our Paul had engaged upon one of our

intermediate fall outs after a drunken New Year's Eve scrap and tussle.

I still loved my family, though; you only get one in your life so you have to live and let live and make the best of each other. But, during those times, we were light years apart and the days of our 1970's family communal spirit and all being in it together were a thing of the past, well as far as me being a part of it anyway. I suppose I appeared strange and uncompromising to most family members

and we just couldn't relate to each other's ways. We simply did not share any of the same interests within our lives anymore at all. Sadly as a result, I drifted apart away from them more and more: nobody's exact fault, I suppose.

By 1982, our pal, Barney had veered into a new hybrid of punk v Mod v proto-Goth v owt else that appeared offensive to public taste. One day he called for me wearing a tartan kilt, a woman's wig (I never dared to ask where he had got it from?) and a kid's pedal car wrapped around his waist. When I answered the door, he gave me a soundtrack of "Vroom, Vroom, Vroom." On the way to the shop he caught sight of the Lollypop woman and went and stole her lollypop stick off her and ran up the street with her chasing him. What a sight he looked! We laughed non-stop all the way to the park. Barney managed to outrage in new ways each time we met. He created walking anarchy and belly-laughing insanity wherever he went. And to think, up until me and my mates had got our hands on him a couple of years previously, he was an everyday school swot-styled kid who handed his homework in on time and never got into any trouble. What crazy monster had we created?

Old 80's Rotherham

A Golden Wonder van passes the old corner paper shop where present-day Boots now stands. Below: a busy early 80's High Street

Barney not being fazed by anything; sending him to the chemist for some Johnnies would only cost a bag of Nibbets for him to munch on in return. If the chemist wasn't looking they cost even less too! My bravery for condom-obtaining stretched as far as the Marples' toilets on an afternoon and even that brought a certain degree of embarrassment when old blokes in flat caps sat reading the racing page in the Daily express would be nudging each other, pointing and laughing after just seeing me struggling to turn round the knob on the blasted machine in the bog. What was it back in those days with Johnny machines? Why did they have such nasty uncompromising and tormenting handles like Panzer tank wheels, almost aware of your desperate struggle?

We went through a period of drinking in local boozing holes: some of those that would not let us in during the previous year had now let their guard down a little. Of course it wouldn't take long before we would be asked to leave when we had Barney in tow. One day, Barney called for me with a freshly-shaved Mohawk haircut and I just knew that we hadn't a hope in hell's chance of getting served in the local wheel tappers drinking joints. Barney decided, thereafter, to relocate his drinking sessions to the Charter Arms in Rotherham town centre, a pub that welcomed all kinds of cult-led desperadoes, rebels, individuals, punks, new romantics, proto-Goths, Ghouls and alternative misfits. It really was an open-house to the disenchanted and left of centre fashionistas. I ventured there quite a few times too, but never fully joined in spiritually with the apocalyptic Mad Max gang of alternative extras. I couldn't decide who to bloody sit with - or which tribe I belonged with - half the time for a start!

"The revolutions over and we've got to move on – dance to a new rhythm and try another song..... You're all carbon copies, you're all carbon copies."
Lyrics from the song 'Rearrange' (Beesley – 1982)

The second year of the decade would be at an end soon and what an inconclusive one it had been so far. One of my older mates got his bird in the Yorkshire pudding club, my guitar playing was still annoying the neighbours of nearby streets and beyond and my lyrics were ridiculing the carbon copy tribes of punk whilst mates dispersed as we all did our own individual thing. I really couldn't understand why, but I felt a sudden surge of optimism running through my skinny armed veins, rushing along and kissing the inner voices of my self-belief and increasing power of self-determination.

**Circles Records (around the corner from the old Advertiser office)
1982: The Jam's final single poster can be seen in the window**

The year also signalled the end of my treasured band, The Jam. The situation within the Jam camp had not been well since the summer, but only Weller knew it. When it was announced that they were to split towards the end of the year, I felt sad, angry but strangely relieved. I was a massive Jam fan. They had been the main catalyst for my succumbing to punk back in 1977 and I had followed them ever since. But... they were in danger of potentially representing everything that Weller detested in Rock music... ultimately on the well-trodden road to becoming a dinosaur-sized band of 'Madison Square Gardens' proportion. Bravely Weller decided to split and move on and in doing so he left us a legacy of music few have since met, let alone surpassed. But most of all, The Jam left us with a time capsule of memories and experiences that were now history and could never be tarnished by the trappings of fame, mass-adulation and a contradiction of ideals. The Jam meant so much more than that... and still do! I said my personal goodbyes to The Jam whilst watching their new channel 4-launched Tube performance.

It was Bonfire Night and to celebrate the occasion I compiled a C-90 of some of my fave Jam tracks and played it before the momentous TV event. When Weller and co launched into 'The Modern World' the goose bumps were out in full force and it really felt like the end of an era. Switching the telly off as the credits came up for that very first edition of The Tube, I got myself ready to pop over to next door's Bonny celebrations where no-one seemed in the least bit interested in hearing me bang on about the loss of one of the most important bands in music's history. I couldn't even persuade anyone to stick my carefully created Jam tape on to shut me up either.

Paul Weller, 1982: copyright of Pete Skidmore

Around the time of The Jam calling it a day, my dreams of being a musician and songwriter were also briefly tasted. The tantalising thrill of knowing I had learnt a few basic guitar chords and could write a very basic three chord song was a huge step forward. Yet, the reality was less enticing. The bedroom band of mine, Voxx, which we did nothing but create a cataphony-like wall of undecipherable noise (like the Fire Engines covering Discharge after swallowing up a discordant punk version of Chic on speed) survived a few months only.

Terminal Daze (my next loosely pieced together Wire and Subway Sect-influenced band) never did a sod despite some new songs, practice sessions upstairs at the Queen's Hotel pub and the addition of a home-made fuzz box created and designed by my good pal, Julian Jones. I was right back to square one... all on my own, waiting for some like-minded kid to come along and share my vision for the future: some kind of a musical utopia within a journey of individual creativity. Kick down the doors, give us a chance... we wanna be heard. We have something worthwhile to say!!! The only problem was WE was merely I and no one seemed to be bloody listening! OK let's have a re-think... yet again!

Pretty soon I would very rarely see my punk pal, Barney, except for rare gig experiences together: he eventually disappeared for almost eternity into a punk rock time tunnel, or so it seemed. Me and Gaz Stables remained in touch; helped by the fact that we still lived on the same block as each other and always held on to our off-the-wall sense of humour. He would keep me updated on all things punk and manage to drag me along to concerts by Stiff Little Fingers and UK Subs, at which I stood vacant, bored and apathetic... a world of difference to the crazy and excitable pogoing kid of a year or two ago. As for my old mates, Andy and Pete; although we never fell out at all, we were completely off our social radars, rarely crossing each other's paths again. In 1982 local Mod face, Zal (Steve Downing) - an older lad who I had always

Kept an eye on for fashion tips (from punk to 2-tone and beyond) as he was either strolling cockily past (oozing of stylish Weller cool) or speeding by on his Vespa P200E scooter, was involved in a nasty car crash. Whilst Heaven 17's 'Crushed by the Wheels of Industry' played along on their car tape player, Zal (Bottom of photo below) and his mate's lives were changed forever by the car accident. Thankfully he survived but not without serious life-long damage to his legs. One friend in the car did not survive!

Meanwhile as mates of mine fell by the wayside a lad who I had come across numerous times via my travels through school and punk would soon be joining me on a brand new journey. Before the year was out, myself and this sharp-dressed young Mod lad would be creating something we had both dreamed about for what had seemed like eternity.

In anticipation of something good coming together, I retreated and spent hours practising on the guitar to Clash, Kinks and Who songs, dreaming of one day being able to play in a real band of my own! Absorbing (as always) the guitar style and pose of Weller and the attack of Townshend and Mick Jones, I was desperately aching to play in front of a live audience. I had a raw soul vision and it was nothing like Lionel Richie's piss-weak lazy Sunday morning version or Luther Vandross's slick tunes for the ladies: I was fired up, angry and had plenty to prove!

Now that The Jam were gone (soon to be followed by The Clash), it was also time for me to move on: I sold my signed Jam ticket for three quid to go to the pub and gave away all of my Jam cuttings, badges and memorabilia, but faithfully kept a precious hold of all of their records. Despite my passion for The Jam and everything they stood for, I needed to temporarily shed much of my past to move forward into the future. The question being... did I believe in 1982?

Chapter four

A blurred Soul Vision!

In late 1982, I had no job, no money, no girlfriend (except for a lass that would pop round for some heavy petting sessions every now and again)... at least two of my mates had pulled knives on me and I had the status of undesirable alien with almost every member of my family. My D.I.Y fanzine 'Ghetto' had amounted to just the one issue and accumulated exactly 8 copies hot from the printing press of Rotherham library's' A4 photo-copying facility and were now gathering dust above the pile of yellowing Sounds and NME's in the hall, which I often daren't go near if our Tommy was snuggled up on them. In a nut shell my guitar and life was temporarily out of tune!

What had happened to all of that school-leaver optimism, self-belief and youthful bravado of a mere year and a few months ago?

Away from the Numbers - Tony Beesley

To add to my interchangeable frustration and optimism, I held a profound realisation that my obsession and involvement with punk rock had amounted to very little: the original punk leaders and their anti-establishment rhetoric appeared to have mostly surrendered to the enemy and left many like myself feeling bitterly disappointed and living through a period of the Thatcher years in a state of confusion. Even Joe Strummer of The Clash ran off to Paris! The punk bands I had attempted to form myself; a series of non-musical naivety and atrocious noise with plenty of ideas but little platform or talents to create and support them had all failed too, our only achievements being a series of bedroom releases of pent-up energy blasting away our one chord rants to ourselves and a few mates, along with a lesson to myself in how NOT to write songs. I also hated the Top of the Pops club, the pretentious music press and was often well pissed off with my life in general. Perfect material for a future Smiths song then: Heaven knows I could have been miserable now, if I had tried just a little harder. It was autumn, 1982, I was 17 years old and all my plans had basically screwed up. Time for that positive life re-think I reckon!

Something positive did come along and that was my renewed friendship with local punk and Mod face around town, John Harrison, and our consequent determination to create a new punk and Mod-influenced band. We met again through a mutual punk pal, Bryan Bell, over a few pints up at the local pub and before you knew it we were obsessed with the idea of creating music together and began writing our own teenage angst-ridden, politically-saturated diatribes set to some rudimentary tunes and basic chords. Turn up that dial!

To begin with, though, we couldn't manage to project our songs any further than our front room complete with a microphone popping out of a hanging plant pot, lyrics and chords written on sheets of paper stuck together with blu tac to the wall, people walking past and peering in and laughing at us. Well punk was supposed to be all about 'Do it yourself', wasn't it! One day, however … we determined (during a never-ending series of into the early hours sessions of worldly plans, usually spent drinking home brew cider that we had cajoled off the next door neighbour) that we were going to get somewhere. This time next year we were going to be in the NME declaring our punk-realised vision to the whole world. 'This time next year, we are going to be someone. And that really would be a wonderful thing.'

My determination to learn how to play the guitar properly and write songs

was now even stronger: banging and thrashing away all hours at any
opportunity, it's a wonder it didn't drive Cissy Bon Bon next door completely
spare! I suppose her therapeutic salvation would have been her bread cake
baking sessions that were still on the go, as were my Mum's. At my side of the
wall, my initial Clash and Jam obsessive influences had now been joined by
generous helpings of classic 60's Mod bands and the uplifting vibes of
Northern Soul alongside dashings of Ska and Reggae. Me and John had a
vision, a dream with hugely-driven ambitions. Somewhere along the damned
way that very vision managed to become pretty well disjointed and out of
control. Of course we didn't yet know this. We were only just starting out on
our musical adventure and blurred soul vision!

John Harrison was the young Leeds fan who chased
me all over Rawmarsh for liking Rotherham Utd back in
the mid 70's. He was two years older than me and had a
few older brothers and a sister. I knew one of 'em –
Richard (also known as Smiler) from us knocking about
playing footie on the school field and I knew John on
nodding terms and us passing each other in the
newsagent back in the mid 70's– him to collect his
Beano comic and me picking up my Warlord. We lived
close to each other, went to the same school and had
some of the same mates, so we came across each other
fairly regularly, especially during punk when we
ventured to gigs as part of the same gang and sampled under-age drinks in
city centre pubs. John was anti-authority; always wagging it from school,
smoked like a chimney, had been in some spots of bother with the cops and
had a great sense of humour. He was cynical, self-depreciating, cunning and a
bit dangerous, a right good pal for me and we got on well right from the start!

Motivated by punk (and his older brother, Jeff's involvement in it) in early
1977, John took to the sound (and look) of The Jam straight away. Like me, he
had his classic 70's shoulder-length hair cut to mirror his new persona and
the scene was set for his own punk rebellion. Also, like me, throughout all of
his Mod leanings, John was always a punk at heart. It was one of those things
in life that are just meant to be, me and John partnering up, as they used to
say in the old John Wayne Westerns, which John ritually despised.

Reasons to be in Control: 1982 to 1983

**Early Control rehearsals 1982 – 1983:
bottom left photo has the mic and lyric
sheets stuck to the wall in our front room at
no.10 Warren Avenue**

In that sense we were different, me and John. I loved Westerns and War Films
and he (the cynical realist) didn't... not one bit, but we matched up in far more
characteristic and important ways than those Sunday afternoon servings of
Stetsons, six guns and horse shit!

Now, John was just as anti-conformist and piss-taking as me and would rebel against himself given half the chance. Hilariously, he kidded a lad on that Led Zeppelin were to play an open-air concert in our local park and the kid turned up. He was a never-ending trick-up-his sleeve, ducking and diving chancer and simply hated being told what to do. John had some cool Mod gear, had good taste in women, a great sense of humour and had survived a bad trip on magic mushrooms and still read the Beano: We were in for an interesting journey then I reckoned!

John Harrison: left as a young lad in the mid 70's and years later reading the headlines (instead of the usual Beano)

Late 1982 and John was looking up from his bass guitar with an inquisitive expression. What was this new song I had written and been enthusing to him about? The previous night in the pub, I had been giving him a right old earache by going on and on about this new song I had written called 'Just for a Chance.' We would spend hours and all of our usual obligatory 3 quid's worth of beer in the local boozer endlessly chatting excitedly about our plans for world domination. Paul Weller had set the precedent and shown us the way and we were gonna be the anticipated new breed!!!

This new song 'Just for a Chance' was something special to me. It was a breakthrough. It had real proper chord changes and wasn't played at the usual fast speed. I had slowed things down since my Voxx non-musical speeding tickets and this was the result. The words were a typical of the time naïve prognosis of what I thought was a damn good rant against the futility of war, most notably the Terrorist tactics of the IRA and other Terrorist organisations which were always prevalent in the news at the time. Performing it for John on my unplugged guitar after a session at the pub, he was impressed and keen for us to work out a suitable bass line for him to play. 'Just for a Chance' was an apt song title as that was what we were after... a chance to get somewhere: to avoid the rat race and the prospects of the 9-5 grind: to break free and be noticed! As soon as we saw our chances we were gonna take them.

Around this time we were paying visits to the Rotherham Mod events at Clifton Hall and the Assembly Rooms, searching for a drummer and maybe a second guitarist and singer. We had some great nights but never once returned home with a fellow musician in tow.

That late autumn of 82 also saw me begin to attempt to learn how to play the guitar to such songs as 'All or Nothing' and 'Hey Girl' by the Small Faces and the Townshend-penned songs on the Who's 'My Generation' LP that Julian Jones had introduced me to. Each day, me and John could be seen practising in my Mum's cosy front room within our make-shift little rehearsal space banging out our ramshackle versions of 'Dancing in the Street', 'Heatwave', 'Sweet Soul Music', 'Jail Guitar Doors' by The Clash, The Jam's 'Billy Hunt', the Kink's 'You Really Got Me' and The Who's 'Much too Much' amongst others. If we reached or surpassed our expectations then we could retire at 9pm to watch Minder... if not it was time to sit and bloody sulk, have a re-think and then start all over again.

We had written our very first song together earlier that year, almost immediately after meeting up, a catchy little simplistic song called 'Reasons'. We would later laugh at that song writing attempt, but in hindsight it was a decent little debut song. By the onset of the dark nights (Chestnut weather I would warn John) we had a set of covers half covered and a sprinkling of our own crude but enthusiastic songs. 'Happy People' which we would perform at our first gig a couple of years later, 'Just For a Chance' and 'Shout' which was an up-tempo Soul shouter betraying my ever-increasing affliction towards Soul music.

'All Mod Cons' Jam LP-influenced collages me and John put together and my H/H Combo amp

My proudest song writing achievement came along not much later and was inspired by a girl I hung out with called Alison. One rainy night, Alison had called around appearing troubled and upset and in obvious need of a shoulder to lean on for a couple of hours. Me and Alison were good friends. We did have a bit of a thing for each other, a lot of it remaining unsaid and unacknowledged, but mostly we spent time together laughing, snogging, fondling and listening to music, be it round at her house or in our front room, or straggling through corn fields in torrential rain after midnight. This particular night, I listened to Alison's problems and after she had gone, I had my song writing Eureka moment. Alone in the house, I quickly scribbled the words down to a song I would call 'It's OK' alongside some simple major chords "It's OK, the things you say when you talk to me, it's alright, I understand the confused words you spoke last night," the lyrics went. The finished song, which I recorded with a microphone on my music centre on an old cassette and dated it November 1982, was short and very Jam-influenced. "Wow, I have accomplished something here," I thought. I kept playing the tape back and pinching myself into actually believing I had written a real proper song of some worth. My earlier songs had been honest and raw, this was passionate and real and my best one yet. The next night Alison came around and I decided to play it for her. I couldn't wait to test her response.

First I bravely went straight for the emotional pull at the risk of making a right pillock of myself. I told Alison that I had written a song for her... fully expecting either a fingers down the throat motion or a straight laugh in my face. I followed this up with "Here let me play it for you." I picked up my guitar, plugged it in and stuck the lyrics on top of the coffee table, then proceeding to sing and play the song all the way through for her. I never faltered once which was bloody amazing as I was nervous as hell. It was one of those moments in life when you just go for it and think 'oh well... sod it, what the hell.' Before she could comment, as soon as I finished the song, I pressed play on the tape section of the music centre and last night's recording of the song came on. We both sat and listened to it again, me looking away out of embarrassment. I mean, I had told her that the song was for her. It could have been a big no-no! When it was finished, my face glowing red with a sudden onset of shyness, she looked straight at me and remained quiet for what seemed like eternity. Then, she said "Tony, I am so amazed and can't believe you wrote that song about me. It's great... I love it... I don't know what else to say." My moment of fame had arrived here in our good old front room. I had performed my great signature tune to an audience of one... a real self-composed song to a girl called Alison... to the soundtrack of the kettle whistling in the kitchen and our insane cat wailing outside. Wow... this is my purpose and calling in life... to entertain people. That dark winter night of 1982 was a defining moment in my life. I now truly knew what I really wanted to do with myself. It was no longer a faraway dream, it was confirmed. The punk years had truly done the trick. They had fed the breeding of my future adult psyche and the metamorphosis into the real me. Can you see the real me... well can yer!!! CAN YER?

Not long afterwards, I fell in love with a dark purple Hayman guitar that a lad just around the corner from me was always taunting me with: somehow the poor-action, battered, bruised and paint-flaking Woolies guitar of my punk-spawned guitar playing days seemed so lacking and I conjured up an agreed higher purchase agreement between me and the lad (him throwing in a box of original Tamla 45's to seal the deal). When I arrived in our front room and plugged the Hayman into my 50 watt combo, I felt a million quid. I stuck the obligatory 'Carnaby Street' sticker on its body and belted round for John to come to come and have a peak at my prize. A few weeks later I also gathered myself a whole £100 (don't ask how!) and upgraded my crappy little 50 watt temperamental combo amp to a classic 100 watt H/H combo (from a gigging late period pub rock band at the Commercial pub in Parkgate) with 4 inputs and a gain that enabled me to boost my guitar sound to almost Who-like volume - at least in our front room anyway. I had earlier failed in an attempt at purchasing a pure white Gibson SG semi-acoustic guitar from a music shop in town, when I had took our Paul along as guarantor. I had dreamt about the instrument for weeks and on the day of decision was turned down flat by a man with a sad moustache in a dodgy suit. I seriously considered throwing the guitar through the window I was that disappointed as I left without the guitar.

In early 1983, time went backwards for a few weeks when our Glen moved back in to our house, with wife, Lesley and their two year old toddler, our Darren in tow. They had lived up Kimberworth from getting married in June 1979, but had now bought a house on Chapel Walk, Rawmarsh and were in the middle of moving and renovating their new home. It seemed strange and if I am gonna be honest, though it was a novelty, it did infringe on my independence little: but then he did bring along his VHS player, which was a revelation and an exciting one at that. My very own film season was now ready to begin then!

Our Glen had been amongst the very first people in Rotherham to get himself a VHS player and it cost him an arm and a leg for it and also to join Chantry videos in town. Amazingly back then, a blank BASF cassette would knock you back about £18! Nowadays people throw them in the bin! Anyway, for all of the disadvantages of being stifled with a family home once again, I soon took advantage of having a video player in the house. Me and my mates rented 'Quadrophenia', 'Rude Boy', 'Mad Max', 'American Graffiti' a load of war films and a spaghetti western that had the 'News at Ten' music as its soundtrack? We pissed ourselves laughing at Miss Ballbreaker in 'Porkies' and laughed even more at some of the dodgy cheap horror films that were making their way onto video. One night me and our Glen put on 'Halloween' as a special treat for Mum when she came back in from the bingo. She was scared stiff and suffered nightmares at the thought of Michael Myers's face. She wasn't impressed one bit when I went and pressed play on the huge top loading player as she walked through the door to the sounds of the 'Halloween' theme. It didn't help that she had lost at the bingo again either and truth be known when my Mum hadn't won for a while, it would have been Michael Myers running off if he had clocked her bingo-failed chops!

Inevitably, the temptation of sneaking in some naughty video porn reared its filthy noggin when Clarkey came round with a so-called gangster movie called 'Baby Face': that's what we told my Mum when she asked what we were gonna be watching while she buggered off to the bingo for another defeat her saying 'Not heard of that Jimmy Cagney one?'. 'Baby Face' was full of sexy mature women being rather naughty and gave us quite a buzz, but was kind of ruined by the moustache-wearing Burt Reynolds and Magnum P.I look-alikes dishing out all the pleasure on screen and our Tommy's face glaring at us on the settee. Maybe he was jealous, or maybe he had seen it all before?

As I said, my independence in the home was now potentially at stake and it wasn't long before the good old infamous Beesley rows made a much belated revival. Lesley wanted to watch horrible Dynasty on a Saturday night, my hidden crisps and chocolate were going missing; our Darren wouldn't shut up while I was watching The Tube and I wouldn't turn the records down when everyone wanted to get some sleep. I won't lie to anyone, I was a bit of a git and my home turf, which had been a free house for me and my mates for so long, was under a 'Code-Red' threat. It didn't help when I went and had a bit of a party while everyone was out and when the family returned a little bit early to the stink of dope and a house full of strangers it didn't go down that well. I don't know who brought the dope, but I had not yet touched the stuff and was a bit of a drugs virgin: outrageous stuff indeed. Although it was not such a huge deal, I did feel that it was wrong when my family was around. So, I got rid of them all, except for one lad who stopped over, and that was that!

Soon, the novelty and inconvenience of having a full house like the good old days had worn off and we were all getting under each other's feet far too much. Before things got out of hand the move to their new house came into place and we all moved on with our lives ahead of us.

In 1983 a new disease called Aids further put the jitters up the promiscuous, the gay community and the clap clinic clientele. Ken belted Mike Baldwin in

Coro and Kids rode around on BMX bikes in place of the classic Chopper bike. Our old punk mate Bryan Bell went and joined the army for a stint too. Our Dave left school and got a job at the Steelworks and we finally got around to getting some central heating in our house after decades of surviving with just the one coal fire to keep us warm. I was digging even more Mod sounds and re-visiting my brother's old Bowie and Bolan records yet again. Remarkably I bought even less contemporary records than the year before, if that's possible, and watched in amazement when a little unremarkable band I had listened to on John Peel three years previously called U2 started to become mega famous. I had bought their 'New Year's Day' double 7" single pack at the start of the year and borrowed their 'War' LP out of the Rotherham Library (something our Paul had encouraged me to do as he was taping LP's like nobody's business and hiring books too until he got banned for not returning them and ignoring the fees). Even our old pal, Barney Rubble had succumbed to U2 fever just before they got famous and went off to see them play at the City Hall with his newly engaged fiancée. Yes, Barney got himself seriously engaged. Mates were now veering off and getting into serious relationships, never to be seen again, and others were embarking on life-time careers as our punk generation finally grows up and becomes domesticated.

By now my days of gig-going in Sheffield were decreasing rapidly. The 2 to 3 gigs a week of the few years previously had narrowed down to a few each month. The Top Rank had passed its hey-day and the very last time I went there was to see Goth stars, Bauhaus. I left unimpressed, catching the last bus home, alone, confused and fed up. The Mod scene was now far more alive in Rotherham than Sheffield and some great nights were had at the Assembly Rooms and Clifton Hall. Mods would travel from all over the region and beyond for these reputable nights. Some Mod-inclined bands performed there too, but it was the records being spun that most impressed me and would help influence my varied musical tastes throughout the rest of the 80's.

Over in Sheffield there was the Limit club, but that had had its heyday and although some great bands would still perform there right up until its demise, the place quickly descended into a club night-themed venue. Consequently, I never stepped into the place again after 1982. The Leadmill was another story. By late 82 and into 83 it was just getting into its stride and some amazing bands performed there. Another new venue had opened too. The old Beerkeller of my older brother's 1970's drinking adventures had re-opened as an off-shoot of the Dingwalls venue of London. Only open for a short period of time, the venue managed to attract some great bands and me and my mates ventured to plenty of their rhythm and booze nights: The Damned, Richard Hell, Hanoi Rocks, London Cowboys and others including a Bo Diddley gig to which I went along pissed up and oblivious. In February 1983, me and Barney Rubble went to see Big Country, the new band formed by ex-Skids guitarist, Stuart Adamson. They had only just released their second single 'Fields of Fire' and I was keenly interested in finding out how they cut it live. I was crazy on the Skids and Stuart was one of my favourite guitarists of the period.

Big Country's Stuart Adamson
Sheffield Dingwalls 1983
(Stuart Sutherland)

The temporary return of Barney saw us get there and bang a few pints of cider down the neck, quickly buzzing with the effects. We tried chatting lasses up, but seeing as we couldn't afford to buy them a drink, we didn't get very far; besides, Barney was now a hitched man and going proper steady, not that it would have deterred him really, though. When two older lads asked us to watch their pints while they went for a slash, we said "OK, no worries... will do." As the fellas, themselves a bit worse for wear and disappeared, me and Barney took one look at each other and picked up a pint each and supped 'em straight down. Right at that moment, Big Country came onto the small Dingwalls' stage and started to play and we got up and shot straight to the front. Turning around, I saw the two pint-less blokes arrive back at their table and noticing their pints were supped dry; one of them had got a bloke by the scruff of the neck, blaming the innocent soul for nicking his beer. It was dark, we were crafty and the other guy just happened to be in the wrong place at the wrong time! The sounds of 'In a Big Country' and Stuart Adamson's almost-bagpipe-sounding guitar sound-tracked the occasion as me and Barney cracked up laughing like a pair of Mutleys of 'Wacky Races' fame. That night we must have nicked half a dozen pints each from people distracted by the music and spectacle of this fresh new post-Skids sound from the Highlands.

Big Country were tartan shirt-wearing Scottish laddies and that night they played almost note-for-note perfect renditions of what would become their first album, 'The Crossing'. They played 'Fields of Fire' and 'In a Big Country' again for their encore after which we were left wanting more. Their set was quick but just enough to whet my appetite for more songs. Thankfully, I did see Big Country again within the next few weeks, at the very same venue and they were just as amazing to experience- sending out a Celtic vibe of anthemic rock n' roll with Stuart even wearing a kilt for the occasion. They soon became a big-selling band with fast selling albums and sell out tours and, along with U2 and Simple Minds, heralded a new era in stadium rock for the 80's. I far preferred the experience of seeing Big Country perform in that small and intimate smoke-filled-dimly-lit Dingwalls venue than an arena, where, for a very short period, their music crossed genres and style and the beer was free! Years later, the very talented Stuart Adamson took his own life and there is never a play of a Skids or Big Country record that I hear when I don't mourn his sad passing and recall those nights at the Sheffield Dingwalls!

1983 was the year of Breakfast TV when a fella called Frank Bough jumped ship from Grandstand to sit on a settee with his TV accomplice, Selina Scott trying to wake up the nation. It was the year that Hip Hop gained prominence and MTV tried to con us into believing that the music video was far more important than the music being played and it was also the year of Michael Jackson's classic John Landis-directed 'Thriller' video, which we waited to watch in anticipation one late Saturday night on BBC2 during a Rock and Pop music TV marathon bonanza called 'Rock Around the Clock'. Paul Weller unveiled his new Style Council with the impressive Pop/Soul of 'Speak Like a Child', the promising but all too brief Positive Punk was launched and sunk and girls wore their hair like the Hair Bear bunch crossed with the Jackson Five as hair styles just grew out of all human proportion. Straight blokes had their hair cut just a bit shorter than their 70's styles on top and up the sides but forgot to tell the barber to whack the back bit off: the result being... the

dreaded mullet... ahhhhh!!! Space Invaders and Pacman amazed us with their
out of this world super-futuristic technology, Betamax tried to compete with
VHS and the costs of a pint went up about 2p resulting in me and John no
longer being able to go out on three quid each for a night out. Some things in
life just aren't fair are they?

Meanwhile after almost a year of beginning our journey together, as John
and I awaited the world stage to embrace us, we embarked upon a great little
summer of (often slightly naughty) fun all the time honing our rudimentary
musical skills to a (slightly) more polished effect, well we did tune up once in a
while!

While awaiting the elusive fame and fortune, I was also forced into breaking
my Dental phobia and paying the old tooth pullers a visit! The last time I had
ventured there was to an infamous Chinese dental butcher when I was about 11
years old. I had been almost dragged there on that occasion and at the last
minute as I saw the WWI gas mask looming my way, I had decided to try and
escape, fists flinging around in an attempt to stop the ensuing gas attack
straight out of Battle comic's Charlie's War. Needless to say the gas knocked
me out, my tooth went bye byes and I vowed never to return ever again!

This time, though, I had a couple of agony-inducing bad teeth, one with
a swollen abscess for company and after a few weeks of hot drinks, pain
killers, whiskey-soaked gums and a 5 pint (potentially numbing) Sunday
lunch-time armistice session with our Paul to Rycroft working men's club... I
was almost bloody crawling to the canine driller!

Unfortunately, my return to the world of fillings, drills, pliars and nasty
gum-attacking needles was no more pleasant this time either. I had a couple of
teeth removed after experiencing a wobbly stroke-like mouth and a swollen
tongue, that was as scared and wobbly as I was... but also experienced the
effects of an allergic reaction to Penicillin... sending me swirling around the
dental surgery like a drunken sailor and sweating ten tons of Penicillin out of
my whole body, what a sight to see I must have been! This was followed by a
whole 24 hours of vomiting to endure on my return home. When my pal, Beanz
called for me to go to the Queens for a few pints, I was puking up before the
bar was even open! Let me get back to my change the world drinking sessions
with good old John... its much safer and a far more rewarding experience.

Following one of these over-zealous alcohol-fuelled sessions and getting

Kicked out of the pub long after last orders, we strolled back to my Mum's house, zigzagging down the hill like over-grown kids and over the junior's school field for a short cut. "Look John, there's the bars we used to play on when we were kids," I said. John made a dash for the bars and started to play dangling Orang-utans on them, 5 pints of beer stripping all the years away since he had spent his childhood on this very playground. As I joined in with him and we hung upside down like monkeys, John spotted a bloke right up at the bottom of the hill in the blurry distance, stood staring down and looking just a little intimidating.

John let rip at the looming figure with a tirade of insults and threats as I realised exactly who it was that he was verbally attacking. When John took a breather from his rant, I said to him "Hey up, John, does tha know who that is?" John's face dropped a mile as I informed him that it was a big lad, some years our senior and known to us and all else as one big hitter! John quickly calmed down and set about making a hasty retreat back to my place for some musical therapy. The bloke on the hill stayed but took note of who had been giving him all the stick! The next day, on our visit to the pub, he let John know all about it and John dodged him and the pub for all of a fortnight or so.

We had to frequent the Rawmarsh Trades and Labour club a bit more regularly for a while. This was an unchanging world of drinking, club turns, card games, darts and dominoes... just like stepping back in time. Had the Second World War ended? Is Elvis famous yet and why is that bloke sat with all of his shirt un-buttoned revealing a massive thick rug of chest hair? There was a selection of each post-war generation of working men on hand. From demobbed war veterans and aging Teddy boys to that fella out of 'Love Thy Neighbour' look-alikes. From 1945 to 1975, they are all here: the national museum of working class drinking in motion. And through the fag smoke and dodgy disco lights for the Saturday night turn, stood me and John at the bar. gaining sneers and comments from the regulars. "Hey up, it's two thirds of The Jam at the bar,"... "Look at this, Monkwood regulars getting tucked into our cheap ale, cheeky gets." But it was all in good taste, or at least I think it was?

One Saturday night visit there saw me turn up looking like a sun-tanned Eskimo with sliced up teenage acne after a session with a cheap plastic Bic razor went wrong half an hour before John called for me to go out. What is it about the trials and pitfalls of early shaving? Why do we cut ourselves so much? So that's why my Dad used to always have tiny bits of the Daily Express stuck to his face an hour before he went out. I thought I had got away with it, this time. No sarcastic comments from anyone. "This is never right," I was thinking. Then I spotted our Paul sat at his regular table and before you know it, he's pissing himself laughing at me. "Look, its Kenny Everett," he shouted over. I was puzzled. Why was he shouting Kenny Everett at me? Then I saw myself in the great big mirror behind the bar. The attempted Bic attack had left me with a purple shadow spread everywhere cross my chops. From across the concert room I looked like I had a Rolf Harris! "C'mon John, we are going up to the Monkwood, no matter if tha gets a hiding off that big bloke or not. It's better than me battling through the gauntlet of our Paul's comments all night," I decided and off we went, no sign of Hot Gossip following anywhere!

Our nights of drinking in and around our quaint little Rawmarsh village were accompanied by weekend days of hanging out and having some good old fashioned childish lad's fun. In-between John worked at the local bookies where he would stick a bet on a wobbly pony and come racing out shouting and diving in the air trying to urge his horse on to win. "Amber Gambler', my mate, Clarkey called him one day as we passed him performing this ritual. John loved betting. He was an opportunist and a gambler, so why wouldn't he?

On hot summer Sunday afternoons, we played games of 3 a side footie to which, it goes without saying, John took bets on who was gonna win, and we paid an old fashioned trip to the park in the hope of catching some scantily clad women sun bathing on the grass. We were paid in kind for our hopes by a sight you don't often expect to see almost 40 years after the end of WW2. Kenneth Moore, where art thou!

Like a surreal-movie-like dream we were transported back in time. We sat bored, thinking of where to go next as there were no decent looking lasses knocking about and we were in danger of getting Rawmarsh sunstroke. We then caught a glimpse of something mighty peculiar. Walking down the hill with the glaring sun behind them was a whole family of 1940's people. Yes... a real proper 1940's family. I nudged John and said "Hey up... look who's here, it's the bleeding Nesbit family." The head of the family, Dad, wore a white shirt with sleeves rolled up and braces whilst his hair was slicked back exactly like Humphrey Bogart. He wore demob trousers and gangster spats and a face that could have been used to promote the George Formby fan club. "Where was the ukulele, then?" Mr 1940 was, unbelievably carrying one of those radios that belonged in a museum and I bet if you had tuned into it, you would have been able to listen to news of the evacuation of Dunkirk. He was grinning a grin like no normal self-conscious adult would dream of creating in the 1980's and had behind him a brood of evacuee dodgers and a matronly lady who could have scared away a whole queue of ration card nominees with one wink of her eye. Me and John took a look at each other and could not believe our eyes. John was saying... "Oh bloody hell, please don't let them come and sit near us." Guess who they parked their bags of dripping sandwiches and council pop next to for a rest? Us two truly! "Christ, get the Ovaltine out, John," I whispered and held my tongue firmly in cheek. John was busting to laugh. Turning the huge dial on the radio, the dad tuned into what sounded like the Glen Miller showcase and that was far too much to take. We ran off up the park laughing in disbelief leaving the wartime family to their picnic in peace. Besides they needed a bit of a break, they weren't sure when the Jerries were gonna invade. As me and John made our way out of the park, I could have sworn I saw a Spitfire doing the Victory roll far up in the blue summer sky of 1983!!!

There were plenty of belly-tremblers that summer, and we took the piss out of all walks of life on a daily basis. From 50's throwbacks singing 'Tell Laura I love her' on the pub jukebox dressed in gravel-voiced real man denim with a fading fast dude's old fashioned hair style - to tough blokes stood at the bar in flares and out of control sideburns, who, had they realised our mimicry, would have knocked us all over the tap room.

Other hobbies we took up were drinking cider with straws to a soundtrack of my Reggae tapes. Whereas proper Reggae aficionados would celebrate the sound of Reggae whilst partaking in a few joints of Jamaican best, well we sat supping a bottle of Woodpecker cider with a straw apiece! Nodding our heads to the heavy duty sounds, we would throw in a Babylonic enthused seal of approval every now and again by saying "Yeaaahhh Maaan!" Also our post-pub hobby of hedge-leaping in people's gardens - to which John once took 'the penultimate ditch' and consequently ended up walking around like a deformed version of Rising Damp's Rigsby for a while. Or chasing lasses but hardly ever catching any with our cross-eyed drunken romantic notions; some of whom would have probably made us turn around and run the other way had they made a determined last stand.

When We Were Young!

Away from the joviality's, I was still avidly collecting records and via the many cheap bargains to be had from the second-hand record shops of Sheffield and the various markets around the area, was cultivating lots of new influences for my song writing. The most profound influence was Soul (I collected the Stax and Atlantic labels religiously), but a new band was being talked about in the music press called The Smiths. Upon catching the band perform 'This Charming Man' on Top of the Pops, I was hooked and yet another influence was born, notably the unique Byrds-like guitar playing of Smiths man, Johnny Marr, who joined Weller, Wilko Johnson, Steve Cropper and Pete Townshend as one of my guitar heroes.

It seemed to take forever; forming a band. Day in and day out, me and John rehearsed our songs in our front room and the school classrooms we rented out two or three times a week, alongside other local bands, with our Steve and his mate earning 75p a week as our official roadies... and humping our gear up to the school practices. We must be on our way to being a proper real band now, having our own roadies eh! It seemed strange, for me, being back in those class rooms, where only a few years previously I had been having lessons and messing about. I would have never dreamt that I would be returning with a guitar a mike and an amp to play renditions of Soul and Mod classics alongside my own partly-formed self-compositions. Luckily there were none of my old much-loved teachers still knocking around by the 6pm start as we arrived back in the school grounds.
Wasn't it about time to hand in my over-due homework now then?

I had left school three years ago, but our Steve (above) was still there and was going through his very brief Mod phase, digging The Who, sporting a Keith Moon hairstyle and borrowing a mate's parka. He was in his element helping us out; having a laugh and listening to us perform imperfect but heartfelt renditions of Who, Small Faces, Jam and Kinks songs.

My mate, local music talent, Julian Jones, also played at the Youth club with his bands Alternative Route and later on Turn the Key as did local Mod,

Karl Haigh and his pals in Suburban Dream. Not one of these bands trusted me and John as we would swipe, borrow or beg (in that order) any equipment of any of theirs left in the lock up cupboard, taking care not to blow their posh amps to pieces with our northern rock 'n soul!. John himself had an amp that his Dad had built for him which was simply an old box with an old speaker and amp fixed in, so the Carlsbro and Fender equipment we borrowed off these proper musicians were a real treat for us, that's for sure and no amount of threatening notes and pleas left on the lock up door could deter us. We were desperate to get somewhere and really did not care how we got there.

Whilst searching for a suitable front man for our act, we stupidly made the mistake of letting daft lad, Martin recommend a friend of his for our singer. One Friday night practice up at the school, me and John waited impatiently for our prospective candidate to turn up. We expected some Weller protégé or at least some like-minded Mod-inclined kid born of the punk generation like us. We went through a few songs whilst waiting for the big moment, our adrenaline on full speed and expectations high. Had we reached that pivotal and life-defining stage like so many before us? A Paul McCartney meeting John Lennon moment... a Johnny Rotten rehearsal to Alice Cooper scenario... Mick Jones meeting Joe Strummer? The excitement was getting too much. "Where the hell is he," we kept asking. Then the door of the practice room opened and from behind that creaky school classroom door, Martin entered followed by our new singer. Cue historical epic fanfare with finely tuned trumpets!!

I looked over at John and he turned to me. Our eyes must have been deceiving us... this couldn't be! The sight of our career-boosting musical mate in future fame was stood before us and we just couldn't believe what we saw. This was no Paul Weller lookalike, no fledgling Joe Strummer or Roger Daltrey and certainly no aspiring Steve Marriott of the Small Faces or a Kinks fan club member either. Jeez, how do you describe it? The kid in front of us looked more like an audition member for a forthcoming Hammer Horror film than a rock n' roll hopeful. Is someone taking the piss here or what?

Dressed in the most unfashionable, creepy-looking, moth-eaten clothes attire you could imagine topped off with a stolen Mormon neck beard worthy of out-cursing the Curse of the werewolf itself and hair like Tinsley Wire, stood this monstrous figure with a Dictaphone (NOT A MICROPHONE EVEN!!!) waiting for us to welcome him into our musical dreams. When we asked him what songs he knew, vainly hoping for 'A Town Called Malice', fools that we were, well he replied "I can do the latest song from Limhal." Limhal? Kajagoogoo? Aaaaaaarrrr... get me out of here... in fact get him out of here!!!!

Me and John went through a couple of my songs I had written, 'Shout', 'It's OK', 'Just For a Chance' and even 'Happy People' the last one being a really simple song to sing. We gave him the words and asked him to have a crack at the songs, not expecting that much really: just some reasonable attempt at singing. "Sure, I can sing those songs, they're easy," he said picking up the lyric sheets. OK then... 1,2,3,4!!! We waited, mesmerised and in disbelief. He stood there, not a muscle twitching without a single note escaping his mouth. He merely spoke quietly into his cherished Dictaphone as some kind of pathetic excuse at lyric reciting! If anyone had have been around with a camera to capture me and John's faces they would have been in for a right old treat. He even had the cheek to say "Is that ok for yer," on us finishing the song. 'This is getting bloody stupid; he's having a laugh at us, surely.' The temptation to go over and pick him up and throw him straight through the bloody window was very high. Me and John took our music very seriously, the rest of our lives were at stake here after all. And this pillock was trying to pass off a message to Peter Cushing on his werewolf communicator as being something resembling singing! It really was too much. He had to go... or we may as well just give it all up there and then. What had we bloody done to deserve this!

In the true tradition of identifying fools and general social idiots, we immediately named him Wolfgang and after half an hour's frustrating interrogation we gave up on him completely. Back to square one. "Hit the road, Jack Palance... you son of Lon Chaney and don't bother us no more." We might as well have gone and asked the Boney M look-a-like fella that went with a lass around the corner from us to join us rather than expect anything exciting from Wolfgang the First! Winding things down, we gave our small audience of well-wishers a look of Oliver Hardy-styled disbelief and decided that a pint or two up at the pub and a few plays of 'Speak Like A Child' on the juke box was well in order and fully deserved to calm us down and refresh our nerves.

The trouble is... Wolfgang followed us around and we couldn't get rid of him for about a month. On ordering our drinks in the pub, there he was. We had to listen to tales of him eating dog food, being the next Rod Stewart and being tougher than Kung Fu for what seemed like forever. We just could not shake him off. We dodged him and ran off from him. We gave him subtle hints that he wasn't that welcome to join us on our drinking sessions and certainly not our band practices. We were rude, obvious and crude, but he never took one blind bit of notice of us. Then one day he was gone.... Gone for good and I can tell you that was something to celebrate! Goodbye Wolfgang!

A new Soul vision? Blimey even Kevin Rowland would have given up on his very own intense and talented Soul vision if he had to put up with our false starts and doomed attempts at creating a musical future; even Rodney and Mental Mickey had more going for them! Now named Control, we set about getting sorted, acquiring even sillier wannabe Rock star hopefuls. "We just want to be part of Control," they would proclaim. "Yeah, and we just want to get someone in who is worth being part of bloody Control," would be our sadly frustrated retort. Often, I let band applicants strum away and sing along happy as larks with them not knowing that I had sneakily pulled out their guitar and microphone leads. John would look over grinning, knowing that it was really the kindest thing to do for all concerned. Now we weren't pitch-perfect singers and perfectly-tuned musicians ourselves but some of the noises that accompanied our songs by these talentless misfits were not human and should never be heard ever again by anyone with a remotely sane mind. How we survived that year or two of all the local celebrities we seemed to attract I don't know... but we soldiered on. Despite everything that was being cast our way to test our endurance, our belief in ourselves was still miraculously unshakeable.

"Is this supposed to be your reasoning, this your perverted war.
Guaranteed a wall of hate, how many dead so far.
Destroy and rule our lives, can't justify your means.
Fear on the street all around ain't got much of a chance
Just for a chance, I would do just anything... to stop this madness... and help
ourselves."
Lyrics from 'Just For a Chance' (Beesley – 1982)

Chapter five

Mods, Miners and meeting Paul Weller!

"No more Wolfgangs in 1984. This was gonna be our year," we declared. We were going to get noticed and this time next year we would be proper musicians... not quite millionaires, as our telly pal, Del Boy would regularly Proclaim to aspire to, but give us time and you never know!

Away from the Numbers - Tony Beesley

Me and my best pal, John celebrated Christmas that year of 1983 with extreme vigour. We partied hard and constant. From the afternoon of Christmas Eve, we kicked off a mammoth seasonal drinking session. Back then the boozers were full to the hilt, even on an afternoon. Blokes would break up from work for a fortnight and they would be straight to the pub with their mates. Couples would be out from Friday night onwards and daft lads like me and John would be out for the whole shenanigan knocking back copious amounts of (any variation of) alcohol available. It was a time of total freedom and constant fun: we didn't care if we were sick, got ourselves arrested or fell asleep in a stranger's house (which we often did); it was Christmas and time to get drunk!

One of the follies of getting so blind drunk is that you do stupid things that you wouldn't do otherwise (I often woke up fully suited on the settee – or sometimes in the bath – wondering where the hell I was). One of the great advantages of being in such a state is that you tend to forget them; that is unless some kind soul is around to observe, take note and cruelly remind you during a later far more sober occasion. I mean there are some spiteful people out there aren't there?

Of what I can recall of that never-ending super Christmas jamboree is getting chased by a police car, John climbing up our drainpipe trying to get in and then throwing up all over and consequently blaming the pickled onions he had consumed round at his brother Rob's party. Also quite distinct in my memory is when we held a rampant, loud and very incoherent Jam session in my Mum's front room in-between an afternoon and evening session. We blasted out every Jam song that we knew on our guitars and mikes and thoroughly enjoyed ourselves. That is one part of Christmas 83 that we both can still remember. However, the funniest event has to be the Boxing day night when John was meeting me in the Trades and Labour working men's club, where we were often banned or told to leave, and on arriving and ordering a drink he ran straight onto the club's dance floor and proceeded to jump up and down screaming "Aaaaaaahhhh" with pure unadulterated abandon! He had reached his absolute peak of euphoria and merely wished to let the world know. My Mum was a part-time glass collector at the club at the time and her face was hilarious on sighting John do his impression of a lunatic's drunken night out highlight. If you had placed a bucket under me and caught the tears of laughter spilling from my face you would have so easily filled it to the rim. You know, as you get older and hopefully just a bit wiser, you look back on times such as these and you have to pinch yourselves to believe it all happened. The Christmas of 1983 was like that and high up there for me as a period of freedom, of not having a care in the whole wide world and not giving a single thought of what tomorrow would bring. How naïve we were!

Care less or not, 1984, that Orwellian threat of a year was now here. Christmas was now a fading and very blurred memory and it was time to get things moving. Let's get ourselves into Control! Talking of control, the stinking Tories were back in for a second term led by their right dishonourable leader Mrs T. On the back of the Falklands War and a nation's mixed up and partially misplaced patriotism coupled with the fact that the Labour Party had screwed up: the Conservatives were once again in firm control of this good island. As the year began, who would have guessed that very soon a whole year of political turmoil and class division would be on our doorstep? Within the year the Miners would be on strike and a new working class struggle would begin. It was to be bloody, tragic and frustrating and would ultimately break the back of the Northern working class destroying whole towns, communities and families. The state of the nation and the future we now know has its political and social roots firmly placed within 1984 and all of its consequences!

Meanwhile back in Rawmarsh, me and John were still continuing our search for a drummer and a singer/lead guitarist to complete our line up. We opted for new even shorter haircuts at Vic the Barbers and in-between our hopeful searches we were still cramming as much fun and boozing in as we could afford and have time for, frequenting the local drinking holes and obscure little clubs such as Parkgate's 'American Graffiti' club. That establishment was a pokey (and rather seedy) little club above some shops where the drinking (and often occasional dope-smoking) clientele of the area met up after normal drinking hours. It was one long corridor-like room with a bar at one end and was as rough as an old tramp's beard. If passive smoking is as bad as they say it is (along with an added mix of the best continental and Cuban grass), you could probably have died on the spot if you had inhaled in a bit too deeply. Faces were often just as rough as the decor and Al Capone would not have felt out of place in there. Even so, no trouble was evident on all of our jaunts there and we fit in quite nicely thanks. Besides we knew about half of the fellas and diamond geezers that chucked their readies over the almost collapsible bar and then pissed it up the totally wrecked urinals of the place. The 'American Graffiti' club didn't last all that long and would have never even existed at all if health and safety had known of it. It was an experience and a laugh and felt just a bit like an old Prohibition era gangster Speakeasy... it fit the bill perfectly for us in our black suits and almost Mickey Pearce social stance for a while.

Not long after our Speakeasy-styled days we came up trumps in another club when we happened to get chatting to the resident club drummer at the Trades and Labour club. We had been rebuked by their organist for constantly

The Deakin

laughing at their cheesy Blackpool organ-sounding musical intro to each act. The drummer saw the funny side of it and had a pint with us and before long he gave us a telephone number for a lad he was teaching to play the drums called Ian.

Ian Deakin was a Mexborough lad and was a fan of punk and Mod music. He in no way resembled Wolfgang or any of the other fruit and nut cases and nice people we had endured and he was also dependable, talented and quite importantly up for a laugh, which is a good job really. We met up with Ian up at the school and straight away we knew he was the one and just right for the job at hand. Before long he was a proper part of the gang and even teamed up with us on drinking sessions, trying desperately hard to keep up with us and occasionally paying the consequences of doing so. Ian did end up looking like a green-faced alien on at least one or two occasions, but he survived, saw the funny side of it and was now a real good mate and the official drummer for Reaction, which was our new band name, by the way.

We took Ian on pub crawls, gate-crashed parties and introduced him to our craziness and almost force-fed him a new musical diet of Mod and Soul sounds. To begin with, Ian sported a college boy-influenced look, which I thought was quite Mod, but we decided that he needed an update on his image

and pretty soon he could be seen decked out in Dog Tooth trousers, Fred
Perry polo shirts, boating blazers and bowling shoes. We bonded via nights of
booze, music and social insanity. Ian would laugh at me and John's crazy
sense of humour and seemed to immediately grasp what was inspiring us in
this world of being young and desperation to succeed.

We got started right away; Ian brought his drum kit up and kept it in the
storage cupboard up at the school and we ran through all the songs that we
had written along with the cover versions we could play. He picked it all up
really quick so things were finally on the up for us. Yeah, and about time too.
We also started to attract a crowd of local Mod kids that had been gathering
outside our practice room to listen to us and who were interested in adopting
us as their own Mod band. Me and John would hang our heads out of the
window and ask them for requests. Eventually the Mod kids would come up
and join us in our room and sit and listen to us go through our songs; The
Jam and Who covers going down well with them too. We continued to tighten
up our set in preparation for our first gig. For a while we were joined by
another bloke on vocals, who was a really nice fella but totally unsuited to our
Mod image and sound. When it came around to us doing the important first
gig he was well excited and up for it. Me and John were not keen on the idea
and knew that we really had to be performing as a three piece. John in his
infinite wisdom bottled out of us both telling the poor bloke that he was out of
the band on the actual day of the gig. John felt that I was best at doing stuff
like that and could put it across much easier than him. Cheers John, leave it
to me to shatter the poor fella's rock 'n' roll dreams!

The deed done, we played our very first gig as support to Turn the Key at
the Rawmarsh Youth club disco, nervously performing to a crowd of clapping
and excitable kids along with some of our young Mod fans. This was what I had
been veering towards all of my life, to actually perform my own songs live to a
listening audience. The lights were now on us and we had no choice but to go
ahead, plug in those guitars and play; to which we did and it felt amazing! Our
first-gig nerves subsided as we soberly performed with surprising ease and
confidence. Our set consisted of some of our own songs 'It's OK', 'Happy
People' and also 'Pretty Green' and 'That's Entertainment' by The Jam along
with The Who's 'I Can't Explain.' Received positively we now felt the relief of
knowing we had performed to the public for the very first time. The world was

123

now our oyster, we were young, cocky and sure of our worth... and nothing could stop us in our tracks, or so we so passionately believed at the time!

Around this time, a young Mod lass called Wendy who had requested us to play 'I Can't Explain' let it be known, via her friends, that she was interested in me. She later told me that she couldn't decide if she fancied me or John, but opted for me in the end. I didn't take it all that seriously to begin with but after me and John literally chased her and a mate up the road and invited them back to my place; we eventually became a serious item later that year after a blossoming and rather innocent friendship turned into something more.

'Café Bleu' by the Style Council was released in March 1984 and it quickly became the sound of Spring. While hordes of Jam fans (many far too hardened by the aftershocks of the punk-enthused mod revival) derided Weller and his new European look and continental approach to music (Modern Jazz, contemporary Funk and Northern Soul being a few small examples of his new musical agenda), me and John fully embraced this refreshing style and soulful offering. The sounds of 'Head start to Happiness', 'Here's One that got Away', the cool-lounge Jazz instrumental 'Blue Café' and 'My Ever Changing Moods' will always remind me of those days of early Spring 1984 when everything seemed to be great in my life and all was finally fitting perfectly together. Later that year, I even fell in love to the sounds of 'The Paris Match' and 'You're the Best Thing'. Amazingly me and John even went teetotal inspired by Weller's new clean living outburst and if you didn't blink too quickly you could have caught us sat outside the Monkwood pub supping a glass of pure orange juice apiece. The abstinence lasted for... the whole of three days! Didn't we do well?

Away from the Numbers - Tony Beesley

That spring and summer was such a great and life-affirming period of my life
so far: the band was coming together and I was confidently writing more
new songs... 'You in One' was one of my best new compositions and then a
Johnny Marr-influenced instrumental called 'Catch That Dream' and 'Never
Too Late' also came along as did more gigs at the Rawmarsh Youth club. I was
on a song writing roll, arranging almost all the musical parts as my influences
expanded (Orange Juice, The Smiths, Weller's Style Council jazz leanings etc.
joining up with my Mod obsessions). As John sat with my Mum watching
comedian Tommy Cooper play out his famous and fatal heart attack-inducing
last stage performance live on TV, I was in the other room writing a new song.

Meanwhile we all made new mates and girlfriends whilst poor old John still
had his good old dependable partner... the pint! The time was a great mix of
music, laughs and parties and it seemed that the good times were never going
to end. Night do's at the Matador (a local for hire venue that did weddings,
engagements and the like), where we danced to Northern Soul with local Mods
and swapped kissing cousins on the way home. I also met my girlfriend's
parents and brother and it soon felt like I had a brand new family of my own,
becoming as close to her Dad, Don as if he were my Dad too. We would go out
for a pint or three, now and again and hit it off from the outset, sharing a
taste for wind-up humour and contradictory chat. Me and her brother Steve
became best pals too and I took him out for his first pint, watched videos with
him, played games of darts and drunken pool, made him laugh when I would
turn up (always in my long green Weller style mac) when falling out with his
sister and even borrowed him my Fred Perry sweaters. We clicked straight
away with our sense of humour, pulled the same daft faces and had some
amazing laughs and piss-taking sessions. It is true that we all seemed to never
stop laughing that summer, one way or another!

During scorching summer days, me and Wendy would sit outside pubs
wearing our best Mod gear. We would share our hopes and dreams whilst laid
in the long grass overlooking a proper local Yorkshire landscape on the nearby
Greasborough tops! Exploring our minds and interests, we cared for no
tomorrows, just the present. The year had been predicted to be an Orwellian
'1984' one? Don't know about totalitarianism and big brother and the like... for
us it was a time of laughs, music, mates, daftness, youthful innocence and life
being... well just great! It truly was a time I used to wish would never end!

Meanwhile the Miners' strike was in full swing. Without getting involved with exploring the history and causes of the strike - far more knowledgeable sources can provide that in more apt places - suffice to say that the region was affected deeply by it all: lives and futures were at stake. Of course, as is the spirit of the working classes whilst hitting hard times, ways and means of surviving were quickly adapted and utilised.

Local folklore stories tell of families pulling together and providing for each other. Our local village may have been old fashioned and contemptuous of the strange, the unusual and the rebellious minded of its youth, but when the crunch came, the socialist spirit and care of our fellow neighbour came into place. The mass materialistic consumerism of later years was light years away and it was share what little you had if and when the going got tough.

The life of being a miner had killed my Dad and good mates of mine were miners too, so no guessing whose side I was on! My mates would make sure that they were not gonna give in to Thatcher's plans and would improvise their means of survival along the way. Coal may have been short, legally, but the slag heaps were abundant and rich pickings. Re-designing lead roofs, relieving scrap yards of their (often) ill-gotten gains and then flogging it back to them were daily occurrences, whilst Sunday morning car boots in the words of one of my good mates "Were like a visit to see Ali Baba and his Forty Thieves!," and inspired the comment "I've never seen as many pit lamps, orange overalls or thermal vests and pants for sale before or since." From ducking and diving in local pubs, selling all and sundry to keep heads above water and all along retaining the spirit of the cause and holding on to its unity... the miners' strike drew similarities to the spirit of the Blitz and, no matter the outcome, there was never a chance of giving in without a damn good fight.

My old school pals, Shaun Angell, Andy Goulty and Pete Roddis were all Miners and out on strike. They had been further toughened up by going down the pit, a place I, personally, have never ventured any further than picking my Dad up from his afters shifts in our Glen's car back in the 70's. But they did the deed and spent their formative school-leaver years down that dark, dust-ridden abyss. 'More pluck than me that's for sure', I would think at the time.

My pals... they were right there at the famous Battle of Orgreave Common, too. As were local legends, Captain Bob Taylor, Shaun Bisby, a lad from my same year at school called Darren Goulty- who became an integral member of the striking miners' comradeship team... and the Wilson brothers (Bruce and Bob also from Rawmarsh and whose legendary 'Battle bus' Triumph 2.5 car was a means of transport from picket line to undercover task). They were all present when Maggie's Boys in Blue charged the strikers on horseback and met them in battle during the famous Battle of Orgreave!

The Battle of Orgreave

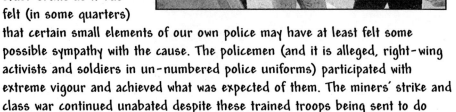

The battle was televised, or at least the edited version minus the off-screen miner-bashing was. During these confrontations with the striking miners, Maggie had hired a contingent of Southern police to crack skulls as it was felt (in some quarters) that certain small elements of our own police may have at least felt some possible sympathy with the cause. The policemen (and it is alleged, right-wing activists and soldiers in un-numbered police uniforms) participated with extreme vigour and achieved what was expected of them. The miners' strike and class war continued unabated despite these trained troops being sent to do battle and (no matter the outcome) the spirit to put up a damn good fight against the planned pit closures never dissipated. Through an undefeatable sense of pride, determination, stubborn nature, adaptability and sharing an unshakeable sense of loyalty and good old northern working class humour, the local miners – with the unrelenting support of their families and friends and regiments of supporters – were set on seeing it through to the very bitter end, and that they surely did!

In-between hiding behind Treeton wardrobes from marauding police riot squads and being given chase by Nottinghamshire scabs, during battle, skirmish, picketing and daily protest the many challenges of the pit-strike were met. From Manvers to the Cortonwood Alamo the struggle continued, a nation awaited its outcome and the future of much of the north and the country itself hung in the balance.

Our house still depended on good old British coal for its fuel and as a result of the strike coal became extremely thin on the ground. Our coal deliveries became sparse and I would stand listening at the door counting the bags brought down the path, often having to say "Alright then, pal... where's the other two bags, then?" As things got worse we ended up with none left to burn and had to do without heating full stop, which was nothing compared with what the lads out there striking were going through. Me and our Paul went out acquiring coal and on one occasion returned with a huge tin of yellow paint instead... don't ask me why? We also found out about places where coal was being secretly stored and with our Glen and his van we went and collected a few self-inviting sacks to put us on. You have to adapt in hard times!

Around this time a new youth cult seemed to appear out of the blue...The Casuals! In fact the casuals had been around since the late 70's, as far back as 1977 in some places. My mate, Shaun Angell was a keen follower of this football terrace-spawned cult and well clued-in on the gear and all of its style and culture.

The Casuals were born on Liverpool football terraces. These floppy-fringed clothes-obsessed football fans (and hooligans) had been flaunting their love of cool trainers, sweaters and polo shirts of designer label origin for some time. Taking a pinch of punk's influence and a dose of 'Low' era Bowie and Roxy Music, the ever-changing styles soon spread to other areas as fans travelled on footie away days. Manchester, Birmingham and later on, Sheffield, soon cottoned on and the era of the Casual was born!

I had experienced the scally pre-Casual Perry's (named after their Fred Perry polo shirts) of Salford and Moss Side while on my Manchester excursions. They were very provincial, violent and not to be messed with. We avoided them! As the Casual style spread, a number of lads around our neck of the woods took it up; some already being veteran Casuals of a few years to start with: often bouts of Mod-bashing became the in-thing in town too.

In 1984, the Casual movement went over-ground in an attempt by music weekly, Sounds to front page the next big thing. They featured a band called The Accent on the cover aiming to give the style a token representative band and giving it all a big push. It didn't work! Even so, the Casual look remained popular and the wedge hairstyle so favoured by most Casuals could also be seen to be adopted by everyone from other football fans and Soul Boys (many of whom had previously adopted the style and been amongst the crowds of early Casuals anyway). Even Paul Weller sported a lop-sided fringe and classic Casual/Soul Boy barnet for most of the 1984 to mid-1985 season. By the time, yours truly had decided to go for the hairstyle in 1986; Weller was back to his short and spiky cut. I kept mine for a while through my hybrid mix of Soul Boy, Mod and stylist and when it got in my eyes too much off it all went and in came a short and dependable Mod style. The Casual style of clothes also crept in to vaguely influence me for a while, but never reached any further than a selection of kagools and hooded James jackets worn with tassled loafers and Dog tooth trousers. If you are thinking now, that the fashion police should have arrested me, well you should maybe have a think at what a proportion of the young male population was looking like in the mid 80's. Dodgy 'Brookside' themed moustaches, permed hair (yes for blokes), the eternally cursed Mullet, short sleeved Don Johnson Miami Vice jackets and Andrew Ridgley copied fringes and many other unhealthy styles and uncool looks that held mass appeal as the nation created a horde of young Kevin Webster look-alikes!

1984 wasn't just casuals, anarcho-punks, Mod Stylists, George Michael wannabees and dodgy-looking straights, though. The new pop of 82/83 had given birth to a widespread plethora of bland pop artists and Smash hits icons. Wham – who I had amazingly quite liked on hearing their first two singles 'Young Guns' and 'Wham Rap', were massive that year and everywhere you went you could hear the sounds of 'Wake Me up Before You Go Go!' on car radios and ghetto blasters. King with 'Love and Pride', Nena's '99 Red Balloons' and still topping the list for making tipsy girls swoon were Spandau Ballet and Duran Duran. The pop culture of 1984 UK was as bland as before punk: it was shallow, meaningless and annoying and driving me bloody mad with its endless mediocrity. Only Indie unknowns in the NME chart alongside The Smiths, Aztec Camera, The Mighty Wah and Weller's Style Council offered any shades of an alternative musical vision; one without Frankie Says!

Frankie goes to Hollywood were the Trevor Horn studio-produced media spectacle that created outrage with their ode to ejaculation, 'Relax', which was accompanied by a suitably seedy video. They did manage to upset the apple cart for a short while - almost echoing the days of Sex Pistols infamy (on a far less dangerous and creative scale, of course) - but that was it... pop music for the masses at the end of the day and nothing more than a few number ones, a best-selling album and half a million T-Shirts ever came of them!

Me and Wendy joined our Paul, Megan, Michelle and Mum for a trip to Rhyl in Wales. And guess what... bloody Frankie was there as well. It was red hot that day and when we got there Rhyl was heaving. We hit the beach and after a traditional paddle and a game of dodge the jellyfish, me scooping up some on a stick and chasing Megan all over the beach with them, me and Wendy were sat gazing out to sea breathing in the fresh Welsh seaside air keeping a listen for some Richard Burton narration, just as a speeding projectile zoomed from behind me and did a u turn as if guided by remote control. Lining up to its target the missile hit me straight in the eye bang on target... bull's eye!!! "What the heck," I said... rubbing my eye and realising a great big fat greasy 'Welsh special' chip had been aimed at me and splattered into every corner of my eye. Wiping greasy fat and potato morsels out of my injured eye, I turned around and saw our Paul laughing his head off, stood a good way behind us and tucking into his bag of chips with the rest of the gang. "I think our Paul's chucking chips at me," I concluded resulting in tears of laughter from all!

Recovering from the chip in the eye ordeal and still finding tiny elements of ingredients from the sea front friary lodged in hard to clean places of my eye, we took a stroll along the sea front. We had a pint outside a sea front bar that was packed to the rim in and out. I saw Welsh rockers The Alarm look-alikes and was expecting to hear the sound of '68 Guns' resound from them; we had donuts, waffles and some had cockles, Mussels and whelks. I fancied a tub of fresh warm popcorn and decided to indulge in some. The trouble is, just as I started to tuck in, a tiny Monkey on a bloke's arm also decided he fancied some too. As we passed the bloke who had two of the little monkeys on his arms, ready for photos taken, I gave one a pat on the head just as the other made a swoop straight at my popcorn. The popcorn went all over the place like a seaside avalanche and the monkey dived straight down and got itself tucked in. What a show! I became a seaside spectacle myself as people passed by pointing and laughing at what had happened. The monkey won, I lost, I should never have indulged in so many Planet of the Apes films and comics back in the 70's should I? It was bound to end up getting a bit too hairy and simian.

Other seaside visits that year were daytrips to Bridlington, Skegness and Morecambe Bay, where I searched for a record stall I had been told about that sold some decent Soul vinyl. There were no chips in the eye at Morecambe, and no sign of Eric and Ernie either (sadly our comedy pal, Eric Morecambe – like Tommy Cooper -had also gone to the great jokers gathering in the sky, earlier in the year), but I did catch the coach home with a bag-full of Atlantic black label Soul 45's starring Carla Thomas, Barbara Lewis, Solomon Burke, Doris Troy and the one and only Wilson Pickett, amongst others! The coach driver must have been on a promise on that return journey as he drove like a possessed maniac on heat blowing everything off the road and taking country lane corners like Skid Solo. When we got off the Grand Prix bus, I kissed the ground like the bloody survivor of a near-miss airline crash.

The summer of 84 was a great experience and in-between fine-tuning the sounds of Reaction and the new songs I was writing (including the Solomon Burke via Small Faces homage of mine 'Walk it Talk it'), I was lapping up being in my longest running relationship so far- one that would last 20 years exactly. It was a time of teenage tiffs and sun-enveloping fun and bliss and learning about life from a vision of two as opposed to one: which meant having to endure episodes of 'TJ Hooker' and 'V' on the telly, unfortunately. It was also a time of parties, music, endless renting of 'An American Werewolf in London' and 'Revenge of the Nerds' on VHS (and why was that bloke with the husky voice always on about some crappy film no-one was bothered about on the start of each video?)... a time of getting chased down the length of Haugh Road by a gang of Mod-hating thugs and of drunken stupors, swollen bellies from Mum's legendary bread cakes eaten from oven to mouth with no journey in-between... and continuously more of the same, all the while laughs coming through thick and fast and continuously. It really was a long hot summer and (despite the hardships of the time) a truly great time to be young!

By the end of the summer the band was ready to gig again. We had spent hours, weeks and months trying to achieve our ultimate sound, though the patrons of the Rawmarsh Trades and Labour working man's club would have disputed that when one week we hired out their concert room and brought back memories of Stukas at Dunkirk for the older fellas and afflicting previously untapped nervous dispositions amongst the middle aged and square and straight remainders. On a quiet night while drifting into sleep, I can still hear the insults, comments and pleas sent our way during those afternoons... "Turn that bleeding racket down, you unmusical cat-wailing nuisances," being the most polite rating we received. To us though, we sounded the best we had so far, but even though we felt confident at presenting our new set to an audience (other than the Rawmarsh cloth cappers and co), I didn't want to continue being the lead singer, preferring to concentrate on the guitar, and so we carried on honing our craft and began our search for a suitable singer.

In October me, John and Ian went to see the Style Council at the Sheffield City Hall, supported by Tracie Young (of 'The House that Jack Built' fame). Tracie would later team up with the band in a Mark 3 version line up of The Way. Another individual that would soon be making an impact upon our musical future was also in the City Hall building that night, Terry Sutton.

It had been ages since we had had our own proper family bonfire just like the old days. It was usually a communal one up at the Marquis or Clifton Park This year was different though. Our Paul and his merry gang arrived at our House on the day just in time for a 6pm kick off with all the makings of a proper good old-fashioned Bonfire. Stood at the gate, I saw a mobile Sherwood forest of wood, branches; bushes and general bonfire mayhem appear at the bottom of the street, (to a rendition of the 'Steptoe and Son' theme tune, in my head). "What tha up to, Paul?" "We are having a bonny, Tone." And a bonny we surely had. In no time at all, my Mum's back garden was ablaze with a towering inferno and, as was the old tradition, Mum panicked and threatened to go to the phone box and call the fire brigade as it was getting far too out of hand. Taters and chessies in the smouldering embers followed a feast of nosh and firework cheating (watching everyone else's). Everyone got the mickey taken out of 'em and all were smiling. If there had been a blazing row between us instead of a blazing fire it truly would have been like the good old days! Still it was great to be back in the company of my family, a situation that occurred far too rarely by that time. Of course it's true that we had all changed a lot, but Bonny neet 1984 proved that we could all get on with each other, forget our past rows and differences and still have a proper good time together. It remains a happy memory of mine.

By 1984 the family tree had uprooted and spread its wings a little and some members (at least the extended ones anyway) were hardly to be seen from now on. Uncle Mick (at one time a regular drinking pal of our Paul's) had married, had kids and moved to the frontier town of Canklow and I bumped into him occasionally in Rotherham bus station, usually slightly abbreviated, but always asking of his 'Lovely Auntie Eileen'. The ones left in my Mum's family resided in and around Rotherham, Ravenfield and Bradford (one family member a fireman sometimes turning up at our house in his fire engine). Mum's sister, my Aunty Amy, was still around and every time we saw each other, we would give each other a great big hug. She never cared if she was hugging a local punk rocker or one of those Mod kids that caused riots at the sea-side... I was still 'Our little Tony' to her. My Aunty Amy was a real character who we all loved dearly. She always made me laugh with her exuberance especially when she would play act situations to describe occurrences. Beneath her everyday innocence there was also a rebel streak still evident within that young school dodger my Mum used to describe old childhood tales of. Her husband, Uncle Eric, had passed away in 1979 after a terrible cancer. The year before, when stood at my Dad's grave-side, he had spoken (as if to my Dad) saying "I won't be long before I join you, Ken." It made me feel sad and sorry for him when my Mum told me and I didn't really believe it would come true, but it did. Sadly other family members were soon to join them both.

In early 1985, as Morrissey's Smiths declared 'Meat is Murder' and Billy Bragg sang poetically about 'Between the Wars' and the blue-eyed soul of Big

Sound Authority declared 'This House is Where Your Love Stands' and Frankie still hadn't quite made it to Hollywood but had recently discovered the 'Power of Love', me and my band mates were introduced to a young lanky Mod kid with a cool Weller-style hair cut in a Mac round at our usual meeting HQ... my Mum's front room, where else?

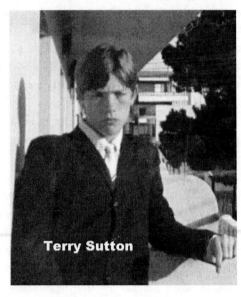

Terry Sutton

It was a Saturday afternoon when we were introduced to our lad, Terry... who, like Ian, was from Mexborough and, quite importantly, also had a Rickenbacker guitar. Myself and John were keen to hand over the singing duties (well around 75% of) and this time hopefully not to someone in the unique calibre of our old begrudged acquaintance, Mr Wolfgang the first. Thankfully, Terry was well up on his Mod culture and music and clothes etc. and most importantly was a very accomplished and talented musician who had already mastered other instruments prior to taking up the guitar quite recently. He was very keen to impress us that day, appearing just a bit nervous but 100% committed to giving it his best as he sped through a medley of Jam songs. As the nervous drips of sweat dripped down his Mac, me and John edged a sneaky wink of approval at each other in recognition that we had finally found someone to belt out the vocals and flesh out our tinny old guitar sound. "Jobs a good un," as good old Del Boy would summarise to seal a dodgy deal.

Before long, the naffly-named 80's Reaction became The Way, Mod targets and power pop art and clobber took over: out went the Paisley shirts, cravats and Fred Perry polo shirts and in came a kind of post-1966 Mod image. I grew my hair out of the short Mod Weller style crop and John remained the second best thing to a real genuine Bruce Foxton in a band. Ian indulged even further into the Mod look and Terry became our young and talented front man: all was stinking of lovely blood red roses and our future in music seemed positively sealed, promised and absolutely imminent. We had finally arrived!

Almost straight away we began gigging. The dependable Rawmarsh Youth club disco, Mexborough Civic (where we did a photo shoot and interview with a local Mod fanzine), Conisborough Station Hotel (a gig that the owners foolishly paid us in beer and saw us almost drink the place dry) and Rotherham Clifton Hall - 'No punk rockers in attendance or bomb scares this time,' though, I mused as I stood chatting to the crowd of Mods in the venue's bar. We received features in the local press, did photo sessions and interviews and wrote a clutch of new songs: myself and Terry quickly settling into a workable song writing partnership as his talents inspired my confidence. We revamped old tunes of mine such as 'You in One' and 'It's OK' and an old Mod beat one of mine called 'Walk it Talk it' and collaborated on new songs 'Days Like--Tomorrow' and the Mod fave; the Tamla beat-enthused 'Sock it!'

In May we recorded our first proper demo tape in a Doncaster recording studio, taking a whole day to put down 3 short songs of ours and what seemed like a month getting the drum sound right. When me and John took it along to local Mod icon, Zal (Steve Downing) who was still getting over the bad car crash he had been in, for his opinion, we were nervous and proud. When he gave us the nod of approval we thought we must be doing something right then. This lad had seen just about every band worth knowing about, from early punk through to the very start of the Mod revival, he had experienced every aspect of growing up in the era and his evaluation of our endeavours was highly rated. Nothing can stop us now! In weeks we had gone from being a zestful 3-piece struggling to get out of playing the local one venue Youth club circuit... into a gigging, recording, local media-covered Mod band with a set comprising our own songs, a selection of fave Mod tunes and a few Jam covers: so yes, overall things were really pretty damn great!

The summer of 85 was yet another fun-packed season of laughs, boozing and music with the extra bonus of being a part of a real band that people were actually paying to come and see. We even had our own small, but loyal following of proper Mods who would turn up to give us support and dig the Soul sounds before-hand and check out our set - to which we added a rousing cover of The Impressions 'Oer the Yonder'. John and me lapped it all up, spending drinking sessions after rehearsals up at the Marquis Hotel and the sparse corners of the local boozer map, sprinting with youthful confidence, whilst setting our sights and ambitions upon making it big... but with a social conscience: what immature sods we must have been? Nevertheless, back in the summer of 85 nothing was going to stand in our way as we finally set off on our path to truly setting the world alight!

Chapter six

Northern Rock 'n Soul

Like a Punk Rock-spawned garage band take of a poor man's Hamburg period Beatles... escaping from the local youth club with an obsessive dose of Mod sensibilities and a lyrical social conscience... we, The Way had arrived. It was 1985, halfway through the decade and nothing in the world was going to stand in the way of our frantic rhythm and blues-energised Northern Rock 'n Soul!

Of course, now that we were a proper band we had to make sure that we had more clothes to intersperse throughout our live appearances. The tacky but (mostly) dependable Mod mail order catalogue of the Cavern Club and Melandi (along with Sheffield's 'Impulse' where I shelled out for pop art shirts, off-the-peg Hipster trousers and 3-button blazers) all provided the staple clothing attire diet. With a wardrobe of button down shirts of all styles and colours along with an array of Small Faces-styled knitted tops and Pop Art-influenced sweaters along with the cool made-to-measure Mod strides off George on the outside Rotherham Market on a Saturday afternoon and the charity shop golden nuggets of undiscovered original Mod clothes we sometimes found, we seemed to have it all cornered.

John was already well clued-in about Mod clothes, when we met 3 years ago, having been through the whole Mod phase from mid-1979 onwards. By this time he was at his casual Mod stage- Fred Perry's, Levi's and his traditional black 3-buttoned blazer. Terry seemed to have a never-ending wardrobe of Mod attire and for a 16-year old lad he was really cool: the perfect front man for the band, oozing with confidence and cocky attitude. Our drummer, Ian also went with the Mod flow going for Cavern gear and a never-ending selection of bowling shoes. The band, in as far as, songs wrote, clothes wore and attitudes extolled, should have been committed to a time-capsule right at that moment - mid 1985!

I loved my two-tone suit. 3 button fitting, 2 buttons on the cuffs, thin lapels, 4 inch side vents, slim-fitting trousers with frog mouth pockets and one back pocket. I thought it was the bee's knees of Mod, when in reality it was quite possibly nowhere near as neat and detailed as any true self-conscious smart (and authentic) Mod's suits. Maybe in some sense of realising this, as the sheen of the two-tone began to wear off, I began to wear the jacket and trousers separately and reverted to my black Carnaby Street suit... but for a short (yet proud) period of time I was the lad in a two-tone suit, ducking and diving through the 80's: a Pete Townshend-worshipping 20 year old Mod lad with a band all of his own. Talkin' bout our generation... indeed!

I was twenty years old and it all felt like a dream come true. The gamble had paid off. Despite being relatively shy in that sense I always had a vision of performing on stage. Right from my early pre-teenage youth of watching Bowie and Bolan on Top of the Pops, I had this secret dream of one day playing in a band and feeling that buzz. Until you experience doing so you really never know what it will be like? For me it felt like

second nature once I had made that initial step of going ahead and doing it regardless. As long as you have that self-belief to drive you on it gets you through, no matter what.

Within a couple of years so much had improved in my life. I had very little money in my frog-mouthed trouser pockets and would struggle to get from day to day; yet amazingly I had just about everything I wanted in life. It all just fell perfectly into place at the exact right time. You only get so many chances in a lifetime: a time when you really can't wait to get up each and every day and live your life to the full: new experiences, laughs, identity, creativity, good clothes and top mates and the thrills of performing. Lovely jubly!

A surge of positive confidence was speeding through me each day. It was a very Mod summer for me, 1985 and it all seemed like it would last forever! However before we knew it, everything would drastically change way beyond repair!!!

In June we all went to the Sheffield City Hall to see Paul Weller's Style Council. We had all seen them the year before at the same venue, Terry being lucky enough to have met Weller. This time around we were all lucky enough to do so too.

The gig was, as to be expected, top class. The Style Council were at their peak with their classic LP 'Our Favourite Shop', Weller's document of mid 80's UK with more than a few political overtones involved. As we all gathered around the back of the City Hall after the gig, to our surprise, we were let in to meet Paul and the gang.

Paul was stood leaning up against the wall with a camera around his neck, looking bloody cool as usual. He appeared taller than onstage and was fairly quiet. Nothing like the angry young man I had felt I had grown up with: my unconfirmed missing twin! He listened to us waffle on about our band and our hopes and dreams, showing interest, and struggling a little to keep up with our Yorkshire accents, giving us a confused look every now and again. Paul could hardly get a word in edgeways for us spouting our Yorkshire pudding lingo excitement about wanting to be famous and play our own songs that would be recognised and loved by the world and hopefully Paul himself? After about twenty minutes or so, the security (as usual) came along and told us to bugger off and so we said our goodbyes to Paul, Mick, Steve and DC Lee. We dropped our tape off with Paul's sister, Nicky, who was running the merchandise stall. Apparently, Paul listened to the tape the next day on the tour bus... I often wondered what he thought of 'Sock it' and 'It's OK' (My 1982 tribute to an upset girl called Alison).

That same month, The Way played the annual Mod weekender in Scarborough. We travelled there in the back of Terry's Dad's transit van, a bumpy ride all the way, with us sat on our Amplifiers and equipment. Terry had got us the gig: he had a very close and keen ear to the ground with regards to getting gigs and the like. We felt just like The Jam with Paul Weller's dad on their first tour. The only thing is, much as I loved the band with a passion and enjoyed playing their songs, I was trying my best to get away from being just like The Jam!

We played that night to a packed venue of Mods (including a contingent of Rotherham Mods), winning them over with our energy and mix of classic Mod songs alongside our own raw rhythm and blues-energised tunes. Right from plugging our guitars in everything just felt perfect somehow. We were nervous yet totally confident in being able to deliver what we had been perfecting for months. The atmosphere was electric and in a way, quite surreal. It felt like we really had truly arrived. As we played our very own songs and The Who's 'I Can't Explain' to these Mods who had never even heard of us before, I gazed around the packed room, looking into the faces of Mods. Close-cropped Mod cuts, immaculate 3-button-tailored suits and Italian knitted shirts galore; only the odd few tickets in view. This was a truly defining moment in my life. It was an epic personal musical bliss and I was hooked. We were shouted back on for an encore of the Batman theme and as I made my way off stage, over to our corner gathering of mates and the cloud of smoke omitting from Critch's extra huge reefer, I was still buzzing with a euphoric inner glow. I now desperately craved the prospect of more!!

Before the gig (which we recorded on tape for prosperity), we did interviews with fanzines, had our photos taken outside the venue and it all felt like the perfect little band. It was one of the best days of my life and I felt totally on top of the world. The next day, myself, Ian and Wendy took a trip around Scarborough admiring the hordes of scooters and taking photos on the beach; posing like the image-conscious Mods we were. The sun was shining that morning and was seeping deeply into my life and every essence of my being.

Scarborough Mod Rally June 1985

CLASS presents
on the

SCARBOROUGH MOD RALLY '85
A SIXTIES EVENING FEATURING

YEH YEH & THE WAY
+ 60's DISCO featuring Tony Class, Shirley & Dom
at
THE SALISBURY HOTEL BALLROOM
Huntriss Row
on Saturday, 15th June, 1985
6 p.m. till 2 a.m.
Smart Dress Absolutely Essential

ADMISSION BY THIS TICKET ONLY

Top: Scooters on
Scarborough's Huntriss Row

Middle: Ian, me and John

Right: Mods watching The Way

Mods at the Scarborough 1985 weekender

Mods photos Courtesy of Steve Peoples

Away from the Numbers - Tony Beesley

June 1985 was an amazing month in my life. Everything was moving fast and totally in tune. I had met my idol, Paul Weller; we had our own demo tape of self-penned songs under our belt and had now performed a life-defining gig at northern Mod's favourite seaside resort, Scarborough. Nothing could spoil the huge frantic rush of life I was feeling! Everything I had been veering towards during those years since becoming a teenager, throughout the punk years and frustration-fuelled early 80's... the whole confusion and indecision had turned into something just right, exactly as I had dreamed of! It tasted bloody lovely and I wanted more! The years of insecurity, false starts and lack of truly rewarded faith had been swept away: here was my reason to be here: to be someone was a wonderful thing! And then it had to all bloody end!

Christ it wasn't as if we were really the bloody Beatles or something! We weren't famous at all. But, during that summer of 85, it seemed as though the world around us was truly ours and maybe in a very small way it was. The trouble is we were young and daft. We had ideas above our stations. It just happened so fast and we peaked far too early... or maybe we didn't peak at all? Anyway, either way, after that Scarborough gig it all went rapidly downhill.

The next gig was in Mexborough and me and John stupidly walked off stage, him treating the audience to a barrage of Sex Pistols-styled verbal abuse. "I suppose you would rather listen to some f*****g Wham or some shit like that.... You're just a bunch of f*****g tossers!!!" We had to grab our gear and scarper pretty quickly that night as the word spread around Mexborough that some Mod band from Rawmarsh had just insulted the entire flower of Mexborough youth. In fact, we were half Rawmarsh and were merely expressing our disdain towards the feeble and un-moved audience. We were young, foolish, and impulsive and didn't care who we upset! Poor Terry got his parka spat on by Mexborough toughs the following day as he ventured out and it would take me years to grasp how much our actions actually hurt his prestige and self-esteem. The seeds of ill-fortune were heading all of our way, though.

The summer continued with us briefly splitting, reforming, and doing local interviews, writing new songs and then a mini riot of a gig at the Rawmarsh Baths Hall. The Baths Hall gig set we played went well, with a great Northern Soul DJ spot as the local Mods all turned out in force. We played our usual set of Mod faves and our own songs and all was hunky dory as Mr Bowie might say! Maybe the trip there in the afternoon with our gear should have fore-warned us when me and John had to get off the bus with our gear cos of the rotten stink omitting from an old fella with an out of control greasy neck beard on the back of the bus: we were almost puking up as we knocked on the door of the venue to let us in, away from the red hot weather-encouraging aroma of the tramp from stink city; perhaps an omen that things would maybe not turn up smelling of roses later on for us?

Following our set and a great night of Mod sounds and drinks to sooth our angry stage personas, we all congregated in the small and cramped dressing room where an argument between the door security that we had employed and our mate, Martin turned sour and violent.

The dressing room door was shut on us by the bouncers as outside a mate of mine, Paul Coggins, from school, hammered on the door saying "Don't hit Beesley, he's my mate." Before you knew it, a punch was pulled and unfortunately Wendy got the back-draw of it and got herself knocked out... and then all hell broke loose! The rest is a blur, a series of fights, scuffles and rows ensued in and out of the venue, as they always do once some bloody cowboy decides to belt another cowboy. As police sirens wailed and cop cars arrived on the scene, all I can remember is trying to revive my girlfriend who was out for the count and in a hazy dream-like vision we caught the sight of John opening up the takings tin (which was my much-cherished saving tin from my kid days) and sharing the cash out. John was the perfect chancellor of the exchequer and came up roses with a pocketful of fivers and quid coins whilst the rest of us got just about enough for a 2-pint drinking session the night after! Never a lad to over-look an opportunity was John. I still have that green cash tin, though. The lad I knew from school who stuck up for me during this Mod mini-riot, Paul Coggins, later died in a crash on his bike, nice lad he was too. I still think of Paul from time to time.

I reckon that The Way, or at least the version I knew of and was a part of, ended that night and my dreams of being a proper song writer got pissed up the wall and were knocked out clean cold too. Within a few months and a few sporadic gigs along the way, we would be consigned to history. The dream was almost over!

Before the dream ended, there was a chance for us to make our small mark in history. Everyone has heard of the famous Live Aid Wembley concert and all of its associated charity merits, and musical grievances and extravagances, but how many people actually recall our own well-intended local version, in which any local band worth their guitar strings (or synths in the Dolls case!), would play for free to a thousand and a half souls on a cold August afternoon and night on Herringthorpe playing fields; the very same place that the Specials had attempted to unify a crowd of brawling skinheads four years previously.

Organised by local musicians Mark Lynam and Jon Ward of our friends, Suburban Dream, the event saw an eclectic bunch of bands perform; including New Romantics My Pierriot Dolls, Psychobilly faves Phil Murray and the Boys From Bury, Traces of A, Kid Salami and the Carboni Brothers, Heavy Rock act Barabbas and (amongst a long list of others) the only Mod band on show, us naughty white Levis-wearing Mod lads... The Way!

All I can recall of the day (our only outdoor performance) was it being really cold and us waiting to go on stage for what seemed like ages. When we did eventually play our set, it was so cold that John's fingers froze whilst playing his (Free-form Jazz) bass line to Wilson Pickett's 'In the Midnight Hour', to which we never stopped ribbing him about. We went down fairly well, but it wasn't all about that - unlike the larger event down south. It was about doing our own small bit to help a good cause. I went home not long after playing, taking off my white Levis and setting about writing some new songs. And that was my experience of the Rotherham Live Aid event of 1985!

In September a classic album was released. It was not the recent Jesus and the Mary Chain punk-styled gig riots and accompanying headlines or the imminent new Clash LP that sparked my interest, but the dungarees-shed, Brooks Brothers suits-wearing Dexy's Midnight Runners. Amazingly, it seemed at the time, that I was amongst a very small amount of people in the whole country that believed in its status and worth. 'Don't Stand Me Down' had taken almost 3 years to complete and also in a way symbolised, for me, the new mood and renewed faith I had in music! I wanted more Soul and R&B in my music, less Rock, less punk and fewer guitars. I was also massively into the Gospel Soul of Al Green after picking up his 'Gets Next To You' LP of his at a record fair. I felt stifled within the safe 4-piece structure of The Way and none of my ideas, plans and musical influences fit appropriately within the agenda at hand!

The new songs I was writing - 'Love Becomes Politics' being the only new one that was ever performed live, which was at our final gig at the Rotherham Arts Centre (for a while the accepted showcase for up and coming local bands) - were nothing like the stuff we had been playing, being more contemporary Weller, Soul and folk influenced and (lyrically) personally, rather than directly, political. It was true; I did have a new musical vision, a dream, maybe even a fool's dream. I truly believed that I could achieve it all too. In October I had also convinced John as well. We had been falling out with Terry on and off for a while, we even had rows before going on stage. It seemed that we were all pulling in different directions. I felt that we had had our day and foolishly wanted to start all over again. One dark and rainy winter night at our front door, me and John told Ian and Terry that we were splitting the band (Ian was more than welcome to come along but in our hearts we knew he would stick with Terry). And that was that: we closed the door on Ian and Terry and began a new chapter in our so-called musical career... or so we naïvely believed!

Around this time John got booted out of his parent's house and came to live round at my Mums'. What started out as a novelty and a perfect excuse for me and him to create our new musical vision as we had done before soon turned into a friend-testing and patience-stretching nightmare. Pretty soon we were at each other's throats. True, we tried to create a new sound. I wrote plenty of new songs and was as keen and determined as ever to get things off the ground. John soon got his foot under the table and you would have thought he was the son and I was the lodger within a matter of days. Then again, he did get on like a house on fire with my Mum - who always had a soft spot for him too. They would sit and watch Blockbusters and the rest of the telly programmes together, while I tried to write new songs in the other room. He soon set up his own gambling nights in the room too and as he had his own key he would piss off into the early hours getting pissed and then turning up waking me up. He took over the bloody telly with marathon sessions of Horse Racing and one afternoon I got so fed up that I threw a cup of tea straight into the middle of our blazing coal fire with the result being a mushroom cloud to rival Hiroshima! As the dust and debris from the fire enveloped the entire room, my Mother ran in going mad with us. The fall-out began to clear and John just sat there and said, "Umm, so that's how you summon a Genie then!" Covered in soot we looked like we had been subject to a controlled demolition of the local cooling towers and sat through the middle of it. On hearing John's characteristically dry assumption, I tried desperately to hold back the laughter: I couldn't. We both burst out laughing in hysterics. "Say Stanley, it's just like the talcum powder episode all over again isn't it," I said to John in my best Oliver Hardy voice. John tickled his head in classic Laurel mode and replied "It sure is, Ollie, what happened!"

John eventually buggered off. He somehow got himself a flat nearby. We stayed mates but had realised that it looked very unlikely that anything could ever come out of us spending that much time together again. The end was also here - before it had really even begun - of our next musical venture. I was struggling alone, taking on musicians of every description, but never managing to even come close to recapturing our glory days of that summer.

In 1985, a new record shop opened up on Frederick Street across from the old bus station: Laser records. The shop was massive and had an Alternative record cave upstairs which was a Goth-styled thing with Simon out of local band Spring Heel'd Jack running it. The shop stocked hundreds of records, had DJ's playing there and wasn't that expensive, if I remember right. The trouble is, they sold a load of crap and most of their back catalogue stock was faulty seconds, a dead giveaway being the unpeelable white faulty stickers stuck straight across the front of the LP sleeves. I got that excited about it being a new Mecca for vinyl addicts such as myself that I walked straight into the massive front window, nose first, knocking myself straight to the floor! I had thought it was an open door, the window was so clear. Brushing myself down, I got up hoping that no-one had even clocked me doing my best Norman Wisdom impression, but as I dared to look around I saw a pack of teeth-clattering Rotherham monkeys all laughing their noggins off at me. "Oh, bugger it... just laugh along with 'em," I thought and set off home to write a new song and have some Paul Weller style streaks put into my hair!

The first lot of streaks I had done looked pretty cool. The second dose did too. By the third lot, something drastically wrong occurred. It was a Thursday and the lovely kind woman who had, so far, done some successful haircuts and streaks in my hair arrived with her bleach and streaking cap. It was always a daft experience having to sit with a plastic cap on my head while strands of my hair got tugged through tiny holes and were then smothered with bleach: I would dread the prospect of John or our Paul calling around and catching me in this uncompromisingly pathetic state. Luckily they never arrived and unfortunately a proper streaked hair style didn't either. Whereas my previous streaks had looked cool and nowt to be embarrassed about at all, this time something serious had gone bloody wrong. I looked through the mirror and saw not a scattering of random silver blond streaks in my hair but a collection of inch-thick orange patches!!! "Oh shit!"

The rescue attempts lasted all day. I had more doses of blond applied to my hair than Billy Idol on bloody tour. We even ran out of colour and I had to run round to the chemist for some more, looking like an escaped leopard on human legs. I could have sworn I saw the chemist practitioner sneakily phoning the zoo up to enquire if any new rare species of leopards had escaped. Anyway, I got back without being shot with darts and had yet another go at sorting the barnet out. By early evening my hair was that fragile it was in danger of breaking off and we had to leave it as it was, part rescued, part hilarious-looking leopard man. And to top it all off, it was 7.15pm and John and the mates were due to call for me to go to the boozer!

Would I dare to show my brand new unique hairstyle off to the local drinking establishments and my mates? Yeah, sod it... I went out for a boozing session: my punk days had accustomed me to strange looks at varying hair colours, so why let this bother me. Besides, after tears of laughter from John and the gang and plenty of comments from bar staff who asked if I was allowed out at night etc... the effects of three pints down the neck made me care even less? Anyway, John had his Rupert Bop hair disaster to look forward to in a year or two... not that he or any of us yet knew!

Christmas 85 was - yet again - a time of parties: all-nighters, pub stop overs, house-warming's and all other kinds of parties with not a trifle in sight! Just before the Yuletide celebrations me, John and Ian went to a local lasses' Mod party. It was boring to start off, with us sat looking vacant and watching the Psychobilly kids (actually ex-Mods) and scooter boys dancing to The Meteors and throwing indifferent looks over at us sat on the settee. The fact that we still resembled Soul-focussed Mods as opposed to the now more prominent dressed-down, combat trousers and flight jackets of the scooter scene style that was being invaded with late-punk and skinhead sensibilities was well enough to not have much in common with us. We didn't care anyway! I personally was rapidly losing any affinity with any youth tribe or cults by then.

The parents buggered off, stating in no uncertain terms, that the drinks in the fridge were ok, as were all the bags of booze everyone had brought along... but... DO NOT touch the bottles of wine at the side of the fridge. That was theirs for Christmas. Me and John were sat 'ears pricked to alert' status, catching these last few comments. We never could resist the temptation to steal censored alcohol, be it the traditional barrel of cider we emptied at parties or a mate's homebrew in his shed. Sneaking a look around to check no one was looking, we ventured into the kitchen and grabbed two bottles of best French wine. 'Le pinched punch circa 1985 anyone!!!'

We downed a few glasses, mixed with our cans of cheap 3% lager we had brought along and offered a full glass or two to the young Mod lad stood near us, who we knew full-well had a reputation for not being able to hold his drink. He lapped the wine up in no time and in two shakes of a drunken kitten's tail, he was lathered. The (so far) quiet and boring atmosphere of the so-called Mod party was constantly being interrupted by the lad's loud and very drunken nonsense. His face was glowing with the effects of another couple of glasses and he was starting to stagger around. Me and John were nudging each other and tongue in cheek were getting more and more amused at this party spectacle. Things were looking up. Someone put The Jam on and suddenly the atmosphere eased up even more. Now this is more like it.

Just as we were starting to laugh and relax, we turned around and saw the drunken Mod lad's face turn pasty white and his eyes start to glaze over... yet he was still laughing. He made a grab for a door, fell down and then stood up. He then threw up: then again and again, before turning around, his head rotating in full circles replicating a Quadrophenia version of the Exorcist, and spewing up like a bloody lighthouse all over the place!!! We ducked as it went flying all over, just missing us. We then stood up to see the human lighthouse launch yet more psychedelic wine-reeking projectiles all over the show. Kids were dodging him, lasses were screaming, his mates were trying to push him to the toilet and we... well we sat there in hysterics, tears dripping into our cheap 'Challenge' lagers. Everyone was staring at us in disbelief and disgust. How can they sit there laughing when chaos and puke were being spread all over the room? The lad finally made it into the toilets and then settled down to a night with his head over the bowl while we sat laughing, guzzling booze and wondering what the poor lass's parents were gonna say when they returned home. Puke all over the show and their best nowhere to be seen Christmas wine to blame and a pair of empty bottles as evidence. Well before they were due to arrive home, we too were nowhere to be seen either!

1985 ended! The year of Live Aid and the Miners' Strike! The Miners had been defeated (but not without a momentous fight), the Unions were castrated by the struggle and the pits began to close one by one. Our community soon began to feel the results of the pit closures as whole families were devastated and left out to dry with job losses and poor prospects of the years ahead. In ensuing years, the Steel Industry also partly collapsed before reaching privatisation as did many local business and factories. In 1985, there were hardly any drugs, except a slow but steady flow of marijuana in circulation, within our Thatcher-wrecked town. Within less than ten years, though, drugs and its associated crime were rife and nothing would ever be the same again!

Back in 1985, I was still hanging on to the false hope of becoming a musician. My guitar playing had improved and I was now influenced, not so much by Mick Jones of The Clash or Dr Feelgood's Wilko Johnston, but by Nile Rodgers of Chic and a whole host of funky players many of whom I had discovered via the eclectic tastes of my hero Mr Weller. As 1986 arrived I was buying records by contemporary bands such as punk/funkers Black Britain and Jazz/Soul lovers, Working Week amongst others. I also had an incredibly naïve dream of grandeur of actually forming some kind of musical coalition, not unlike the Style Council collective of musicians of Weller and Talbots'. The major difference is... they were hugely talented... I was a council estate kid with a chip on his shoulder with a rudimentary knowledge of how to play Funk Soul on a Fender copy guitar. Big dreams for a kid out in the suburbs, eh?

My old pal, John Harrison stuck with me for a while but deserted the sinking ship after being offered a place back in the ranks of our old band, who were now swiftly moving up the ladder with their revised line-up and a distinct influence of politically-tinged Northern Soul pop... not a little unlike the Redskins. John was doing well for a while and travelled to London with The Way for a 'Morning Post' interview and extolling the virtues of socialist pop whilst performing numerous gigs at venues such as Rotherham's Assembly rooms and Doncaster Rotters and experiencing a near-miss record contract with Go-Discs (who signed up the Proclaimers instead). He eventually got the sack and of course, it was obligatory for John to leave the fold owing cash to someone. Meanwhile, I was now down to a one-man band, continuing my futile auditions and managing to look forward to a regular morning session with two lovely looking lasses who were born twenty odd years too early for the X Factor!

The sessions put me out of breath with these two aspiring Pepsi and Shirley's. I could only manage to perform so many continuous renditions of Barrett Strong's 'Money that's What I Want' in the front room couldn't I? They were a tidy little duo, full of excitable enthusiasm... and it all made me feel just a bit embarrassed. Besides I had a very strong feeling that one of them fancied me, which reached its unconsummated demise when they realised I was already hitched up. One morning I dragged myself out of bed to be met with a message stating that they had been enjoying the rehearsals, but they were packing it all in. Bloody hell... even the front room Bananarama wannabees had now washed their hands with me. So... back to the drawing board! I had tried out countless musicians (and ideas) ranging from a meek and mild spectacled bass player called Ken with a friendly love and knowledge of Soul, a manic Jazz drummer who was just perfect but predictably unreliable... to a number of

loose and undependable budding musicians, non-starters and idealists.
Thankfully, the legend that was Wolfgang never returned. I couldn't have taken
that. He would have ended up wearing a set of guitar strings for a beard
instead of his John Landis-influenced werewolf neck growth.

   I went back to the Rotherham guitar shop that turned me down for a new
Gibson semi-acoustic guitar the year before where a member of local Soul
covers band the Internationals worked and asked him if I could audition for the
band as they were advertising for a new guitarist. I gave my best shot at
scratchy funky guitar playing but I came out without a new guitar or a new
band membership. I also went along to Barnsley to audition for a working club
act. They picked me up and took me along to their rehearsal room, which was a
fair-sized one with huge amplifiers and PA system, a far cry from the school
classroom I had been used to rehearsing in. They managed to persuade me to
play along to songs by Bruce Springsteen, Fine Young Cannibals and even
Queen, me improvising rhythm guitar. They had a complete line up, singer,
bass guitar, drums and a really talented coloured girl on backing vocals... but
no rhythm guitarist. On the way home in the car, they spoke of touring
Germany and the rest of Europe, performing cover songs and being paid
generously for their troubles. They offered me the job... which was quite
surprising. Apparently they were impressed with my quick ability to adapt and
keep up with songs I had never played before and the fact that I could
improvise as I played along... just what they needed. Maybe they intended
turning down the volume dial like I had so mischievously done to some of our
cling-ons a year or two previously? They were not impressed, though by my
objections to performing Springsteen or any other 'over the hill Rock music'
and the fact that I was wanting to play guitar for a band with Soul not rock 'n
roll as its blueprint! Lead balloon fast approaching time again... then!

   My dreams of a live Soul revue had ended now for sure, it seemed at the
time. I was never gonna be a new Paul Weller, a fledgling Kevin Rowland or
even a cheap part-time club act. My days in music, or at least performing it,
were over which was hard for me to swallow. It is true that some of the wrong
turns and downright refusals to conform and play the game were also my fault.
I just couldn't bring myself to grin and bear it. I had to search for the
alternative option, but the trouble is, I was never sure what it was and where to
find it.

At the start of the decade, I had dreamt of playing in a band and to get halfway to where I had been would have been a dream come true... but now I had let it all slip out of my hands. The punk ideal, the Mod sensibilities and the prospect of ever performing on a stage ever again: all were now held into question. The dream was now truly over and I tore up one of my suit jackets in a fit of rage in response!

That year a part of me died with those dreams as my walls came tumbling down hard and fast, yet, strangely, another part of me was re-born. The crazy anti-authoritarian out for a laugh chaotic piss-taker was given a new lease of life as I found more time to have fun, new mates to get drunk with and a whole life ahead of me wondering which path life was going to speed me towards next. As 1986 and the rest of the 80's replaced the euphoria and musical dreams of 1985, only one thing was sure to be in place - as I cast my guitar aside - I was gonna have a damned good old laugh... anyone care to join me? Let's backtrack a little and see if the bar is open!!

"Confide in me, please, confide in me in everything that you see."
Lyrics from 'Love Becomes Politics' (Beesley – 1985)

Chapter seven

Two Pints of Lager
and a bag of nuts pal!

Throughout the drinking years... we were daft as owt, me and John. If we weren't going to set the world alight with our musical talents and spleen-venting attacks at the system via our songs of political poetry... then we were surely going to get plastered and have plenty of fun drowning our sorrows. Two pints of lager and a bag of nuts, please... pal, and hurry up, we're thirsty.

Me and John shared and experienced life together just like proper mates should - just like a 1980's version of Laurel and Hardy to be honest and just as daft and accident-prone too. We shared the same dreams, the same aspirations for bettering ourselves (in a socialist non-capitalistic way of course)... we shared the same dodgy pub jukebox, the same clothes when skint and the exact same zest for living our lives whilst embracing as much care-free hedonistic booze-fuelled fun as we could, or something along those lines.

We first became mates with pints in hand, me and John. Frequenting the local boozers kicking off orders at the Monkwood Hotel and onto the Earl Grey, The Crown, The Star, The Queens and the Marquis Hotel, we would drink until our cash ran out: often John's would deplete half way through the evening from his fruit machine habit. He had once gotten into trouble at a local pub for trying to empty the fruit machine via a scam of his, but his love of gambling never abated. It was one of his passions.

To begin with, we were both still dressing as ardent Mods and my Weller-influenced Soul stylist look had not yet made an appearance. Wearing our blazers, boating jackets, bowling shoes, Ben Sherman button downs and sporting neat French crop Mod hair styles (John's always a little bit longer), we stood out like two great big sore thumbs in the hard-hitting white shirt-wearing mullet-attired pit village of our home turf - Rawmarsh. Luckily, between us, we knew most blokes or were on (sometimes strained but just scraping in) nodding terms with the local tough nuts. The odd comment thrown our way, "Look here comes the Small Faces," or "He thinks he's Paul Weller" never bothered us one bit. We were at times arrogant in our own way, but didn't mean to be and certainly never meant anybody any harm at all. I was almost 18 and fiercely anti-racist, anti-complacency, anti-blood sports and anti-vivisection... I was pro-Soul, pro-attitude, pro-vegetarian and pro-drinking. Aping my idol, Paul Weller from his attitude-laced gum-chewing expressions and sense of cool to the size of my trouser creases whilst taking great influence from John's knowledge of Mod attire... I thought I knew it all, but in reality, I really knew bugger all about the world and its goings on.

Being Mods and standing out of the crowd also meant the positive notion of getting noticed by the girls: something we set out deliberately to do and every night we went out in hope of pulling the magic one. To be fair, though, me and John's pedigree of 'getting off with the girls' would have made a great script for 'The Likely Lads'... always starting off well yet ending up as pear-shaped as that bar-maid's arse I was looking at. Don't get me wrong about the shapes of the other sex; the long, the short, fat, thin and the tall... I loved 'em all. Life would have been perfect if the enthusiasm had been as zestful in return. But, like all young lads with so much to learn in life, we screwed up, double-booked and pissed up many a healthy option and came home hand in hand with a nicked pint glass instead of the intended lusty girlfriend fantasy.

After a couple of pints and a good chat about music and who John had conned of late, we would always be up for chatting up the fairer sex. Now, years of memory loss, not forgetting the drinking of the time, has eroded much of those times... some thankfully for our benefit, I would imagine, but here are some highlights (and lowlights) of those rampaging sex hormones being let loose in the faraway days of the early to mid-80's set to our soundtrack of The Jam, The Who, Small Faces and the sounds of Tamla Motown with a menu of Carling Black Label, John Smiths Bitter, Woodpecker cider, tatty roll ups and endless amounts of packets of crisps... oh and don't forget another bag of nuts pal, while yer at the bar!! It was a great time to be irresponsible; there were no smoking bans, health conscious rulings and a spade was still firmly a bloody spade, no matter which way you looked at it or used it! Fools we may well have been, but we had nothing to worry about and our world was... well cool.

On one drinking occasion, as me and John had just started chatting to two very nice (nowadays we would say fit) birds with lovely sixties-styled bob hair do's and were actually getting somewhere for a change, even getting invited back to a party they were going to, well we noticed a mate of ours called Martin enter the pub. Now this guy was a pal of ours but had a knack for wanting to shock, talk dirty and outrage the girls as his chat up strategy. Sid James had nothing on this lad: just what we needed at this crucial point of almost cracking it with a lovely couple of young hot women, then! Let me tell you the outcome.

"Don't look now, John, but guess who has just come in," I craftily whispered in John's ear. John couldn't help but look; he had the curiosity of an extra-nosy cat. "Oh Christ, all we need... just ignore him and he might piss off, with some luck," he reasoned. The pub was packed. It was a typical busy Friday night in The Crown with Spandau Ballet's 'Gold' and 'Do You Really Want to Hurt Me' by Culture Club on a seemingly endless repeat play from the DJ. The drinks were going down lovely and we still had enough for two more. Most importantly, we had two very interested and lovely-looking sexy girls with a very inviting sparkle in their eyes. What could go wrong then?

"What do you two do then?" Asks the dark-haired one with the coolest sixties Bob haircut. I fancied this one the most. I had been watching re-runs of 'Ready Steady Go' on Channel Four recently and had a thing for Swinging Sixties sex siren and Mod's great female icon, Cathy McGowan. Being only born during the mid-sixties, I had missed the promiscuous decade and birds that looked like Cathy and Emma Peel of The Avengers (another of my teenage fantasies after I had moved on from Kim Wilde) so was aiming to make up for it tonight. John also had a lovely-looking blonde flashing her eye lashes at him and his eye brows were going up and down like Groucho Marx' as he became more excited and openly keen. "We play in a band," was my choice answer and hopefully one guaranteed to impress. "I am the guitarist and (uh hum) sing a bit and he plays bass guitar just like that fella out of The Jam," I followed up, my heart beating like mad with an unwanted voice in the back of my head, sat like a devil on a parrot's ledge throwing bricks at my sudden surge of confidence... wondering where the hell it had come from. "We write our own songs too," I threw in the winning goal. "Oh right, blimey, proper little pop stars," they giggled with each other. "What do you write about, then?" came the quickly followed attack. "Oh, you know, Margaret Thatcher and all that." "Eh!!!!" was the look on John's face... "You're buggering it up." Shit... I had to answer quickly... "What I mean is... we write about how that old cow, Thatcher, is wrecking the country and all that." Is that better, I thought? "We are angry and pissed off with the world, basically," I concluded, putting on my very best Paul

Weller-styled cocky grin and stance most likely coming off more like Rodney Trotter on a date. "We want to carry on where punk rock failed and change the world, don't we John?" My vitriolic agenda crept through the cracks. I thought I had left it at home filed away under the first Clash album, but seemingly not. John was looking the other way, hoping that we hadn't been chatting up two young conservatives and that we might just impress them with our young rebel stance. "But we are up for a laugh, we aren't always spouting on about the state of the country yer know," I chipped in to even the balance a little. "Anyway, let's talk about you two... and what time's the party? Can we get going now, then?" I said. "Yeah, that's a great idea," John added as he looked over my shoulder and saw our unwanted guest approaching our small gathering. I could see John's eyes dying and the previously excited sparkle in them fade away in a space of 2 to 3 seconds. "Oh shit," I thought... "Please not now... please don't do this to us." And, like a rotten old unwanted penny good old 'Carry on slap n' tickle Martin' craftily turned at the bar and spotted us!!!

The lad appeared and tapped me on the shoulder. I enacted a look of bewilderment and reckoned to have as little affinity with our conversation interrupter as I could muster. "Oh hey up, we are just off. See you around," I announced. "Hey, I say luv... do you know if they sell shorts at the bar?" Martin jumped in, directing his words to the nice blonde lass on John's arm. "Oh no... don't do this to us." The horror surged into my whole Carling-soaked psyche. The lasses looked at him in disbelief. "Oh, it's just that as I walked in... I shit myself and need some shorts," he followed up with the killer line! The girl's faces dropped. I picked John's up off the floor and mine must have looked like a replica of Captain Hurricane out of the Valiant comic. "He did it... I knew it... he's ruined it for us." As the pennies dropped, the atmosphere rapidly changed from a promising loved-up night for four to a searing cold North Pole blizzard of a sexual encounter failure Mark 25. He just had to hammer the nail firmly, squarely and unashamedly into the coffin. One designed by the undertaker specifically for two pathetic ex Romeos in a world of chat up failure!!! Carry on Bozos... episode 23!

"Oh did they tell you, I am in a band with these two, I'm the main man... the pin up, you know, we write about how much we hate Thatcher." Our faces could have now been peeled up off the floor and pasted onto the wall for cheap wallpaper decoration. It was over... he had done it: Mission successful for the sod. No leg over for us tonight. "No, wait he isn't in our band, he's just a drinking pal of ours, he's having you on, come back, let me tell you the score," I foolishly tried to dig ourselves out. Too late, they were gone like lightening. They had just met two pop star wannabees with a great line in Mickey Pearce chat-up lines and a leader of the band with the charisma of Selwyn Froggit on magic mushrooms. Like I said the Likely lads had nowt on us!!!

We got our own back on Martin many a time and so he did on us too. I cruelly took my revenge during the following summer as John and him went on a week away in Cleethorpes and while they were away eating cold baked beans in a falling to pieces Arctic caravan at the seaside living out the deleted scenes from a rejected 'Likely Lads' script, I was having it away with Martin's all-too willing and able girlfriend every night of the week. Ha bloody ha!

It had all started a few months before. John and I were invited to a party by a lad we knew. As soon as we walked in, Steve (the party host) said "Just hold the fort, we have got to pop out for some more booze and pick some mates and lasses up. We won't be long." We were keen and early and with 'The Who's 'My Generation' LP we had brought along and a full barrel of cider on tap by the side of the record player we were proper sorted. I shoved the record on the turntable and as the sounds of 'Out on the Street' and Townshend's guitar kicked in, me and John both looked at each other and our minds read each alike as we both grabbed a glass each and turned on the tap and let the cider flow. Woodpeckers in motion! Wurzels nectar!!! Umm!!!

It was a Thursday evening. We were feeling on top of the world. Our world was all just perfect. In an alcoholic slumber, me and John sat laughing, bleary eyed and on a 'cloud nine' - with no sign of the Temptations. We had been tempted more than enough, I suppose. In the space of around half an hour or so, we had emptied the whole barrel of cider and there was no alcohol left in the house. When Steve and a whole house full of lads and lasses appeared with extra bags of booze, we just kept quiet. Maybe they would never think to try and have a glass of cider. They might all think the barrel was an ornament or something. Anyway we got away without any grief or reprimand and the party soon got into full swing. It was a full house and we kept putting our 'My Generation' LP on which brought some welcome respite to the Michael Jackson 'Thriller' album that everyone was so obsessed with at the time. As the drinks continued, we set our eyes on a gang of lasses sat upstairs chatting. It was dark, we were pissed, they were pissed and we were interested. "Let's go and chat 'em up, Tony," John opened up. We barged up there and got chatting, pushing two lads aside who also thought that they were in with them. We got the lasses' phone numbers, a snog and then John started scrapping with one of the lads who was also sniffing around the girls. John laid the boot in him as I went and gave one of the girls a last minute snog and told her that I would phone her tomorrow. "C'mon John, that's enough, leave him mate," I said trying to calm him down. We ran down the stairs, picking up my Who LP on the way and into the cool dark night to the sounds of kids shouting and swearing on the inside and cars screeching on the outside. Cars emptied with an assortment of Kimberworth toughs who had also been invited to the party and as they all fell out of the cars, on seeing us, they stood to attention with fists at the ready, why I know not?

Me and John walked straight past them and expecting a punch at any moment... we calmly said to them "Hey up lads, I would hurry up if I were you lot. There's a massive barrel of cider in there on the go and two twats are aiming to sup it dry." One lad faced up to us, but party host, Steve came out in the nick of time and said "Leave 'em alone, they are mates of mine." So he ran and followed the rest of them and joined in the fracas and general drunken mayhem going off inside, replicating that scene in 'Only Fools and Horses' when Mental Mickey gets left behind and charges back into the scrapping foray. We set off back to my house. "Is there some cans left in your fridge," John enquired. "I don't know mate, but there's certainly no cider left in the barrel there and I reckon we have got out at just the right time, let's piss off," I answered, us scarpering off around the bend of the road.

Away from the Numbers - Tony Beesley

The next day we rang the girls up and arranged to meet them. We did meet them and in the cold light of day they really weren't what we expected. Bloody hell, blame the free cider. Anyway, owts better than nowt so we took 'em out and made the best of things. Somewhere along the line, following a fair few dates with them, our mate, Martin ended up with one of the lasses. He knocked her off for a few weeks while we left him to it and hoped for better things.

John and his mate went off on their holiday for their Carry On styled fun. I was bored and still after revenge for being upstaged that time in the boozer. I asked his girlfriend, Shaz, to call round and see me. I just rang her up out of the blue and said "What you up to, do you fancy coming round to see me and have a few drinks tonight." She would call round every day and we would wait until my Mum had gone out to work at the club. Before that, Shaz would be slobbering all over me while my Mum was still in... embarrassing or what! I got sick of telling her to wait, but she just couldn't help herself. I tried to take my mind off it while watching re-runs of films such as 'The Vikings' on the telly and when my Mum went through the door I would say "Right then, how about I wait here while you go in the other room and get naked." Unbelievably she did and one thing led to another.... every single night of the week!

The lads got back from their disastrous holiday: they had been skint for the last half of it and been sat like miserable gits all week waiting to come home. I don't think either of 'em pulled at all. Did I feel guilty? Did I bloody hell like. John pissed himself with laughing when he found out what I had been up to. "You swine, you absolute swine," He kept saying. In the pub, that night, I told her part-time boyfriend what had been going off. He wasn't happy, to say the least, but took it on the chin like a man. He was a good lad like that. Revenge tasted a bit less sweet cos of that, though. The thing is Shaz wasn't exactly a real catch, though I had seen far worse... but most importantly, she was nice-natured and game for a good time. She got on my nerves a bit but you know beggars can't be choosers. Predictably, I soon got bored with her.

One night we had one of our regular parties at our house. The music and booze flowed and the lasses were in good spirits. A new friend of our female friends called Donna had come along and she got all of our interest. About halfway through the night, I decided to go and chat her up and leave Shaz to the delights of her ex instead. We hit it off and buggered off to the shops out of the way for some more booze and then came back and went upstairs. Shaz was crying in the arms of her ex, once removed. Then as he was pacing up and down the room, steam bellowing out of his ears, I couldn't help but burst out laughing. John, who was with the other lass, was laughing too. Just deserts for messing up our chat up lines, we both agreed. We meant well, though. We were only young, competitive and daft and none of us bore any grudges.

On another occasion Martin really shook us up by announcing that he had a date with one of the best looking most gorgeous girls in our neighbourhood. We were having none of that and were devastated that he was actually putting us to shame. "Drat, drat, drat. Do something to stop this.... now!"

He had announced to me and John the night before after a few bevies in the local and when we met up the next day, we looked at each other and weren't sure if we had dreamt it all up. "Nah, he can't possibly be having a date with saucy Suzie... nah, surely not," we reasoned. Suzie was a rock chick I also knew. She was classed as a real catch. Long dark wavy hair with inviting cute lips and a body to die for, she had always been out of bounds for courtship as far as I knew. I think she may have gone out with some older lads and ventured to the Rock clubs of the steel city such as the Wappentake and Rebels, but am not sure. No matter what, though, she was also a very nice lass who always said hello and remained polite and unpretentious in the knowledge that she was one of the best looking lasses in the whole of our area. And here we were, hearing that sex-mad Martin had gotten himself a date with her. It must be true, though. We had both heard the scandalous news. We can't have both had the very same dream, well nightmare could we, surely?

Correctly, we both also recalled the exact time and place that the date was to take place. Bad news for laddo! Ethically sound and correctly so, we also turned up at the exact same time eager to spoil his fun and prospective date... in fact, so keen we were, that we arrived even earlier than him, knocking on the doors of the pub before opening time. We passed time on putting much-needed ten pence pieces into the pub jukebox listening to the sleep-inducing sounds of boring old UB40 and Billy Joel's 'Uptown Girl'.

The uptown girl's prospective date arrived early too; his face dropping when he clocked us two sat there supping our pints and grinning, masking a severe streak of jealous insecurity whizzing through us. But he soon gained a confident and cocky allure when he consoled himself with the fact that he was meeting Joan Jett's little sister and not us. His stakes had been upped.

Away from the Numbers - Tony Beesley

"Hey up, look he's got his hair done in the old 'Stop me and buy one 1920's style'," John laughed. Barely holding back our laughter, we watched Martin go and order a pint and then come and sit near us. We questioned him, whilst attempting to not show too much of our envy. He came out with some typical daft Martin lingo and we laughed at his confidence. "Geer oer wi yer, She's not gonna turn up pal," we said, hoping to hell she bloody well wouldn't. "She will, you see, then you two won't be taking the piss... she's got to turn up, I have had a three hour bath and washed parts I forgot even existed just for the occasion," he nervously answered. John and I looked at each other and our faces barely hid a look of 'If she turns up and meets him and they get off with each other, that's us two done with.' "Anyway, what time did tha say she was meeting you? Its 8 'o'clock already and she is half 'n hour late." John went over to the juke box and put on The Jam's 'Absolute Beginners' while I went and got me and him another pint each. The show continued.

By 9.30pm it was painful to watch the ditched prospective Romeo and his still never-ending watch-checking. We could now breathe a sigh of relief and our prestige, whatever bit we had to our name, was still well intact. She had kidded him on and jilted him... ha, ha, bloody ha! Phew! Poor lad... we bought him a pint to cheer him up and he soon got over it and saw the funny side.

Our escapades with the opposite sex were usually the stuff of fumble, grab and get what yer can. We would try and get off with any game lasses we came across, especially after a few bevies. Behind Walsh's sweet shop (the old last destination of the Northwest passage of my red chopper days) we would take lasses round there and get a snog and an all tentacle hands thrill, or stop lasses and ask what the time was and then uncouthly say "My place or yours luv?" usually to a well-aimed slap on the chops. We managed to get off with the big-nosed, the rattle cans, the 'can't stop giggling' gigglers, the teasers, the already spoken for and the rejected cast of Cinderella's lovely sisters meet the She wolf at Midnight... but it was all worthy of great fun!!! It was all good and well especially when we were in it together, rejections or conquests, but let one of us step out and go it alone and the game was classed as unfair.

When I got bored with the company of John and Martin and their constant flow of roll-ups, John Smiths bitter and moaning of being skint, on one occasion I left them round at mine playing records and cards, I decided to go round and see a lass I knew. As I got there, my luck was in as her brother was out with his mates and her Mum was away for the night somewhere, so a few hours on their settee was up for grabs. When I returned home around 3am, I couldn't believe it when John and Martin were still there and had the right mug on with me. The shock and disgust they threw my way for abandoning ship was formidable... Christ we shared a lot of things, but I had to stop somewhere. "Who was it you have been with, anyway," they jealously enquired. "Hazel O' Connor" I kidded them on. Coincidentally the lass, who I regularly saw, did look a bit like Hazel O' Connor. They got over it, eventually... the cheeky sods!

The Way (without Tony Beesley – it states) in local paper, The Advertiser; they would soon also be without my pal, John.

When me and John parted and he went back to a revamped The Way, our buddy buddy time together took a temporary vacation. While he was off doing interviews in London and recording new songs, I was doing my own thing, writing, interviewing and making a few pennies selling Populist Blues. Before 1986 was out, though, John was once more out of The Way and back on Civvy street again so It was inevitable that, before long, our drinking sessions and the accompanying chaos and stupidness would make a predictable revival.

Our starting off place was still always the Monkwood Hotel local boozer, where an assortment of characters and mates would all meet up, some going off on their own jaunts and others joining up with us. The pub had been an old haunt of my Dad's back in his day and was still a frequent stop off place for a beer-guzzling session for our Paul and the gang, though, we mostly kept to our separate social circles. Looking around the place, which was usually packed-out with regulars most nights of the week, you would spot a lovely old mix-up of colourful characters, all forming in their own little pockets of alcoholic resistance, fighting off the daily onslaught of the working grind and life's troubles. Ex-miners out to graze talking, laughing and wheezing off years of underground working activity-my Dad, himself, should really have still been around to join them, but the rotten pit had claimed him nearly a decade ago. Steel workers, some of the local Dale Farm Yoghurt factory gang, an old D-Day veteran who we warmed to and listened to his war stories in-between pints and larking around. There was the Bonanza man, Herman Munster, the Bruce Forsyth fan club, the man in a book, a Dickie Davies off World of Sport lookalike and Ginger the RAF man who never once shot out of the pub at the words 'Scramble!' Then there was General Custer, the famous Indian fighter who would sit for hours with his pints, fags and daily paper, often looking up with an amused grin at our antics. One day, there was mention of a gold rush down in Rotherham Market and he was never seen again! Yes, there was plenty of colour, character and individuals to take in at our local boozer and then there was me and John and our lot. The wild bunch, the hole in the broken wall gang out for a beer and a fruit machine robbery!

Within our gang we had the salt of the earth outlook of the two Gary's, the one young Nicky Ferret, filth and sexual obsessions from our old pal Martin amongst other upstanding characters... all of whom provided hilarious laughs along the way. We ventured in every boozer in the area and when flushed we would go to the town centre and every rough house boozer you could name, sometimes being chased straight out if our faces didn't fit! The fuel had lit our fires of craziness and youthful abandon and anything went... for a laugh anyway! We snogged lasses we had never met before, laughed at blokes big enough to eat us up alive and me and John followed the Morris men around the square doing our own pissed up shambolic dance just like Laurel and Hardy's jig in 'Way out West'. What a pair of plonkas!

Me and John drunk ourselves silly with little encouragement, but the best Times were the annual pre-Christmas piss-ups. A good crowd of us would turn out for the festive frivolities, including our Dave and Steve and some of their mates (and sometimes girlfriends) plus us lot, the prospective brother in law, Steve and his girlfriend and mates. We would get lathered and end up in good old Tiffany's nightclub and dance to Deacon Blue, New Order, The Style Council and smooch to 'Eternal Flame' by The Bangles. Sometimes we may be treat to the rare appearance of a classic Northern Soul tune or maybe 'This Old Heart of Mine' by the Isley Brothers to strut our drunken stuff to.

Tiffany's was a nightclub legend in the 1980's. Now, don't get me wrong, I was never a regular night club townie, but when we ventured to town it would usually end up with a session in Tiffany's, especially during the Christmas drinking season. It wasn't hard to get in there, even though we were boisterous and usually already well-drunk. As long as you looked smart and wore trousers you were ok. On one occasion, at a different town centre nightclub, John was refused entry cos he had jeans on so he asked someone to borrow him a pair of trousers coming out of the club. He walked in with an over-sized pair of Chinos on and once he was in, took off the trousers and put his jeans back on and passed the trousers to someone else going out to give 'em back to their rightful owner. John was always resourceful like that.

Tiffany's was a big place, really. Its palm trees and décor resembling a pretend Miami club (remember the Don Johnson led TV show, Miami Vice and Gloria Estefan's Miami Sound Machine was all the rage at the time). If you peered into the corner you might spot the real Scarface Tony Montana planning out a job on some local gangster. Its dance floor was always full. We would get pissed, lark around and dance to Shalamar and Swing Out Sister with lasses with big tits, lovely backsides and lipstick-smeared lips topped off with big and bouncy hair: proper Rotherham lasses all out for a laugh. When the DJ changed the pace a little with a playing of 'Happy Hour' by The Housemartins, me and John would leap about like two escaped lunatics to the amusement of the 'dance around their handbags' brigade. A great time was always had by all. No matter who you were out with - mates, girlfriends or relatives... there was always genuine fun to be had. We would also occasionally pay a visit to the Adam and Eve nightclub, which was a bit more liberal with its music policy and if you asked politely, the DJ would spin some Indie stuff such as The Smiths and please the small up and upcoming crowd of Goths in the dark corner of the room with a medley of The Cure, Bauhaus and Siouxsie and the Banshees. The bouncers there were a bit over-keen, though, and when some fella took a proper hiding that was reported in the local papers, the lure of the place gradually lost its already limited appeal. Besides we had plenty of drinking holes right on our doorstep.

One of those was The Star pub in Rawmarsh! The first time I ever went in there would be 1982 when it was still an old fella's pub, complete with flat caps, betting slips and that Bavarian fella in a hat with a feather in on the beer mats along with no jukebox and no disco of any sorts. I once went in and they had a tiny record player with 5 watt speakers for the musical entertainment. I didn't laugh and spoil the Charles Az-no voice Pickwick choice LP!

By 1987 The Star had re-opened and upgraded its DJ equipment and was added to our rota of drinking holes. It was packed out most nights with a regular booming 80's disco. It quickly became the local fun spot and there was a time that we seemed to know, either by name, shoes, face or haircut, every geezer that set foot in the place. The lasses were loud and fun and salt of the earth and knew how to party hard. By the time Christmas had arrived, the place would turn into a Christmas Eve Wild West saloon and no Dodge City re-enactment could be complete without the obligatory Wild West brawl. That first Christmas of 1987 will always be in my mind as the very first time I saw a genuine Cowboy saloon fight in a pub. Chairs were flying through the air, bottles being smashed, punches rotating all around and lasses pulling hair, dragging fellas off other fellas and the DJ carrying on playing his favourite Pet Shop Boys track. As I stood watching in bewilderment, luckily avoiding any projectile or free-to-a-good home punch and taking great care to not get my beloved Mod suit damaged in any way, I saw the wall that separated the lower and higher sections collapse and everyone pile over onto each other all landing in a heap. The scrap continued until everyone was exhausted and the night ended with the sounds of the new song by the Pogues - featuring Kirsty Macoll 'The Fairytale of New York' being played. We were in the drunk tank indeed... it was now time to say "Happy Christmas, my arse," to all of the injured, unhurt bystanders and everyone you knew. Time to go home... the last stage has left town so it's a case of stumbling across the old Oregon Trail back to Fort Beesley!!!

Those times were the peak of my drinking days... no responsibilities, lots of great mates, a regular girlfriend and some great boozers to go in. We rarely got into any proper trouble, all considering. Scrapping it out on a Saturday night was never my style anyway, though I knew and saw plenty whose idea of fun was to bang it out with some drunken stranger and go home covered in blood, piss and sick and barely remember a thing the next day. Instead we just lost our memories for a few days and had to wait, nervously, for someone to remind us what we had got up to during the venture. The only spots of bovver I ever got myself into was arguing with a muscle man and pulling him over a table and running off before he could catch me and the occasional taxi-dodging scuffle.

Most nights ended up with a late round up and number count back at our place and further indoor daft antics. Me and John had regular post-pub food fights and we would often end up covered in beetroot and orange peel stuck to our faces and necks or head to toe in talcum powder, looking like confused and intoxicated Homepride men. I half food poisoned him many a time too, threw his tobacco on the fire when he got on my nerves and when we got stoned on blow one night it resulted in us having the best night's sleep apiece that we had ever known since the days of Rusks and rubber dummies! That night was the result of indulging in the spicy roll ups of an associate of ours who was a regular connoisseur of the erotic smoking habit. Coming back from the pub one night and falling all over after partaking in some of his special flavour of the month, I was so stoned that I couldn't make us anything for supper without giggling non-stop, dropping oven chips all over the floor and gaining a puzzled look from my Mum before she (wisely) popped off to bed out of the way. One night, John was so pissed he woke up (apparently sleepwalking) and ran like mad across the landing and barged into my Mum's bedroom saying "Give me a go on the bandit." The stuff my Mum put up with... she truly had the patience of a Saint!

Following these nights out on the lash we would fall through the door, laughing and larking around. As is the tradition with nights of inebriation we would get the munchies. John had long since developed a persistent distrust of my late night Diner openings offering strange concoctions of food that you would never see on any restaurant menu. He had tried my Shreddies with dried peas and Cottage cheese mixed with toothpaste so wasn't daft enough to sign up for Tony's £1 after midnight treats, and I won't even mention the home brew bottom of the bottle sediment that one lad partook in (and enjoyed!). To this day John won't accept any form of food served up by me, even if it's sealed in its original packet. Fortunately for my charitable enterprise, other kids did make food orders and to this day some of my old mates don't realise what they actually have eaten on those nights, being too pissed to even bother to question the ingredients. John would sit there laughing as they wolfed down sandwiches containing the most unlikely ingredients. When one daft bugger foolishly asked for some late-night nourishment, John sat amazed as I went right to the back of our fridge and produced the greenest piece of (formerly) red Cheddar you could imagine and said "Here yer go, get this munched on, if you're hungry mate." The silly twat even asked for seconds!

It was a sign that things had to calm down when I woke up, alone on the settee in the early hours to a scene that looked like the aftermath of a battle; the room and kitchen completely full of smoke, telly still on and the back door still wide open. I had put myself a garlic baguette in the oven and fallen asleep on the settee leaving it to cook and almost burn the house down. When I was disturbed and saw the smoke and a scene like the battle of Stalingrad, all I could say was "Where's my supper?" The said food dish was burnt to a crisp. Our times boozing (and having as much unpredictable fun as we could) continued and time seemed to stand still for what seemed like a decade, but which in fact was a few years at the most, after which the hard boozing began

to fade away and our pub meetings decreased to once or twice a week and often less? Kids got lasses pregnant; others fell out with each other, whilst a few carried on boozing to the limits! But we were all ok, I suppose. I mean, some lads we knew had ended up going completely the wrong way and were serving time. You would never have guessed it would you, when you're a kid at school, kids you knew turning up on bloody 'Crime watch' and 'Crime stoppers'! My Mum even appeared on Crime stoppers when she was stood right at the side of dodgy fella trying to cash in a fraudulent cheque in the bank. Every time she came on the

telly, I would laugh and give her some stick and she would sometimes get the face on and chuck the choice weapon of hers, the dish cloth at me. My own biggest crime was the frustration of not knowing which direction to take in life. For a long time, I somehow would always end up taking the one way street to skintsville, but at least I wasn't in a prison cell and none of us ever hurt anyone.

The boozing years were fun while they lasted and I wouldn't really wanna swap them for a shirt, tie and a dose of respectability in exchange for my early 20's. We got ourselves banned from pubs, escaped blokes after our blood cos John owed 'em cash and I lost count of the times that John would come speeding down our path on the run from some money lender after his blood; he once hid under our bed for half an hour and the minute he went back up our path the debt collector was there waiting for him. Luckily, it was only our pal, Martin that time. We dodged the occasional boot and fist in pub 'free for alls' and wild west brawls and chased every lass in a skirt that would run off from us. We had pissed up food fights, grabbed desperate kennel wives at 'Grab a Granny night' at Rawmarsh Cricket club to the sound of the Roger Brooks' band and swapped jackets and trousers like Laurel and Hardy. We were chased up the hill from Sombreros – the dodgiest 80's nightclub west of Denver, took the mickey out of anything and anyone within our vicinity and had a great musical soundtrack to it all. We even managed to fit in time for our own band for a few years too!

Those days were like a separate chapter in my life. There was hardly a thing to worry about in the world. Pain and heartache weren't a part of life for me yet, though I had experienced loss and grief. Times were profoundly different then. That sense of dread and negative vibe so prevalent and largely unavoidable nowadays was simply not around at all. Blimey, we still left our back door open right until it was time for bed. Neighbours would stroll in for a chat or to borrow some sugar and teabags or to wish you Merry Christmas or just say 'How do you do?' We still used outside lavs, an over-sized Ghurkha styled blade to cut the Malayan back garden jungle with and none of us had ever heard of hydrogenated fats and such like. Body language was a cheeky dance and chill-out was stood outside in the freezing cold... and as for money? Well I was so skint at one point that I walked into Halifax bank and closed my account just to draw my last quid out!

Against this quite simplistic and irresponsible way of living and surroundings and of living life from one day to the next, me and John cast our caution to the wind. We threw ourselves into drunken daftness without a damn care in the world and fun it sure was! All great things have to come to an end, though, I suppose, and it would soon become a time of choices. Do I carry on down the path of two pints of lager and a bag of nuts please... or do I shape up and attempt to be responsible?

Chapter eight

Frustration!

I smashed up my record player and ripped off all of the strings of my Hayman guitar, throwing it across the room; I threw my razor at the wall, shattering its every piece... and I smashed all of my old Showaddywaddy and Mud records into tiny splintered fragments. Frustration and anger were flowing through my veins like a speeding locomotive. I had sampled the taste of escaping the rat race and being a part of something special; being in a gang, a proper Mod band, which I screwed up big style! I then continued to appease life's meaning by being a part of a gang of beer-swilling mates and, as great fun as that had been, now my path was jaded, at a stalemate and my destination unknown.

This daft and naïve lad with a yearning to be someone in a band, the punk kid with a mission to change the world: well now the dream was lost, and it was my own bloody fault. I now realised what real proper frustration actually felt like. I was 21 years old and did not have a clue on earth what I was gonna do in my life. Is there a way out? Can I pick up all of the shattered and confused pieces: how long will it take? Who exactly am I? I felt as confused and despondent as Jimmy in 'Quadrophenia'... Is it in my head or is it all just a bad dream... a cruel joke that has fallen on an un-responsive clown!

'Well go 'n get a bloody job then', Maggie and her legions would proclaim. Well, I tried that too. I did contract work, leaflet delivering, and agency work and quick fix college course. I signed on and signed off; was an odd job man, postman and produced my own self-financed and created fanzine. 'Populist Blues' was the zine in which I interviewed bands in upstairs pubs in frontier towns, printed poetry and art and (alongside the most left-field of modern pop and Soul) tried desperately to represent the ambitions of a miss-placed local generation; something I so wanted to achieve. Kevin Rowland turned me down for an interview, though the lost hope of 80's Mod-Soul, Big Sound Authority and Go-Discs record label (home of the Housemartins and some years later, Paul Weller) did write to me with interest in my writing venture. I trudged all over trying to sell the magazine and all of its 4 issues selling them to all and sundry (years ahead of The Big Issue maaan) but ultimately I arrived at a junction called nowhere and the real issue was 'where to next?'!!!

That place called nowheresville was a regular feature for me for a while during my mid-80's post-band period. I seemed to be going around in never-ending circles. My aspirations of making my mark in the world and trying my damnedest to avoid the dead-end pitfalls of life's preordained chosen path and all of its potentially soul-destroying effects all seemed to be failing. Playing in a real working band and writing my very own songs, creating my own enterprises- be it the fanzine, or selling records to all and sundry like a door to door salesman, searching for the perfect little niche in life away from the numbers... they had all ended up exhausted, one way or another: and it was starting to really piss me off... and YES, I was bloody angry with myself for it!

Populist Blues fanzine front covers

Populist Blues was my mid 80's fanzine and was painstakingly self-created via a 100 year old typewriter, plenty of Tipp-ex, a pair of scissors and plenty of naïve ambition

The Young Soul Rebel - 1986

John was angry too. One night, he went and attacked one of the new town home's brand new fences. He went crackers pulling it to pieces and then pulled the house drainpipe away from its fittings. Luckily no one saw us and we never got caught for that one. It was wrong and well out of order, but was a sign of our misguided frustration. This was the Thatcher years and the class division was in full swing and creating resentment. Our lives were a recipe boiling over and seething with anger, disappointment, insecurity and extreme frustration!!

I was at a very mixed-up cross-roads in my life and mourning the loss of playing in a band. John was as un-focused as I was, maybe even more. His outbursts of anti-Conservative rhetoric were not altogether rare, though he mostly managed to avoid being sent down or receive any notable severe recrimination. The closest he came to prison was an escapade involving a mate and Halford's Cycles in town. He planned on defecting to the Soviet Union so convinced was he that the pair of them would serve time for that one.

Now don't get me wrong, John was a good-hearted lad and even though he wasn't adverse to the odd misdemeanour and wouldn't turn down a hooky barrel of beer or a ton of unpaid for fags (even Rick Buckler of The Jam parted with his fags to John during a Jam gig sound check), he never meant anyone any harm: unless they had given him some grief. My Mum used to say you can't trust John with yer cigs or yer money but he's just a loveable rogue and you can't help but loving him. It's true you couldn't dislike him. He could con yer, get you into bother and annoy the hell out of yer with his trickery, but at the end of the day he was a good mate and a right good laugh. Anyway, who can truly put their hand on their heart and profess to being squeaky-clean during the wild and formative days of their youth? Who can throw stones at glass houses without holding one back for their own cracking window pane of hidden half-witted mistakes in life? John had some issues, I had a few too... we belonged to a generation of disaffected youth that usually had some issue or other. We would have carried the flag for a street-based revolution at a whim, or more the case we would have liked to think that we would have, but we wouldn't hurt anyone and the greatest harm that we ever did was knock back far too much beer, shirk our responsibilities and take the piss that bit too much. No amount of confidence-destroying hard times and misguided wrong choices in life could eliminate our kindness for those we liked. We loved our parents, pets and friends and you could have taken any one of us home to meet a well-respected lass's parents and we would have charmed and impressed them enough to warrant a second visit... but just don't ask us to conform to what's expected of us. I can't, won't and never will.

The Thatcher years were now at their worst. You couldn't get away from the evil woman, she even turned up on Saturday Superstore to give her arch-enemy, Paul Weller's new Style Council single 'It Didn't Matter' a slating. The miners had been forced into subjugation and the dole would become a way of living for a proportion of our generation. Personally, during my signing on days, I felt it was demoralising and confidence-destroying. Being on the dole is one savage circle... it chips away at your confidence and sets you apart from those that are lucky enough to have a job... you hate not having a job (even an anti-9-5 ideologist like myself), and you start to feel worthless and lose confidence. Add to all of this my rebellious streak and anti-conformity and my search for a proper job became even harder. 'I will work things out', though, was my self-reasoning determination. It all happens for a purpose and maybe one day I would see that. I determined to make something of my life and would go down fighting whilst trying if not!

Throughout this very same period, whilst doing odd-jobs and a bit on the side painting and decorating here 'n there to help make ends meet, I had been holding down a fairly serious relationship that was starting to get more serious as time went on. I was in my 20's now and I didn't want to carry on pissing about down the boozer - fun as that was - and dodging the possibility, if not certainty, of getting locked up while pissed up with my mates.

The year 1986 marked a full ten years since the advent of punk as celebrations were held with the NME running specials on punk, Channel 4 broadcasting a superb special 'The Way We Were', and the release of a seriously flawed (and annoying) film called 'Sid and Nancy', with Gary Oldman's authentic Sid Vicious performance its only attribute. I was at the height of my anti-rock fervour period and digesting a musical template of Soul and Funk with the odd scattering of anything of note on the Indie scene. My interest in punk still remained, but as an ideal, a mind-set and the occasional nostalgic trawl through the old records. It all seemed so long ago: a different time in so many aspects and as though it had even not actually occurred and had been some kind of a dream. But dreams were all we had for a while during the mid-80's; they held misfits such as myself together with a ray of hope!

The rebellious Tony was still rampant, though... but was much more manifest within a naïve and misguided doctrine of political sloganeering and trendy left-field militancy borne of my misguided inner anger. From beneath the floppy Soul boy fringe and casual James jacket, penny loafers and sta-prest trousers came forth a selection of political verbal crap that I soon came to realise was nothing short of frustrated nonsense. I was no Paul Weller, Billy Bragg or clued-in Paul Heaton by any stretch of the imagination or even a Blow Monkey sweetly proclaiming... 'It doesn't have to be This Way'.

I could be found from time to time in night club corners sneering at drinking crowds that were performing cheesy air guitar theatrics to Bon Jovi (perish the thought!) and spouting (to anyone who would listen) the relevance of the European-influenced Mod stylist look with a compulsory punk attitude and socialist set of beliefs and conscience beneath. Luckily I came across a like-minded soul in Shaun Price, who had tuned in perfectly to the Style Council's music and ethos. Falling out of the Adam and Eve nightclub Sean and I enthused non-stop of our love of Weller's songs and contemporary funk and Soul: a refreshing change from the usually unenlightened club outings.

Following a trip into to Rotherham town centre wearing my 3-button jacket and accompanying Mod attire, I was stopped by a young Mod who recognised me from The Way: he wanted me to post him tapes and info on the now defunct Mod version of said band. I was both flattered to be recognised and slightly annoyed that I was still being seen as a 60's Mod revivalist-styled Mod lad. I was desperate to move forward away from that well-trodden path; instead I aspired to be a Mod stylist, an individual with suitably cool tastes and attire to suit... to be someone set apart in the lost youth landscape of the 1980's! I had never been keen on remaining entrenched with the clichéd media-informed Mod look anyway. I hardly ever wore a parka at any point of my Mod recruitment either. It's all about good taste, but I suppose I only had myself to blame.

I took to immersing myself even deeper into Weller's Euro-Mod approach, wearing the appropriate clothes and jewellery (as he did), the garish colours, turned-up bottoms Levis, cardigan tied to my waist, tasselled loafers, white Levi jeans and a Weller-endorsed much-loved Herringbone long coat. I went through stages of greasing back my hair just like Paul Weller, to which our

Paul said I looked like Alfalfa. I watched (and frequently nodded off to) French-subtitled new wave films for cultural influences and I cast aside all forms of Rock music! I almost became some kind of a fire-breathing Soul puritan for a while!

At home I would blast out the fast-paced vibrant modern Jazz of 'Killer Joe' by Tommy Chase amidst a soundtrack of hard funk and 70's Soul. My new musical heroes were the Modern Jazz Quartet, Working Week and Animal Nightlife and the 60's Hammond Jazz sounds of Jimmy Smith and Jimmy McGriff that sat in my record boxes aside 60's Mod beat and blue-eyed Soul.

In 1986 as Argentina beat Germany 3 - 2 in the World Cup making a star of fat Argie, Diego Maradona and Phil Lynott of Rockers Thin Lizzy, Pat Phoenix and my Dad's old movie fave, James Cagney died... we got a cat called Jerry – a timid ginger kitten that lived in fear of his older feline brother! My Mum's favourite TV comedy, 'Bread' made its debut as did the Dexy's theme-tune-led 'Brush Strokes'. But does anyone remember 'Albion Market' the doomed (and extremely boring) soap that lasted just one year? No, thought not!

My favourite TV show of the mid 80's was 'Prospects' starring Gary Olsen (who later starred in 2.4 Children and sadly died in 2000 of cancer, aged 43) and Brian Bovell as two dodgy-dealing entrepreneurs trying to make money through various scams and schemes in and around the East End dock yards. Not that unlike the recent years of me and John, really. Typically, in the show, Hazel O' Connor made a guest appearance as a singer. The series only lasted for one 12-episode run but accurately captured the mood of mid-80's Thatcherist England. The other great quality TV that year was The Monocled Mutineer starring Paul McGann as a First World War rebel who took it upon himself to impersonate officers. I still related very strongly to rebels even those in stolen officer's uniforms that only existed upon the TV screen.

As for the cinema, I ventured to see the most-talked about film of the time, 'Absolute Beginners' which flopped famously and failed to capture the essence of the original Colin MacInnes novel that it was based upon. Despite all of its wide-spread criticism, it did have some great music (Style Council, Working Week, Ray Davies, Bowie etc.) as its soundtrack (that, unsurprisingly I bought). Unbelievably we still had two open cinemas in town in the 80's and I would frequent them both from time to time to munch on sticky popcorn to films such as Brat Pack goes Wild West actioner, 'Young Guns' and grinning girls-favourite poster boy and top gun, Tom Cruise in 'Cocktail' and his two critically-acclaimed movies 'Rainman' and 'Born on the Fourth of July'.

Down the road from the cinema the Rotherham antique market was also a fantastic place for lots of interesting and very cheap bargains. Opening up to a collectors' market-oblivious public - hordes of video rental-grabbing customers criminally over-looking the vinyl artefacts to be found beneath that battered once-loved 'Bat Out of Hell' LP - the two-level bazaar for Wednesday's bargain hunters was simply perfect for a rare record chasing magpie such as myself. I used to arrive home with bags of great bargains including whole goldmines of 70's Soul, rare Funk 45's and superb original 1960's vinyl. Back then not many people in Rotherham seemed to be collecting the Mod and beat stuff I was so fond of, so the pickings were mostly mine. I captured singles by The Action, John's Children, Georgie Fame and the Blue Flames, ST Louis Union and original and rare early Tamla Motown records, along with a 50p costing (original red Decca) Small Faces 'From the Beginning' LP and original (Plum label) Sam and Dave, Otis Redding and Wilson Pickett LP's. If I already had some of these finds, I sold them on at Record Fairs. The traders knew me and would save me interesting stuff, but why one fella called Andy insisted on asking me (almost every week), if I wanted his latest Gary Numan rare picture disc, I will never know. Numanoid stalking aside, vinyl was mine for the taking for a good year or two at this new Rotherham antiques bonanza... Meanwhile someone decided to build something called a Retail Park down the road at Parkgate, which was opened that very same year by someone from Eastenders, no sign of Dirty Den, though.

That March, my mate, young Mod, Darren was gearing up for going into the hospital for his big operation: one he had seen coming for a very long time. Darren was a lot younger than me and I had known him by sight for as long as I could remember. He had entered my life as a fan of The Way and would come and see us play regularly, hanging around with me going along to Mod parties with me and John. We would chat about music and listen to records. The lad could rattle for England and once encouraged it was hard to get him to calm down, he got so over-excited! He went and watched 'Back to the Future' at the pictures, maybe six or seven times, coming back just as thrilled each time. He was a poorly lad, though Darren. He had some kind of a heart defect, quite a serious one in fact. Throughout 1985 and into 86 he was a constant visitor of mine and to be honest I got to thinking quite a lot about him. He had started to get into early punk music too and would arrive at the door waving a fiver and saying "Tony... how about me giving you this for your Johnny Thunders LP so you can go out to the pub with it." He knew that he only had to entice me with that prospect and the records would be his. The crafty little tyke coerced a double figured amount of old 77-78 Punk vinyl from me. He would depart half an hour later beaming like a kid on Christmas day. "I'll be back for more, in the week," he would laugh. He never stopped laughing, Darren... almost as much as 'Laughing Boy Julian Jones'. I had to admire his positive attitude and exuberance; he never let life get him down and hardly gave up pestering me for records either.

At the start of the year Darren (pictured left following a few drinks at one of our Mod nights) began to anxiously tell me about this big operation he was due to be having. Apparently he had been told for years that when he reached around 16 years old he would be requiring this operation. He also confided in me that on one of his pre-op test hospital visits, he had over-heard the Doctors talking about his case and admitting to each other that they didn't expect him to survive it. Understandably he was scared and very anxious. I would try and cheer him up and tell him that he would be pestering me for some more of my records in no time at all. When we parted, at our back door, he was still laughing but written all over his face was a clear sign of worry and impending doom. I have to say, what he had told me did trouble me too, but I tried to shrug it off and convince myself that he would be fine. Surprisingly, Darren had his operation and it was a success, or so I heard. The Doctors did everything that they had pre-planned and it had all worked. Tragically Darren still passed away!!! The poor lad's heart just gave way under the strain.

Those words he had told me that day haunted me for quite some time afterwards. I had to break the news to Wendy who was as upset as I was. We just couldn't believe it. How had this happened, a young life cut so short so early and so quickly? It was hard to comprehend. I was thinking back to that previous Christmas and him laughing his head off with us at Del Boy in the Christmas special of 'Only Fools and Horses'. It seemed so unreal. We went to his funeral and it was a real tearjerker. I still miss my mate, Daz!

There had been other bereavements too, one of Terry's Mod mates, Mark Ely, who regularly came to watch us practice, sadly died of meningitis. There were family ones as well. Uncle George, who had been so kind and accommodating whilst listening to me chuntering on about 'one day being a proper musician', passed away after losing first a toe, then a foot, then a leg, then both legs due to late-diagnosed Diabetes. Our next door neighbour also passed away in 1986 and before long the whole street I lived on was a street three quarters full of strangers. The classic characters of my 1970's childhood (Old Brynner included) were dropping like flies and unexpectedly, death was now not just something that happened regularly in someone else's world or on the telly... it was right there, almost on our door step, whispering cold and unwanted words to us. But life goes on and people adapt and carry on.

That June, our Paul and his family whilst passing through France by coach to their holiday destination of Cla Llevado in Spain experienced a potentially fatal accident. Paul was one of the passengers who realised that something was not quite right after smelling smoke and so then began to encourage the driver and other passengers to start

evacuating the coach as a safety measure. A few minutes later the coach completely exploded into flames. A very nasty outcome was avoided by quick thinking and good sense. Our Paul, his family and over 60 other passengers lost all of their luggage and travel documents in the blaze. The story hit the Rotherham Advertiser front page for their June 27th 1986 issue. It could well have been the prototype script for the future 'Only Fools and Horses' episode

'Jolly Boy's Outing' in which Del and the gang's coach also ends up going up in flames. It never deterred our Paul and the gang from their annual holidays abroad, though, and the world's tourist attractions have had to endure the Beesley clan for many more seasons since: our Glen even getting stuck in the States on that infamous date in history, 9/11 some years later.

I hadn't been abroad at all so far. It was still weeks and weekends at the good old-fashioned British East Coast for yours truly for a series of Mod visits, piss ups, 'Kiss Me Quick' dirty weekends and the traditional stick of Rock day trips with any club I could scrounge a trip off! Bridlington, Skegness, Scarborough, Cleethorpes and Morecambe were the destinations where you could still feel that 'very cheeky postcard British seaside vibe'. Whilst some people were now taking their hols over at the Costas' Brava and Del Sol... our trips to our own charismatic coast could still be just as fun-packed.

One red-hot summer weekend saw me and Wendy almost sup Scarborough dry. We stopped in an Hotel, where we were informed by the proprietor that John Peel post-punk faves The Au Pairs regularly stayed, which was a great little curio foot-note for me. That brought a smile to my face, but the evacuation for a fire drill did not! Whilst in a mid-afternoon post-boozing session slumber and laid out on the bed half-naked, I was just dozing off when the Fire alarm sounded off like a wartime air raid siren! We threw all of our clothes into our suitcases and flew down the long-winding stairs of the B&B like crazy, hearts beating like mad and in a state of disaster movie frame of mind shock, expecting the jerries to be returning to finish off their infamous WWI Scarborough town shelling only to be told that it was just a drill! "Right, let's get back out to the Pickwick Arms boozer on the corner for a beer then."

That long and boozy weekend we managed to soak ourselves from head to toe in the sea while trying to man a blow-up Li-Lo. We sat drinking next to Fishermen with seamen's pipes and white beards and amazingly I did not blurt out the words 'Captain Birdseye' even the once (though the temptation was high), we had our drunken portraits sketched by one of those invisible magic artists in a photo booth and we ate sugar-covered donuts, sticky candy floss and saturated fat cream-soaked waffles until we felt sick! I ran all the way up the eons of steps from the beach area to the town at the top without stopping or being even out of breath (such is the exuberance of youth). For my traditional coast visit souvenir I even managed to accumulate yet another bag of Soul 45's for my record collection. Life was really good again for a while during these fun-filled ventures and my inner frustration was soothed by copious sessions of alcohol and genuine belly laughs proving life was not so bloody bad after all. OK where to next... Bridlington for the week? That will do. Hopefully bug-free as well this time, unlike our memorable 1970's debacle. Was this the long-awaited replacement holiday after all of those years then?

Bridlington offered us a backstreet B&B for the week and a lovely British sun, sea and booze week; time well-spent away from my post-band insecurities and a place that me and Wendy could forget all of our troubles. We sampled just about every drinking establishment to offer. From the rolled up sleeve belters of rough house 'Sonny's, the cosy seafront old timers bar The Marine Bar, The Greyhound, the Harbour Lights and a dope-intoxicated dive that looked as though a battle and accompanying explosions had taken place within called Beau Brummels... we partook of them all, along with scores of other drinking holes in-between. On re-entering the outside world and seaside daylight of that establishment, we must have looked like nocturnal vampires on wacky backy! Oh well... on to the next boozer.

Throughout our week, we ignored contemptuous glances at my Mod-like Stylist appearance from the Harbour Lights resident biker squad, celebrated my birthday with a flow of Vodka and the sounds of Soul and the Style Council on the nightclub dance floor and stuffed our faces while contemplating a trip on the Yorkshire Belle, deciding to opt out of throwing up a whirlpool of waffles, chips, donuts and Carling Black Label over the side! Glancing at a harbour wall plaque I noticed that a certain T.E Lawrence - more commonly known to film goers as Lawrence of Arabia - had taken an anonymous harbour job following his famous WWI exploits. I wonder if Lawrence managed to do the Yorkshire Belle trip... we never did that year! We came home from Bridlington dehydrated, sun-tanned and smiling.

In 1986 my 21st birthday arrived and I was given a bash at the Rig Dyke pub where most of my family and mates turned up for a traditional piss-up. My birthday present from John, Terry and Ian was a demo tape 'Strike to Win' - 4 brand new songs they had written and recorded as The Way: I wasn't sure (at the time) if they were rubbing my nose in it or not, possibly not but it felt like it and in all honesty it totally ruined my 21st birthday, reminding me of how much I had let slip out of my hands the year before and how irrational and foolish I had been.

THE WAY
HULL UNITY CLUB

THIS IS the way we clean our teeth. With plagiarism being the flavour of the month, The Way stretch the definition to its limits with a sound and style that has dropped directly from the anus of the Redskins. But there's nothing wrong with influence, especially when the inspiration is provided by those sadly-missed, number one pop Bolsheviks. Remember, take no heroes, only inspiration. I looked away when 'Kick Over The Statues' was covered. My spine tingled with nostalgia as I swear Mssrs Moore, Bottomley and Hookem had sneaked upon the pulpit. But far from being merely Redskins' copyists, The Way's own material stands proud in its own right. The jerking funk of the Woody Allen lookalike bassist and the brash brass section complemented by the Motown backbeat, perfectly suited the grit of the pit-village vocals on the imminent debut single, 'Train of Revolution'.

This boy, singing from the heart, is but a mere pup but has the voice of a hardened soul dog. In comparison he makes this year's glove-puppet, Rick Astley, sound like Paul Young with his scrotum in a vice. This is Northern Soul from the heart of South Yorkshire, Mexborough. For me, if the Housemartins are the flagbearers of the proletariat, then The Way are its poles. This is no bric-a-brac from the independent scrapyard, this is definitely anti-grebo, this is a positive assault on the hearts and minds of the nation's chart watchers. This is The Way we wash our hands of all the crap.

Swift Nick

Mods at Rotherham Assembly Rooms

I took it firmly on the chin, took the tape home and listened to it with great interest. They had engaged a Brass section, which was right up my Soul Street, taken on a huge influence of The Redskins (which was not to my taste) and come up trumps! I would be a complete liar if I said I didn't harbour at least a degree of envy: they had truly done good and I was proud of them, but I was secretly wishing that I was still a part of it all. If only I hadn't took that decision the year before and had persevered with the band, I too might have been part of an NME write-up. But, life is full of lessons, as everyone knows, so no good crying over spilt lager and torn beer mats. I decided to exorcise my almost visible inner insecurities by supporting the band, interviewing Terry in our front room and sticking the band on the front cover of my fanzine 'Populist Blues' and then going to see them perform live at old Mod haunt the Assembly Rooms later that year; a gig packed with local Mods and Southern ones where more than a hint of rivalry pervaded within the air on the night.

The lone guitarist- 1987

The Assembly rooms gig came not long after an Art Centre visit I attended by Californian country-Soul busker, Ted Hawkins; a rather tame sit down concert appropriated by mostly academic intellectually-minded comfortable musos taking notes and a million miles away from my vision of Soul. Still I couldn't help but feel a sense of wonder that this grizzled and tough white-bearded singer with untainted and genuine talent had served on a real American chain gang. No party of fun I am sure. Perhaps I would end up busking one day too?

There was a fair few parties on the go in 1986, one unfortunate surviving party memory I can drag back to mind is of a rough barrel-shaped woman getting the hots for me and continuously gyrating and thrusting her cheeky dance in front of me to the sound of 'Word Up' by Cameo; earning my total disgust and fear of being forced-fed her passions. I tried my best to ignore her but ultimately the only thing I found to take comfort from was a non-stop flow of vodka resulting in me waking up in the early hours whilst the party was still in swing and my unrequited admirer was snoring off lashings of Lambrini tucked away in a corner. As I rubbed my eyes in a Vodka-induced stupor, I glanced upon a blurry vision of a man in a black uniform to whom I enquired "Any post for me pal." It was in fact a copper joining the party after his shift and still in full uniform! The next day I couldn't decide if to watch 'The Secret Policeman's Ball' or 'The Postman always Rings Twice' on our new gigantic paving slab-sized VHS recorder.

That very same VHS re-conditioned Radio Rentals one was always breaking down and requiring me to request an almost permanent in-house engineer to look after it, something (due to a slip of words) I asked for one day when my patience finally ran out. The looks on everyone's faces was hilarious when I requested the Radio Rentals video babysitter to fit us in to look after our temperamental video recorder.

As 1986 ended and 87 beckoned, I looked back at my first half decade of the 1980's and what I had achieved. The band and fanzine had left me financially and artistically bankrupt and every song I wrote meant absolutely nothing to me anymore. So much so, that I struggled to even write a song anymore. Every job I had tried so far I had despised. Even the magazine, Spiral Scratch, never responded to my review of The Smiths 'Queen is Dead' LP I had sent in hoping for a paid job as a reviewer and enabling me to embark upon a writing career. I had brief ambitions to be an actor until I realised that maybe I didn't have the qualifications for that either. 'Is there a pattern in all of this somewhere', I was trying to work out that New Year's day lunch-time drinking session of 1987 while sat in the Monkwood pub nestling a pint of lager? "Oh well, go on, Paul, get us another pint in, then, just bugger it all." "Get stuffed and get thee own," was his (not entirely unexpected) answer!

Our Michelle (Paul's daughter) was 16 in 1987. Chelle was like my little sister and I looked out for her. When lads were hanging around, I would tell 'em to bugger off and when I caught her swearing like a trooper, I gave her a proper telling off. When she came to see me and her Nan on Sunday afternoons, crying after falling out with her Mum and Dad, or getting a roasting off our Dave for having a party while the grown-ups were away, we gave her a shoulder to cry on, a joke or three to cheer her up and a plate of Mum's home-made chips and Sunday special bread cakes. It mostly did the trick. She always came back to see us for more saying "Whatever you do, don't put Freddy Krueger on and don't mention the ghost bat at the top of the stairs."

What Ever Happened to the 1980's?

From the top – our Glen and Paul (New year's Eve 1981), Our Darren and Michelle (1982), Mum, our Sheena and Mum's best mate, Annie – when neighbours still socialised on the front wall (1982) and me and our Steve (1987)

The same year (1987) Mum was 63, our Paul was 40 (and counting down his days until his retirement from the steelworks), and our Glen was 33 and I (the young Pup) was 22. My brothers were both married with kids and holding down serious proper jobs and relatively settled lives. The world of having kids seemed a million years away from my irresponsible lifestyle. However, I had been in a relationship for a whole three years now which seemed unbelievable for me. As the compulsive argument years were mostly a thing of the past by now, we were thinking of getting our own place sometime in the future and maybe, just maybe in the distant misty future, even have a kid while we were at it, you never know? Baby in a two-tone romper suit, even!

My love of music showed no signs of abating either, continuing throughout the decade, the Mod influence and punk idealism and accompanying attitude being integrated within my ever-changing tastes in style and music... and I still occasionally wore a dependable Mod suit for special occasions, the latest one being one off George on Rotherham market which took me weeks to save up for. My silver-buttoned navy blazer was worn with the obligatory carefully-placed top pocket paisley cravat or my white Levis jacket sufficed for everyday wear. I had ditched the James jacket and plastic casual wear, leaving those with far more savvy and dedication to that style to continue the Pringle and Lacoste-sponsored fashion crusade.

The 1980's was also the time of our very own Video Nasty seasons! Since having a VHS player which thankfully by now was beginning to shrink in size and had switched from being a top loading monster that could have been mistaken for a Chieftain tank to a front loading one, the era of renting out videos by the truck load had arrived. Everything from 'Stand By Me', to The Terminator' and 'Friday the 13th' was being rented in those huge rental boxes all obsessively lavished upon for our own cinema reproduction nights. And who can forget the antics of 'Ferris Bueller's Day off' or the 80's feel-good youth movie that was 'The Breakfast Club'.

One night, while watching yet another showing of 'The Thing' starring Kurt Russell, I fell asleep and was nudged by Wendy insistently to get my attention. "What's up...? I am knackered, leave me alone", I moaned. "Someone's in the kitchen", she whispered. And true enough there was. As I stood up, the creak of my Mum's recently bought highly inflammable settee spooked our intruder who managed to scarper like mad out of the house and up the path, welcoming in a new era when we would now have to keep the door locked at all times.

Around this time crime had started to slowly show its ugly, unwanted face around us. Previously, the news of a burglary would have been rare and drug pushing was something only associated with the music scene and the cities. During the late 80's the seeds of the future were being sown. Thieving, muggings, regular burglaries and drug dealing were on the increase around our area. Old Nick the bag of swag, stripy shirt-wearing old fashioned burglar of old had progressed into a drug addicted, knife-carrying vagabond.

The year previously had seen a hint for the future of music: Marrs 'Pump up the Volume' arrived at a time of the (Hip Hop meets Rock) Beastie Boys and the declining years of the post-Live Aid pop aristocracy. Soon the influx of dance floor-destined House and Garage music would swiftly step up a few gears with Acid House. By 1988 and the following year, Acid House and a whole collection of Dance music spin offs had begun to take over.

Right from the start, Acid House hit the headlines; its music and air of adult-allergy idealism were refreshingly appealing. Illegal warehouse parties were being held up and down the country and a whole generation of loved up, 'E'd up kids (often ex-punks) began a journey to their own personal ecstasy or the alternative drug hell! I have to admit... I gave the whole drug culture aspect a miss. I embraced Acid House as a new music culture but the path of drugs was not up my street one bit. Apart from the odd dabble of Whacky Backy and a pill or two, I remained totally clean and drug free... unless you count booze and fags and counter-culture rock n' roll that is! 1987 may have seen the birth of Acid House, Smiley culture and the first signs of the social change that was to come, but a third term of Thatcher had kicked us firmly in the balls the day before my 22nd birthday, itself putting paid to any optimism that we had been desperately searching for.

From the mid 80's I was also pals with a young Jam fan called Digga real name Simon Dixon (Right) and we would embark on seasons of pub crawls and chaotic nights out. Digga was a bleached-blond lad a few years younger than me and was also mad on Weller, The Housemartins and getting pissed- and even purchased a pair of my two-tone trousers once they had shrunk a little to fit. Apart from very vocal debates in the pub as to what was the best Jam single or whose round it was next, we largely got on really well and had our fair share of laughs... despite getting ourselves thrown out of the Star and temporarily banned. Besides, he was a budding bass guitar player, so it was once again a case of... "Umm, I wonder if we could form a band together." We held a few unorganised and ultimately unfruitful get-togethers. Me with my Antaria semi-acoustic guitar and Digga with his Fender Squire Bass, but, nothing came of it and we never got past the opening bars of 'Billy Hunt' by The Jam

The Style Council released a new single 'Wanted' in 1987 and along with a flurry of TV pop music shows, announced a new UK tour. In no time, Digga and I acquired tickets for their Sheffield City Hall gig and on the day we set off with his brother-in-law, Chris and Wendy in tow. Following a few obligatory beers in the pub beforehand and a chance meeting with old band-member Terry Sutton in the City Hall bar, we set off upon another of Weller's Council meetings, a more than decent outing but - despite a positive soulful vibe and a scattering of Council classics - an air of tired apathy omitted from Weller and co. His post-Jam venture would soon be winding down.

We managed to meet the band afterwards... which was a real treat. There he was Paul Weller stood looking as cool as ever. I had bought a whole plethora of Council merchandise, programme and posters and whilst having it all signed we made the most of making conversation with Mick, Steve, DC Lee and of course the man himself, Paul Weller. As me and Digga chatted away, competing for attention with Paul, we were soon joined by Terry Sutton. I felt a sense of sadness in the air. Paul's genuine friendliness and interest in our conversation betrayed an inner vibe of boredom with his art, as it did on stage, and as we spoke I kind of somehow felt that. Still my own insignificant small town mojo was certainly not in full working order either so who was I to complain!

Style Council tour programme
signed by Paul Weller backstage
at the Sheffield City Hall, 1987

I hung around with Digga for a year or two. We were good pals and our avid worship of Paul Weller continued unabated. When Digga was courting we went out as couples and when he weren't he brought a mate (usually Cliff Prenton) along instead. He was/is a great kid; a little volatile it's true, but always up for a laugh. His Mum and Dad were a lovely couple as was his sister, Sharon and I used to have a laugh and a few beers with his older brother too some years before-hand. Sadly their Mum passed away a few years later. She was a kind and thoughtful lady who always had a smile for you and she always made me welcome during all those times when I would call around with my Style Council and James Brown records and guitar... making a racket with her son via our music, amps and loud antics! Mums were made of good stuff back in those days, putting up with us and our noise and musical growing pains.

Over at our end, my Mum was having to divide her time between working at Hilliard's supermarket and chasing me around trying to belt me with a dish cloth for taking the mickey at her verbal dictionary of words that would have shut down 'Countdown' in seconds. That and daringly joining a work do to Cresta's nightclub at which she charmed the protection of the bikers in the place and drank real mucky beer with the right down to earth Rotherham lasses she worked with. At her much-cherished bingo (that she allegedly never hardly went to still) she stated that tough old boot, Bea out of Prisoner Cell Block H wouldn't have stood a chance with half the Gala bingo clan when she did a celebrity event there: my imagination kind of convinces me she might have been right. I have seen some of those hard-core bingo addicts, with their chain-smoking leather faces and six gun side-arms, cheating, cursing and pushing their 1950's gambling afflictions into the 1980's and beyond.

My Mum also still had to put up with a revival of the traditional Beesley fall outs season. From a knackered old cassette player came forth me and our Paul having a Beesley showdown and squaring up to each other in the Monkwood pub garden like proper pillocks. We were gonna have a real fight over on the top field (at 4 o'clock I must add for a genuine authenticity... but it was true!!!). I mean how daft is that? What plonkas we were! Falling out over a stupid old broken cassette player and wanting to belt each other over it. It could only have been the Beesleys! I suppose we were holding up a long-standing tradition of the family that went back decades right back to my granddad's Queensbury rules thumping sessions with any brother, Uncle or passing drunk who would accommodate him. It probably went back even further, truth be told, right back to our Irish ancestors. Never mind the infamous 'Michael Fish' hurricane of 1987 when the whole country came to a stand-still amidst a hurricane of Hollywood proportions, we could still kick up our own spritely storm ourselves back in the 80's... too much pride and Beesley stubborn hormones to keep in check for much peace and quiet to be the safe and constant medium for too long.

We never did manage to hold our great showdown, even though tickets were starting to sell quite favourably. Instead we ended up keeping out of each other's way for a while and as is also our tradition all was forgiven and the world was to blame instead when we next both bumped into each other at a family birthday bash or mid-campaign amnesty. That's often the Beesley way!

The 3-piece 1987 line-up of The Way

The year of the famous 1987 storm - when trees uprooted, impaled and shattered people's homes, cars and even lives - also saw my very last attempt to be a musician when I was invited to re-join my old band The Way. Since I left the band, Terry had kept in touch with me and I always tried my best to remain honest and impartial when hearing his new songs something I think Terry respected throughout that time.

Me and Terry met up in the pub and discussed ideas for songs etc. and then we went over to his gaff and played through some songs of his and mine. No more Billy Lonesome sessions with a guitar and a mike for company... I was back in a band. I was over the moon, ecstatic and felt a huge soar of confidence reappear out of the blue. 'Have You Ever Had it Blue' proclaimed my mates, The Style Council? Well yeah, sure I have, but not any longer!

Rehearsals with the rest of The Way were sorted up in Terry's attic and I attended a fortnight's practices. The new bass player was John White (later to be Stan White of Groove Armada and Magazine fame) and I have to admit that it did seem strange it not being my old pal, John Harrison there on bass. We went through Terry's new songs 'Stand Up and Fight', 'Underneath the Arches' and others which all went fairly ok, me adding my trademark rhythm guitar style to the songs... often improvising as we played, trying to find my way around the song structures: but something just didn't quite feel right. Maybe it was me... the odd one out in an updated version of the very band I had formed? I dunno... but something didn't quite fit. At the end of the fortnight, I was informed that I was no longer required to be in the band and that was that! Some things just are not meant to be, I suppose. Yet it was one huge final whack in the face for me; cruelly reminding me of the excitement of playing in a band again for one last brief and tormenting time and then slashing it aggressively short for eternity! I yet again had to retreat to lick my wounds, feeling hurt, betrayed and unimportant. Maybe it was payback time for that Mexborough gig two years ago... but I somehow doubt it. To be honest I would rather not know the reason for my un-required place within a band I so much wished to be a real and crucial part of again.

Some of my (never to be heard) songs I had been writing whilst without fellow musicians to play with, were fierce rants against the increasingly prevalent onset of mass USA saturation. I guess I was soooo bored with the corrupt USA and its stifling capitalism. As the creeping signs of the Americanisation of our town and surroundings arrived with a frontier town MacDonald's and an American-themed diner (complete with wagons to eat in) across from Woolies, people soon began to talk in American slang, the influence of watching far too many Hollywood films and episodes of 'Taxi'. Soon the total immersion of American culture would have a permanent influence and place within our precious little England! My main Americanisation (aside from my love of Soul music) was being obsessed with the actor Robert De Niro. It had been The Way drummer, Ian who had really introduced me to the actor's films. That and a late night showing of The Deer hunter back in Christmas 1984. It didn't take long before I was hunting down all of his films from 'The Last Tycoon', 'Bang the Drum Slowly' to the immortal 'Taxi Driver'. Travis Bickle (De Niro's 'Taxi driver' character whom I briefly copied the hair style of) was pinned up as a poster on my bedroom wall and it even got to the point of me standing at a bar and saying "You lookin' at me?" when some gullible stranger peered my way. Luckily, I never got punched for it and most lads would usually join in and answer "Well you're the only one around here... so?"

Around this time, I was introduced to a real live gum-chewing American via Wendy's sister Angela's soldier boyfriend, Duane. They came visiting from Germany where they were based to see us all. I couldn't resist the temptation of tormenting Duane and enticing him to say things like "Would you like a cookie?" in his best Ohio mid-West accent. We had some laughter-filled nights trawling the local pubs of our home turf and the following year (1988) we decided to go and visit them over in Heidelberg, Germany- this finally being my first time out of the country and visiting foreign shores!

We embarked upon a 24 hour train and ferry journey to get there and I travelled, for the first time, on the London Underground. I was mesmerised by Kings Cross and couldn't help singing 'Down in the Tube Station at Midnight' by The Jam in my head and keeping an eye out for that fella mentioned in the song: maybe I could help him get away from those right-wing thugs who had been giving him a right old pasting for every play of the song since 1978?

Passing through Kings Cross, the scene of an horrific fire tragedy the year before which killed 31 people, we took a train to Dover, again passing by places of cultural note to myself. Travelling through Brixton I peered through the window, my mind visualising The Clash circa early 1977 on those very same stomping grounds and kick-starting my volatile imagination into gear. Sat in the train cubicle that day, I was almost back there and in the distance I could hear the voice of Joe Strummer screaming "Loooondooon's Burning' to a frenzied 100 club punk crowd!!!

Boarding a Hovercraft type ferry we passed the coastline of Dunkirk. My over-active imagination once more kicked back in, helped, I am sure, with the onset of the duty-free Stella-fuelled euphoria: this time evoking images of the great WW2 Dunkirk evacuation. I squinted and could almost see the rotten Stukas zooming in and bombing the thousands of British and French soldiers on the beach, explosions of sand everywhere while the brave little boats came

in regardless and rescued our soldiers who were giving it the V sign and a
barrage of choice words directed at the despicable Nazis. The sound of
machinegun fire in the distance spelled the ever-approaching German army
getting closer. "Hurry up lads, get off the beach and get off home to fight
another day," I was shouting over at them... a shell burst right next to me as I
went flying through the air landing on a small fishing boat... and then I woke
up to a voice beside me enquiring "Would you like any more refreshments,
Sir?" which must have meant "Have another Stella lad!"

The blazing sun transported Dunkirk all the way back to 1940 and we
arrived at the Belgium Port of Ostend, opting for a few time-wasting drinks in
a local bar with no signs of Belgium chocolate sellers anywhere. In the early
hours whilst passing through Germany, I saw a speeding man running at the
side of the train and nearing our destination we saw train fare-dodging Turks
get on board who sat staring at us (Had they never seen a Mod before?) who
then disappeared when the German Polizei with their huge guns and Gestapo-
like hats got on with their German Shepperd Dog accomplices to check
everyone's I.D. Visions of WW2 'Great Escape' P.O.W's rushed into my psyche.
As they reached us (and I prepared myself for a spell in Colditz) they merely
glanced at our passports. The two mysterious Turks were nowhere to be seen,
though, and escaped the clutches of Hans Gruber and Fritz Wanger!!!

During that fortnight of Germanic holiday celebrations of picturesque
litter-free Heidelberg, we took in as much sights, fun, culture and booze as
possible. We shouted 'Howdee' to US army sentries, met our host's German,
Irish and American friends, played drunken games of darts without anyone
receiving a single dart attached to their anatomy, sampled the delights of the
famous German Beer Festival (where Bavarian shorts-wearing Fritz's with
silver moustaches and stubby legs walked around with Steins in hand singing
"Frankfurters are Vunderbar") and we went ventured into the hills to the
ancient Roman Coliseum which was still remarkably intact with Gladiator era
Lion cages. To the fanfare of the theme tune to Spartacus, I could see the
images of Kirk Douglas look-a-like Gladiators tussling like mad with Clarence
the cross-eyed Lion who had paws the size of their shields... all to the delights
of Roman Intellectuals and politicians who, with baskets full of juicy red grapes
at their disposal and villainous bitches at their side, dribbled with excitement at
the blood fest. 'Wake up, Tony.... Slap slap slap'!

Beside the River Rhine and Black Forest – Germany 1988

My 'Billy Liar' styled fantasy-inspired mind also struggled to comprehend that those smiling and accommodating Germans we met were the descendants of a race who had welcomed in Adolf Hitler and his treacherous Third Reich only a few decades before? Those Jew-hating fascists and jack-boot wearing monsters who had sent its armies sweeping into just about every country in Europe in an attempt to conquer the world with their military might and Aryan supremacy? Those Airfix baddies I had shot, flame-throwered and tortured during my childhood on a daily basis? As I looked into the eyes of the smiling Germanic lady behind the counter in the bakers and the sexy waitresses' as they brought us our drinks over, I quickly reaffirmed to myself that people are alike all over. Those Seig Heiling crowds could just as easily have been in any other country, given the right circumstances, even our very own.

In the town we frequented bar after bar, meeting US Generals (possibly related to Generals Patton, MacArthur and Custer) and went on excursions to Manheim (where me and Angela held a long and thirst-quenching celebratory debate on the merits and relevance of The Jam) and Strasbourg in France where I stood in the exact same spot I had seen Hitler stood in an episode of the World at War on the telly in the 70's. This was followed by the famous Black Forest which played host to the most eye-catching and awe-inspiring scenery I had ever seen in my life so far and a welcome antidote to good old smoky, grim and not quite so picturesque Rawmarsh back home.

Home seemed a million miles away to be honest. All routine, cash-flow struggles and indecision was left back there as I revelled in the surroundings of beauty, relaxed attitudes and scenic landscapes. My European Mod dreams of clean living under (less) difficult circumstances awoke right before my eyes. All northern grime, class struggle and 1980's bad taste were dissipated and cleared out of the soul within this clean-aired paradise. I took note of the cool dress sense of clued-in European stylists; how they wore their clothes and hair, integrating it all within my own style. Passing by German hardcore punk rockers, I felt no affiliation at all with their dressed down proto-crusty grime. One night we got refused entry to a local nightclub when Angela (whom I soon came to think of as like a real sister) indulged in a hilarious drunken rant at the doormen calling them 'Nazi bastards!' Whoops, let's make our departure!

Feeding my war obsessions we visited the Heidelberg War Memorial which had all the same names of those lost in the two World Wars. The assumptions that the Nazis were all dead and buried was put slightly in check when we said our goodbyes in the Railway station on our way home and came across a reminder of Germany's shameful past. Whilst stood around saying our goodbyes to Angela and Duane we were interrupted by the voice of a man straight out of an old War Film. 'Ver are you going, Mein friends.' This German man of around 65 stated to us in his best Nazi party voice of cold steel discipline that only those of us with blond hair and fair complexion were of any use. In perfect Third Reich spiel he announced that we would have been sent to a concentration camp back in the war and still would be if he had his own evil way. He ranted on, proclaiming to have been in the SS during the great conflict with Bolshevism and the Allies and had survived the Post-War Allied War Criminal purge. He was clearly drunk and down and out, but looking into those mad eyes that early morning, I was convinced that he truly meant what he was saying and more scarier... actually still believed in it all! Umm... we had not truly been completely spared of the Nazi past of Germany after all. We gave our final hugs to our hosts and got on the train which as it pulled out; I saw the figure of Grupenfuhrer Helmut Muller waving his angry iron fist at me. "Auf Weidersein Dumkopf," I lip-synched!

Away from the Numbers - Tony Beesley

Back home I continued my zest for German-sized Stein double pints of Lager on Wednesday's new Pop Quiz and cheap Stein night up at the Monkwood pub. John would join us for a drink or three and we had some great mid-week nights there during the height of the local pub days: times when blokes would religiously spend their evenings in the same seats with the same friends and sup the same brands of beer year in year out. We always had a shot at the quiz, but very rarely (even when cheating and glancing at other people's answers on the way to the bar) actually won it. There was always a small gathering of know all Henrys' stood over at the bar who had an encyclopaedic knowledge of everything and they would win just about every time. One day, however, no comprehensive 'University Challenge-Bamber Gasbag' could have beaten me to the DJ who caught my attention by saying "OK, for a five pound beer token, who can name the artist and song for this next one... the first one here with the correct answer wins." The first three guitar notes of 'All or Nothing' by the Small Faces came on and I jumped over every stool like an Olympic athlete on extra-strength amphetamines to get there first... earning my fully-deserved free beer token. If I had been beaten by the Henry's that time I would have never shown my face in the place again for the shame of it! As I sat smug in my well-deserved win, I cast my mind back to Scarborough, 1985 and our onstage rendition of that very song to that enthusiastic Mod crowd.

1988 saw Paul Weller's Style Council release their follow up to the critically-maimed 'Cost of Loving' LP of the previous year. 'Confessions of a Pop Group' was an under-rated and brave song writing epic, one part quality Weller-penned Pop songs for the 80's and one-part classical pop concerto. Weller and Mod was still an influence on me during 1988 as I still retained a distinct continuation of the Mod look: the occasional Polka Dot shirt and Ben Sherman joined forces with the staple Polo shirt, Harrington's and Levis in a post-stylist kind of way. I was still heavily influenced by Weller's ultra-cool style and attitude to match.

Just like any other self-respecting 80's Mod, whilst keeping an eye on what to wear and listen to and buying records on vinyl plunder trips to record fairs and shops such as Sheffield's Amazing Records (with its huge a-z of 60's Soul), Kenny's on the Wicker and Spin City - where Northern Soul expert and connoisseur, Andy would entice me with rare and obscure vinyl nuggets to add to my collection, I also had to find some income to fund my life-style. Clearly the chance of being a musician - which was poorly paid anyway - was no longer a viable option.

Like my pal, John - who when he wasn't walking straight over resting black Labradors in dark pub entrances or re-emerging blind-drunk was trying his hand at working for a living and usually failing miserably or collapsing with heat exhaustion or lack of liquid refreshment - I too was out of work. So I decided to do something of my own and, like a proper old Del Boy, started my own Independent Trading market stall on the old Rawmarsh Market, back when it was still a relatively busy going concern. Myself with the help of 'her indoors' set it all up and we sold anything that wasn't nailed down, with little exception. Unwanted Rod Stewart records, books, toys, comics, music papers and heaps of my old Mod clobber got itself snatched up by the young, the old, the decrepit and dudiest of our local clientele and I often wondered what some of them would have looked like in a pin-striped button down shirt and Sta-Prest trousers topped off with a Paisley Cravat! I mean some of those people had no teeth and what hairstyle they had had gone out of date with the advent of rock n' roll! Bless 'em they were some of my best customers... the Liz Dawsons, Mrs Dreadful, Jumbalow Bill, Bob Hope man and old Mother Broken Cupboard. 'Half price', Get 'em while you can ladies and gentlemen' and 'Just because it's you luv, I will do this set of brass muskets off me Mum's room wall (while she's at the bingo) for a fiver.' On one occasion, when the rent man appeared, I ran off and hid in the toilets until he had gone, leaving a crowd of false teeth-chattering, bow-legged bargain hunters fleecing through my stock like a gang of locusts.. John would occasionally remark "And tha calls me a conman, Tony!"

Con men or not me and John couldn't con, cajole, chase or convince our old ageing (though not yet retired) serial killer cat Tommy to part with his captured hostage of a mouse he brought into our house one day. He took it under our table and after crunching away on the victim's bones and swallowing every morsel; he bit off the tail and left it for us as a parting gesture! Get it cleared up, John mate.

As you may now know, Tommy was no simple old domestic friendly cat. He was a law unto himself, like cats mostly are, but he was meaner than most, if not all. During his years as a feline outlaw, he came home scalped like he had rode through Apache territory, he puked up an Alien tape worm right in front of us while we were watching the telly and eating our tea... he presented us with over-sized bruised paws the size of a boxer's fist and set his (already) broken tail alight in our coal fire while asleep. Like all cats, he was a natural born thief too and he stole pork pies on a plate on the settee right under John's nose. Tommy's rib felt like it was hanging out, his ears were torn, his teeth were loose and his eyes often red and looking like they were the wrong way round in his eye socket. But each and every time, Tommy got back on his paws and recovered and meowed to be let back out into his feline world of adventure, brawls, thievery and lawlessness. He was a legend, our Tommy... and still is in some towns south of Dodge City!

We also still had our dog, Sheena. She used to follow us all over the show, never taking a blind bit of notice at my commands of "Jet Black." When me and John took her for a walk to the no longer in use old Stubbin pit; we stood around admiring the view spotting a army troop carrier with armed soldiers diving out. "Hey look, Tony, it looks like there's gonna be a fight," John proclaimed in true Stan Laurel homage voice. The soldiers spread out. It was becoming quite clear that they were partaking in some kind of a Military manoeuvre. "This could be interesting," I thought as we stood watching- waiting for some action to commence. I held Sheena in check. I didn't want her getting us shot. Then I glanced over at the long grass a few feet away from us and saw something moving. As I nudged John to look, I saw the muzzle of a gun sticking out of the grass. Then we both looked around and spotted hidden figures all over the place, all carefully concealed in the grass and bushes. "Hey up John, it looks like we are gonna be in the way, mate.... look down there, it's a soldier. There's soldiers all over the place." We were right in the middle of their manoeuvres and like Laurel and Hardy and a scene from their 'Great Gun's' film we were making proper fools of ourselves. In fact we were nearly giving the game away as the concealed soldiers began noticing us pointing at them and started waving at us to get out of the way. "Look, Tony, the place is full of soldiers," John suddenly noticed. "Yeah and we are gonna get our sens' shot for giving their positions away in a minute if we don't bugger off," I answered. And so we departed laughing, signalling the end of the 'Operation

Stubbin Pit' a location just south of my childhood Coral War adventure.

Around about that time Sheena sadly went missing. She went out one day and we never saw her again. It was sad losing Sheena. Especially since we had no idea where she had gone or what had happened to her. There were rumours of dogs being nabbed for dog fighting which worried us and one day, months afterwards, we were told by a neighbour that she had seen what appeared to be the double of Sheena lying dead across from the Star pub... in the snow. When we eventually got there the dog had been removed so we never knew if it was her or not. We had had Sheena since 1977 when my Dad was still alive. Over ten years she was our pet. She was as soft a dog you could ever meet and wouldn't harm a living thing; a temperament belying her craftiness, anarchic-house-wrecking, cake-stealing, Hay Fever tablet-chewing, kipper fetish true nature of old. Her loss did prey on our minds for quite some time!

One escapade with a dog was a different story, indeed. On the way up to see our Glen, one evening, a Doberman Pincher leapt straight out of its garden and ambushed me. I had been nervous of the bloody thing for some time, now, as it always got itself into a bit of a foaming at the mouth frenzy every time I passed its garden. I was counting the days down for when it would make its tactical move and attack me... the slobbering get! Well, this lovely summer's evening, me minding my own business, it finally made its move. I was trying to hide behind a car as it manoeuvred from side to side making sure I couldn't make a run for it. My neck was pulsating at the prospect of being ripped to bits by this Rawmarsh Cujo! Also, worried that my nice and pristine 3-button blazer would get a good seeing to as well, I was psyching myself up for making a run for it. Just as I put a few steps forward and the beast put a few paws sideways to try and block me, the owner came running out of the house and called it back in, to the clichéd words of "He won't hurt you, he's a big softie"!!! "Yeah he looks a lovely natured lad doesn't he, with his snarling teeth and Omen look in his eye... have to agree on that one, pal!" When I got to our Glen's, heart beat just about slowing down, our Paul was there and on telling him about the Hound of the Baskervilles extra, he bravely declared "Gee 'oer, I would have gid it a right good boot up the backside, it wouldn't have scared me." A few weeks later, he had his chance to show his dog wrestling skills when the very same hound ambushed and chased him all the way up the road. Our

Paul has never run so fast in his life, his legs resembling a cartoon, dust-kicking Flintstone being chased by a dinosaur.

He had his fair share of mishaps, our Paul. He came off his moped, one year, and slid half a mile down the icy road past gangs of kids laughing at him and his rendition of 'De-biking on Ice'. When his said moped got nicked one day a few years later, he was sat in the lounge of the club having a pint when some kids went past on it being chased by the cops. "Look, Paul, isn't that yer bike?" one of his mates pointed out of the window to which another pal piped up..."No, it can't be, it's doing more than 5 mile an hour."

The 1980's was the decade of regular tragic disasters and they seemed like an everyday occurrence. The Herald of Free Enterprise, The Bradford Fire tragedy, the Hillsborough tragedy, Hungerford Massacre, Kings Cross underground fire, Piper Alpha oil rig fire and a despicable terrorist-bomb explosion on a plane over Lockerbie in Scotland. Apparently the plane was actually running late and if it had been on time then it would almost surely have exploded mid-air right over us here in Rotherham with a certain John Lydon on board as he had booked a ticket for the very same plane journey! The 1980's could fall well short of a settled and safe world regularly. When two unfortunate out-of uniform British soldiers were horrifically surrounded and summarily executed by an angry Irish mob live on TV, it just went to show how little the human race had improved and progressed in the 20th century.

Not so far from us a serial murderer, the evil Antony Arkwright, slaughtered three people including his grandfather on a two-day killing spree in August. He was convicted of all three murders and sentenced to life imprisonment the following year and also suspected of a fourth murder committed around the same time. It was an occurrence that shook the region dramatically. Those things (in those days) only ever seemed to happen much further afield, now it was on our very own door-step. The day Arkwright was sentenced, I happened to be passing by the court as he was led out declaring 'I'm not a killer, I'm a poet' to an understandably angry crowd. I shudder when I think of seeing that (and the other tragic incidents) of that time. The Hillsborough disaster was close to home as I had mates who were there, luckily escaping what happened to 96 poor souls who tragically died and the 766 who were injured, let alone those who were left permanently traumatized on that tragic day; all awaiting some sort of explanation as to why the tragedy had occurred. It all made me realise that my small and crazy journey through life was largely insignificant, yet also spurring me on to try and create something worthwhile in my life.

Laser Records shop ad and our cats Tom and Jerry

What that entailed, I simply had no real idea of? I had exhausted almost all of my options. My crusade to avoid the perils of life's mundanity and what was expected of me led me straight up the garden path... and guess who is on the way down the bloody path? My old band mate, Terry Sutton waving another demo tape of newly recorded compositions for me to listen to and give my opinion of, myself being the balanced critic of his songs regardless of being ousted the year before. OK, get the kettle on then and let's have a listen.

Also far less important in the grand scheme of things, my childhood much-cherished Victor comic tragically lost its roots and went all football-saturated. Don't get me wrong footie was great in comics. I loved the Roy of the Rovers and Tiger comics and Shoot was ok, but Victor had been a war-themed institution ever since its 1962 inception so this was sacrilege as far as I was concerned; and what would Captain Cadman make of it if he ever came out of hiding. Ruining my fave much-trusted kid's comic! That was inexcusable, but I suppose it was a sign of the times. The 80's were often ruthless like that, you know!

Away from the Numbers - Tony Beesley

Like some constantly on the go drug dealer, I was now selling records in Record Collector magazine and onto dealers at record fairs at the Leadmill, Polytechnic and other venues. It became a bit of a lucrative business side-line, really: duckin' and diving around flogging records and stuff- making cash; Kenny's Records, Hitsville, Amazing Records, Rare 'n Racy no shop was spared, and if I wasn't flogging 'em records, I was bloody buying 'em to fix my own addiction; accumulating yet more legions of sixties Soul 45s on labels such as Wand, Hickory and Sue, sometimes from the guy on Rotherham market who specialised in Northern Soul. These were joined by 70's Soul and Funk and even a box of underground 70's Disco... a guilty pleasure you may well assume?

I had always sold things; it's in my nature. There's a little bit of a Del Boy in all of us Beesleys, not least in our Paul too. Right from being a kid, I would sell toys, books and anything knocking around. My Mum and Dad would laugh at my front room sales of toy soldiers, comics and anyone's unwanted gifts all for sale out of a suitcase on Sunday afternoons. "What yer selling now, Tony... that's mine and it's still of some use too," they would protest, Mum chasing me out of the house and lobbing a dish cloth straight at me, always missing and hitting either the dog or cat (Tommy would throw it back if you threw it at him, I would swear). Nowadays it was bootleg tapes, records and back issues of the NME that were available to pre-order on Tony's bargain, cut-priced lists! Del Trotter would be well proud.

I had to make some cash somehow anyway so when I had flogged every record I had been inclined to sell and all other available booty within my immediate surroundings had almost all dried up, me and Ian (the Deakin) went on our own Jarrow march for proper man's work after hearing about some jobs at an Attercliffe brewery. Somehow, instead of pleading for a position within the brewery, we found some far more comfortable positions supping pints of beer in a nearby pub with our last few quid, aiming to continue our work-attaining venture at some later date. Product knowledge tha knows!

Soon the Beesley enterprise would be back in style folks and no matter what was around the corner in the Thatcher-wrecked 80's my punk-instigated sense of free-spirited individualism would ultimately provide. Now what about flogging old memorabilia? Years before eBay and the like, I was selling old artefacts from the accumulation of years of dipping into one or the other obsessive collections. Airfix sets, mass regiments of Waterloo-defeated

Away from the Numbers - Tony Beesley

Napoleonic regiments in miniature, collectable comics, tea cards, old toys, stamps, old Dr Who front cover Radio Times, posters, fanzines, more music papers... you name it I sold it! Back in business then!

Around the same time, I also started to fancy writing for a music magazine and began sending my gig and record reviews out to the music papers such as Spiral Scratch (again) and Record Mirror etc. It was yet another of my dreams but unfortunately none of my reviews impressed enough - or rose above the budding writer's swamp - to achieve even a reply. But I wasn't going to lose heart and give in: some other time maybe?

Even the legendary Joe Strummer of The Clash offered to give me a helping hand in entering the starting laps of music journalism - punk style. Following a gig in Brodsmoor, Doncaster where my old band The Way supported Strummer, was a date at Sheffield Leadmill. After a superb gig of Clash classics and Strummer anthems, my old band pal, Terry Sutton of The Way led me down to the backstage area to meet up with Joe Strummer, have some photos taken and then take off to the after-show party. Film director, Alex Cox was sat with us, though I was far too mesmerised with being in the company of my punk hero to ask about anything celluloid-wise. I was only watching Alex introducing his Moviedrome film season the Sunday before, but that all went out of the window now. I was edging in on Strummer for a real good chat and ask a whole list of Clash-related questions and the like!

After a few rounds in the Hotel bar we all ventured up to the room upstairs for more booze and a few smokes. The room and adjoining one were packed with band, road crew and mates and the beer flowed as fluently as the conversations that sped by like the sound of the west-way itself! For a good few hours, me and Joe sat chatting like two old war comrades who had just met up again for some old veteran's reunion, me elaborating non-stop of my love of The Clash. It was then that Joe was impressed enough by my naïve enthusiasm to make something of myself out of the rat race, and an agenda that involved writing about my passion for music, that he offered to put me up and introduce me to some of his contacts. "You really should come down to London, Tony," Joe enthused - eyes beginning to mist over from the enclosed vacuum of heavy duty smokes - "You should come down and I will help you get sorted, its where you need to be." I never dared take up Joe on that kind offer. I was tempted though, but only through the haze of a Holstein Pils and a

Mellor reefer's false courage as it engulfed me. In the cold light reality of the following grey day, it all seemed surreal and out of my existing world.

The night previously I had been sat like best buddies with the lead singer of The Clash and now I was popping out to the shop for a pack of fags for our lass and a bottle of sparkling cola to quench my hung-over desperately seeking gentle karma thirst! "Anyway," I reasoned, "I would have probably only ended up down and out in the streets of London paved with mould." Back to reality... but maybe one day, I may just go ahead and do something like that?

The Punk and the alternative scene of the 80's was spread far and wide across countless spin-off cults, styles and scenes. From Goth to Pyschobilly, hardcore to indie... the journey from year zero had continued. Sheffield was now a haven of alternative shops and 80's post-punk autonomy and yes it all caught my curious attention, though almost all of the punk-era shops I used to once frequent were long-gone. Even though I had left behind the fashion style of all that a long time ago, assimilating my Mod stylist approach along the way, I had always kept a sense of punk's do it yourself spirit firmly at hand. It's what got me through the decade and beyond. It's a constantly evolving part of me.

Even so, it was now time to start thinking of the future. What did I really require from my life? I reckon I had crammed well enough into the decade so far and experienced plenty, but I was ready for change and taking a few well-placed steps forward. I had to leave my briefly tasted dreams behind and move on. Neither could I continue to take the piss out of the world and its occupants indefinitely... surely not? One day a great big warden of the civilised and respectable scheme of things would come along with my name, number, rank and a long list of misdemeanours and give me one huge epic clip around the lug 'ole, demanding my imminent contribution to the world of adults, seriousness and responsibility– forcing me to knuckle down to be a useful, hard-working, boring and soul-less drone with all notions of youthful nourishment drained forever! I suppose I could take all of this if I really seriously had to: my apprenticeship of defiance and shooting at the stars of life's possibilities was rapidly losing ammunition... but please don't offer me a soddin' mortgage. Not just yet, anyway!

As 1988 drew to a close, with our traditional Christmas piss ups, pub crawls around every drinking hole in town, along with the legendary annual Christmas Tiffany's bash, there was a sense of 'This is all going to end soon'. As we knocked back the drinks, laughed ourselves into 1980's hedonistic oblivion surrounded by the crowds of mullet-wearing blokes and dodgy Carol Decker gingers and Kylie wannabee girls of 1988... I was looking around, wondering what the next stage was set to be. As John threw his cash over the bar amidst screams of lasses pissing themselves laughing with alcohol-induced euphoria and dodgy jokes told by dodgier fellas in far too dodgy silk shirts all around the packed boozer, an inner voice in my head was bellowing to me "Tony... it looks like it's about bloody time you started to grow up son!"

Chapter nine

Heaven knows
I'm responsible now!

"DEAR TONY - what happened to that idealistic young punk kid that wanted to change the world... have you given in and somehow conformed... finally?"

It had been a long and eventful decade really: a rapidly-changing and maybe, in some ways, more life-defining and momentous one than the 1970's? I certainly felt profoundly different as the decade came to a close; no longer the young teenage punk rebel with a suitcase of hang-ups and angry questions to throw at the adult world. The spikey-haired teacher-defying kid with a cause of many colours! The kid who had turned up with green food colouring in his hair for his final school exam almost at the start of the decade was still in there, but a hell of a lot of outer layers had been painted onto the inner cream of the cake since 1980. The present seemed light years ahead from those days!

We had struggled with fragile home-taping back in 1980 which we played on small top-loading cassette players, these now being replaced with huge Ghetto blasters. Down the road a local music studio had unleashed the abysmal Jive Bunny onto the world and somewhere along the line, our local boozer's jukebox had been modernised with a CD playing one: the death of the 45 rpm record in the pub... truly shocking eh... be banning smoking in pubs next!

All around us changes occurred, some of importance others not. In a TV world cliff-hanger, Bruce Willis had managed to shag Cybil Shepherd in 'Moonlighting', Baywatch had replaced the A Team on Saturday evenings and Werewolves in London had been replaced by rock music vampires with that nasty lad out of 'Stand By Me', Keifer Sutherland leading The Lost Boys. The Berlin Wall was coming down and world politics were rapidly adapting, whilst I started to notice a new word called the internet cropping up in the NME of all places. As for the fashions of 1989... go ask Madonna or the Stone Roses!

The snotty young punk version of me would not have recognised the end of decade version, thanks to the Stone Roses and something called Baggy. By late 89, I was wearing huge wide-flared jeans for the first time since the summer of 1977, along with hooded tops decorated with rainbows and Egyptian shapes upon them. The youthful spikes and Mod triggers were long gone and had been replaced by a short back and sides swiftly growing into a poor-imitation of Shaun Ryder's curtains. A fascination with Reebok trainers had replaced my love of Clark's Desert boots and Weller styled bowling shoes and the sounds on my record deck were spinning more and more rapidly to the new House sounds of Chicago and Detroit proto-type techno. Phuture, Acid Trax, the Funky Worm and Rhythm is Rhythm's 'Strings of Life' had temporarily replaced my long-time love of Soul and gritty rhythm and blues. Friday and Saturday night pints were knocked back to the populist House sounds of 'Ride on Time' by Black Box, Bomb the Bass and Theme from S-Express. Oblivious to my musical past, I surrendered to a trance-like state at various Rave nights in and around Sheffield and Rotherham. I could be found amidst an explosion of artificial smoke, strobe lighting and spaced out Ecstasy pals at Rotherham's Shipmates club's House nights- totally immersed in the sounds of a new pulsating dance beat. My whole world had spiralled into a parallel universe. Will the real Tony Beesley please stand up?

Away from the Numbers - Tony Beesley

The year had started off well, but all thoughts of me performing in a band were now out of the equation. I even sold my last remaining guitar, a semi-acoustic pride of joy, to the next door neighbour, Graham, who had now managed to learn to play the guitar and had finally got his Bob Dylan LP's back off me. My amplifier, the good old H+H 100 Watt Combi that had been my dependable gig buddy for all of my band performances, was long gone as were my mics, guitar leads, guitar stand, spare sets of Rotosound strings and plectrums. I threw away my fuzzbox as I certainly wasn't gonna use it anymore! There was no trace left at all of my musician days: the hopes and dreams of being a part of a band were dead and buried forever. Me and John would sit re-visiting those days of playing to enthusiastic Mod crowds many a time, all bleary-eyed and nostalgic over a few pints, sounding like two old codgers retracing the lost days of their youth. No, the end of the 80's, for me, was not about playing in a band, and were also becoming less of a time of drinking myself stupid in the boozer. Inside, I felt an inner urge to search for something else in my life: a step forwards onto a new level; yet again. I just wasn't sure what that may have been, though. Soon, I would find out.

I suppose at the start of the year of 1989, I had reached my cultural low in some ways. My tastes in music remained quite open-minded, but image-wise I had lost myself. The Mod stylist look had almost disappeared and would not return for a while. I tormented myself with a short series of boring and drab styles of 80's looks: a neat and boring quiff hairstyle that was as far removed from my punk rock spikey dishevelled self or Weller-styled Mod cut as was possible for me, adjoined with a wardrobe of army surplus shirts and dodgy jean jackets ahhhh!!! It pains me to recall the alternate mirror-image of who I truly was underneath. Before I tasted the buzz of Acid House and entered another fashion bad trip, I took a few steps sideways (maybe backwards) first.

The late 80's gave a twenty-something punk-evangelised lad such as myself a sugar-coated glam take on garage pop with a trio of blonde girl-fronted bands reminding me just a little of how I used to feel as a young under-age gig-going kid. The Darling Buds gave a superb packed out Leadmill a gig or two on red-hot summer nights, whilst the Primitives arrived crashing into the University with their tales of 'Thru the Flowers' and being 'Sick of it all'. Far more bubble gum and destined to wilt just as quickly as the other two one and a half-hit wonders were Transvision Vamp who kick-started their career with a sickly rendition of Holly and the Italians' 1980 punk/pop near miss 'Tell that Girl to Shut Up' and were fronted by an outspoken cut-price Smash Hits version of Debby Harry in Wendy James. For a few months the ghost of Blondie reigned supreme and the pogoing kid of my past was briefly revived until the tides of Acid House swept the blonde ambitions away forever! The punk nostalgia circus was only just around the corner however!

The year probably saw me buy the most vinyl since my peak of Soul record searching of a few years previously, storing my expanding record collection (carefully placed) within our front room wall units: vinyl replacing ornaments and photos of Paul Weller and The Clash framed inside the glass cabinet as opposed to previous past years of Mum's best cracked china and posh glasses. Along with all the latest Indie releases (usually bought mere weeks after release for 10p from Circles Records cheap box) and an amazing album by XTC called 'Oranges and Lemons', I was amassing 12" records on the new Sheffield-founded Warp label. Warp had its own shop on Division Street and also sold all the latest House and early Techno releases from where I bought a handful of compilation albums with the latest sounds from Chicago spread across them. Even my old hero, Paul Weller had digressed into the House scene with the last proper Style Council single 'Promised Land' - a cover of a Joe Smooth single that I already had in my collection. Unfortunately, Weller's new guide to Modernism via the influence of House and Garage music became his undoing as flocks of his, by now, frustrated fans simply stopped buying his records and his record company ditched him, consequently it taking a few years and a scent of wild wood for the modfather's critical return.

Along with House nights at the Leadmill, I was still catching some of the latest Indie styled bands during their early stages there. This was the famous venue that would later win awards for best venue in the country, despite having the lack of insight when turning down Madonna for a pre-fame gig. That spring and summer of 89, the biggest band on my turntable was the Stone Rose debut LP. Released in May, I went crazy on the record, playing it non-stop all through the hot summer evenings, in-between gigging, boozing and going to the coast for some fun. 'Made of Stone', 'Waterfall', 'She Bangs the Drum's' and 'Bye Bye Badman' being churned out continuously during the long hot summer nights. What was it about this record created by a young Manchester gang of tykes, former Perry's and quite possibly around when me

and Andy used to dodge their gangs in and around Moss Side at the turn of
the decade. Perhaps it was the element of their sound that reminded me of one
of my favourite 60's bands, The Byrds? Or maybe it was their charm, their bad
boy image, the floppy fringe of Mani that was similar to the one I had myself a
few years earlier? They wrote and performed well-crafted songs with a distinct
psychedelic sway and when played from start to end, the LP seemed to almost
hypnotise me. I would sit in the front room, can of cheap watered-down lager
in hand and become intoxicated with the grooves of this brand new exciting
contemporary record that spelt out 1989 as authentically as The Clash had
epitomised 1977! And they made really cool B-sides too. It was a great year for
music, as far as I am concerned; one of the best of the 80's and the one
record that managed to effortlessly capture the whole mood of the times for me
was the iconic Stone Roses first long player.

1989 saw Salman Rushdie's Satanic Verses earn him a death threat from Iran. I
had never heard of the fella and thought Salman Rushdie was a fast-food fish
restaurant or something. That year also saw the unlikely pairing up, after so
many years of us all not seeing each other... of myself and my old pals, Andy
Goulty and Pete Roddis. I had grown up with these lads and we had shared so
much together. The last time the three of us had shared any considerable time
all together would have been around Christmas 1979 at the height of our punk
years. Throughout the years since I had drifted apart from them both. Andy
and Pete had taken a contract to dig coal down the pit where my own Dad had
endured for all those years so they lived a totally different life to mine and our
great close friendships were a thing of the past. Almost a whole decade had
passed and by trial and error we all agreed to meet up for a few beers and
(hopefully) the grand epic catch up session of all time!!!

We met round at Andy's ditching our pub-crawl intentions and instead
opting for a booze-fuelled, soak the year's away session indoors until the early
hours of the next morning. It all started off well as the first few cans of
Budweiser's went down a treat and the years and memories just peeled away:
we were laughing at the old days in no time. To a soundtrack of compilation
tapes featuring the Darling Buds, Stone Roses, Wire, Morrissey and my old
The Way demos, the drinks flowed, along with our gradually slurring
conversations. "Does tha remember when tha bought Thin Lizzy's 'Sarah'

single three times cos it had three different pic sleeves," laughed Andy at Pete's expense. "What about thee, when I shoved thee over Beesley's wall on the way to school that day," Pete rallied at Andy. "And hey up... can yer remember Beesley when he cut his own hair and looked like Citizen Smith." "What about when you bought 'Sultans of Swing' and thought it was punk, Roddis... ha ha ha."... "Andy, what about that time Fatso got us all boxing and you and the other lads drunk from his bottle of piss that he said was limeade... ha ha." The years of our youth and childhoods all merged together amidst a cloud of alcoholic slumber: we laughed endlessly never running short of anything to say. I had brought a full bottle of Vodka along too and began to down that NEAT!!! We all were soon inebriated beyond the point of no return!

Andy and Pete regaled me with tales of their recent summer fun-filled season work trips to France and of their times down the pit. It was the mention of the pit and the obvious link of the miners' strike that brought the night onto a more serious topic and we left our laughs behind whilst mistakenly indulging in that sworn enemy of drink and a good time... stinking politics!!!

Now we were all Labour, through and through. How could we not be? We all lived in a pit village; our Dads were either pit men (mine and Pete's) or, like Andy's, a steel worker. We came from proud working class backgrounds so the way we leant politically was no big surprise. The thing is, though, they had been through the strike first-hand and shared the belief that, amongst other reasons, the Militant element of Labour were partly responsible for its failings. Don't ask me why, but at that period of my life, most likely through ill-informed politics courtesy of the NME and maybe a dash of Mr John Harrison's influence, I was a bit politically antagonistic: basically in all honesty, I really knew bugger all, but chose to spout (when given the opportunity) some trendy leftist shit that sounded good to quote! A whole load of bollocks to put it simple; so before you knew it we were on the verge of bloody arguing about stupid politics... courtesy of the Russian Front taste of Vodka... and the appetising and popular Yank lubricant – good old Budweiser!

Well, luckily, we didn't fall out; agreeing to disagree followed by yet more neat Vodka leading the way. By the time we had drunk ourselves beyond any more capable alcoholic intake, we were all incapable of contributing anything worthwhile to add. The road had reached its conversational cul-de-sac, so to speak. We all parted our ways and when I got in I collapsed in a heap of a drunken mess downstairs on the settee, getting called something unrepeatable by Wendy upon discovering me. Wow, it had been one hell of a night. Sadly, that was the last of our reunions. We would all see each other occasionally, giving each other the nod or briefly passing the awkward time of day together, but never were we all together at the same time again. Pete moved away down South and Andy went studying; eventually settling down to be a head teacher at a school in Ilkley. One day, you never know, we may all meet up again and have our intermittent catch up session. One thing's for sure, though. I won't be drinking rotten Vodka again. I haven't touched the stuff once since that night in 1989.

The summer of 89! Morrissey was now firmly solo with no Smiths (or blue packet of salt either). Nights at the Leadmill, record fairs, wheeling and dealing with my market stall, my jeans getting wider with each pair I buy and a new brand of street clothes by someone called Joe Bloggs appears in the shops. My mate Ian Deakin (right) was raving about a band he had been listening to for ages called the Happy Mondays... I had never known such a thing as a happy Monday so far! He had an album called 'Bummed' by them, which made me laugh. I had 'Freaky Dancin'' and 'Tart Tart' and consequently went and bought a new club cross-over hit of theirs called 'Wrote for Luck'.

Following vinyl trawls around the still blooming plethora of Sheffield record shops, I would park my arse down in boozers such as the Surrey drawing on smokes of Benson and Hedges with a pint at hand, Stone Roses 'She Bangs the Drums' on continuous jukebox play and poring over bags of House and Detroit Techno twelve inchers, oblivious to afternoon regulars, betting shop desperadoes and lunch-time suits with their 1980's shares and capitalistic dreams. I was happy in my little world of smiley and shiny plastic; no 'E's nor Aceeeed trips, just my pint and a fag to meet my club hedonism ultimate high!

One night in Rotherham drinking den The Charters, the old drunk-tank of my old pal, Barney Rubble, who I had last seen a few years ago when he got

on the bus dragging a huge dead pheasant along with him and grinning from
pierced ear to ripped lobe... well I was chatting to two very young Mods. I was
on my way to a Rave in Sheffield, enjoying a few pre-Rave pints, but on
spotting their parkas and nicely-trimmed college boy Mod styled hair (not
unlike my own of a few years previously), I just had to introduce and acquaint
myself with these two fledgling Pete Meadons. Mods in Rotherham in 1989,
right during the middle of the third (or maybe fourth?) summer of love! It
must have rehearsed like a Pete Townshend meeting Syd Barrett outside the
UFO club circa 1967, except we were not musical pioneers, just mere Yorkshire
lads from separate generations who shared a love of good old Rhythm and
Blues and Soul.

Surprisingly, the lads were really friendly and amiable, especially when our
conversation stepped into 'playing in a band' territory, these two having formed
their own Mod act and happy to listen to my ill-formed advice. We shared
musical heroes - Townshend, Marriott, Otis Redding, James Brown etc. - and
they invited me to check out their stuff at their practice room. Laughing and
drinking for a whole half hour or so, talking lapel size, trouser bottom and
side vents measurements, we shook hands and I made my way out: they must
have pissed themselves laughing at my Joe Bloggs Cutty Sark flared jeans,
maybe trying to imagine my legs in a pair of two-tone hipsters as they once
had been. "See yer, Lads," I parted... "And don't bugger it all up and split the
band, like someone I know quite well did." And off I went for the number 69
bus and my trip to an intoxicated trance-like 808 state!

The approaching end of the decade saw a swift turn in my outlook not long
after that unexpected Mod meeting (I would soon return to my Mod roots) and
my ever changing moods would be held in check with the news of something
quite unbelievable and truly amazing; something that firmly led me onto that
next unexpected level in life; one that I had recently subconsciously been
searching for. During the late summer of 89, me and Wendy could be seen
strolling around Clifton Park... experiencing a mixed up collection of feelings
and expectations. We were partly in shock, excited, nervous, and anxious and
almost in a dream-like state. How are we going to tell our parents? How are we
going to put it to the drinking gang up at the boozer, informing them that our
boozing days of care-free abandon would soon be finally over and the parties
and raves in jeopardy? How are we going to afford it? One big question over-

rode all of these for me in my confused and anxious head and that was ... how I am going to perform at being a DAD!!!

We both had jobs at least, though mine was not permanent. Finally ditching my Del Boy market stall, I had been taken on at the Sheffield Post Office sorting dept., which was a bit of a hike and late finishes: I used to have to run like a bastard to make the second to the last number 69 bus to Rotherham. In truth it was boring and involved working under old fashioned blokes with rolled up sleeves that looked like Captain Mainwaring off Dad's Army dishing out commands at us as though we were bloody kids at school. I had never been keen on the idea of being treat like crap so my instincts were 'This is not going to last much longer, no matter what.' The late evening shifts of throwing letters into post-coded boxes, whilst chatting up lasses who were into Transvision Vamp were numbered. For the time being, though, we were both employed (Wendy worked at the local Yogurt factory where I too would work the following year) so that held us in a false sense of security while we got used to the idea of having to grow up and try and learn how to become parents in the very near future. A new decade was fast approaching and great changes were in the air. The two of us were very soon going to become three! A clear indication of impending adulthood took place when I found myself banging on the window at gangs of misbehaving kids outside. I had to pinch myself and boot myself on the flared-knee caps... reminding myself that not long ago, I had, myself, been part of the street mayhem and teenage anarchy: 'You boring twat', I concluded!

Rotherham itself was also in transition during the 80's. The old town hall, Court and Assembly Rooms, along with the old Advertiser offices and printing press were replaced by new buildings as Boots shifted from its old classic spot on High Street to newly-built premises. Record shops dwindled (our favourite 'Sound of Music' being replaced by a clothes shop and Circles moving on to Wellgate) as other stores began to close. The old bus station was replaced and a brand new shopping experience called Meadowhall loomed over the horizon. Northern Soul hotspot the Clifton Hall would sadly soon become a car park as the town's map changed beyond recognition- all in the name of apparent progress! Rotherham and its town centre were now set upon a journey ahead of uncertainty as its golden era concluded and for many it would never truly fully recover.

Springheel'd Jack

Around this time, I once again went along to the Charters pub for a few beers hoping yet again to find Barney Rubble and have a good old catch-up. The scene of a few 1982 drinking bouts of mine The Charters was still a haven for the alternative music fan in and around Rotherham so I fully expected to find Barney sozzled in some dark corner regaling stories of his punk days to a new generation of studs and leather devotees. Amongst the clientele of late-period crusty attired punks, heavy rockers, Grebos and fully-fledged Goths I never came across Barney... but I did bump into a certain Dave Spencer.

Dave Spencer was born the exact day as me and we had frequented within almost the same punk circle some years ago. He was a talented musician and songwriter- leader of punk band Cute Pubes at the start of the decade and now fronting a band called Springheel'd Jack, who I had interviewed for my fanzine in 1986 in (you guessed it) The Charters. This day (in 1989) in The Charters we had a good catch up and I started to go and watch Springheel'd Jack play in various pubs around town, most notably their resident sets at Elliot's bar. My mate, Ian Deakin ex of The Way, and whom I was knocking around with quite a bit at the time, was now their drummer coincidentally.

I didn't see Dave for a number of years and we both went our separate ways... but he would come to be an important influence, inspiration and helping hand with my writing in the years to come... and we developed a friendship that transcends time, location and circumstance. We also share a very uncanny like-minded sense of intuition and love of music, quite prominently The Clash. He is a huge mine of talent and a whirlwind of creativity and positivity who I greatly admire.

Meanwhile on the relationship front, to celebrate our good news, Wendy and me decided to get ourselves married at Rotherham register office in October and had a grand old piss up afterwards at our local, the Monkwood pub followed by a proper night do upstairs at the Queen's Hotel on Kilnhurst Road me and my mate's old drinking hole and occasional practice room.

The day went really well within a proper gathering of the clans and we drank, danced and laughed in merriment and celebration. Relatives I had not seen for ages turned up, mates came and bought us drinks, my American buddy, Duane was there talking cookie nonsense, our Paul was in fun-loving mood, whilst my (traditionally teetotal) Mum was sat surrounded by her friends and family and copious glasses of sherry - lapping it all up for the occasion. Mother's face was beaming all night. She loved a bit of attention, my Mum and on getting dragged up for the traditional rendition of her name-sake song 'Come on Eileen' by Dexy's she was secretly over the moon. I loved seeing her happy... she deserved it; times had been hard for her over the years.

Looking around that night, everyone's faces were smiling and genuinely happy; even the usual miserable suspects who usually moaned and grumbled about the price of the ale or the size of the buffet sandwiches were beaming. Our Paul said it was one of the best weddings he had ever been to: official approval indeed! Time seemed to stand still for that one late 1980's October night and everyone was content with their lot. It was one of those proper family get-togethers that we all remember. I think I drunk myself sober!

On this night, for the very first time since 1985 (a whole four years, and a long time to us twenty-something's), the full membership of our old Mod band The Way came back together and spent some long awaited time in the same room. My best mate, John was there for the duration, of course. Wherever there was drinking and merriment, John would be there. Myself and Ian were hanging around with each other quite a bit that year so he was there and who should come along as well, but old Terry. The Way line up complete!!! We all got on well too, any differences cast aside as we enjoyed the present, forgetting the past and having a good old laugh with a constant flow of alcohol.

It was kind of strange, us four all sat there. Terry was still a proper musician and song writer as he always would be. Ian was in and out of performing at the time, but was still one of the best drummers in the area (and beyond). Me and John? Well we had abandoned our musical dreams quite some time ago. We wouldn't have believed it all those years ago, though, when nothing in the whole world was going to stop us on our musical quest. Those two young skinny Mods with angry punk rock attitudes had now been replaced by two beer-loving fools without a care in the world. Yet the trouble was that I had to start bloody caring and get myself a responsible attitude, which was not something that I could attain from reading the NME and sinking pints of beer with my mates. I was 24 years old and it seemed that, finally, it was time to start considering growing up and acting my age: did I really truly, insanely, deeply wish to do so, though... that was the question?

The Way 1989 version... minus instruments

My good old mate John was at the peak of his heavy drinking days. Amazingly, considering the lack of employment available, he kept dropping on jobs from time to time, but would usually bugger them up, one way or another, never the one to cosy up to conformity, just like myself. Either that or his aversion to authority would end up jeopardising his work availability. Throughout each and every attempt at becoming even slightly respectable, we both took the piss out of our failings without any self-imposed censorship to hinder the impact of the jest. When working for one notable name business in their store rooms he simply took his Bank Holiday leave without giving them notice, resulting in his dismissal and typical reactionary character assassination which was met by a retaliation of John setting his local MP on them with a threat of suing the company. Good old John... the punk never gave up a fight!

John never turned down a pint either, no matter who was paying as long as it wasn't himself. He calmed down for a while, getting himself a few steady girlfriends and a fairly steady flow of domestic normality, at least as much as could be expected of the one-time Sid Vicious protégé. He appeared content and happy, his demons cast aside before succumbing to his own personal penultimate ditch. Eventually, through a succession of too much drinking, bad luck, wrong turns, gambling, dodging debt and ill-health, John's life began to spiral increasingly out of control. We remained great friends throughout and our bond was virtually impossible to break, but there were times when I didn't feel like I knew him anymore. Our lives would soon take separate journeys and it would take a long time (and profoundly quite tragic circumstances) before the light at the end of the tunnel could be once more be sighted). It took some years for John to re-emerge out of the wilderness and there were periods I had my doubts that he would return.... But he came through in the end!

That October night was the last time that me, John, Terry and Ian were ever in the same room together. It had been a year for last-minute reunions it seemed. It also signified an end of an era for me. The 1980's were almost at an end and so were the best days of my youth. OK, I wasn't prepared to act like a boring miserable old git and it wasn't time for the pipe and slippers out just yet, but I was now planning on making a real proper go at being a good and responsible Dad!

Strangely it all got me thinking about my own Dad. How must he have felt when hearing the news of being a Dad for the very first time all those years ago? What did he feel? How did it affect him? Going down the pit into the dark abyss of the coal face, did he stop to think about these things? Thinking of all of this also reminded me of when he passed away and it did bring back some painful memories of loss, feelings I had kept hidden for a decade or more. Typically, I chose to carry on, business as usual and stored them all back in the deep dark and untidy cupboard of my mind. It's the future I need to be thinking about now was the reasoning. Anyway, what shall we call our kid on the way?

Any notions of homely financial security were washed away when, after refusing to work through a postal strike... ('I ain't no soddin' scab, so don't bother asking me to work it,' I told the frumpy, stuttering fatso that tried to con me into crossing the picket line)... I was told 'There's no work for you anymore here, lad,' at the Sheffield Post Office I had been working at or the Rotherham one either. Oh well, who said life was a bed of roses or even a sack of love letters sent to the wrong address?

I was excited about the prospect of being a Dad, though, and nothing, not even the loss of my job could taint that nervous excitement. I honestly couldn't wait. We didn't know if it was going to be a boy or a girl, but secretly, in my heart, I wanted a lad. I was hoping for a young mate so that I could drag out the last remaining sets of toy soldiers from the cupboard and play table top battles with him. I was planning on buying him a Scalextric for Christmas and couldn't wait for the day when he would be ready to listen to the 1st Clash LP and watch 'Only Fools and Horses' with me and simply spending time being daft and having a laugh together. To show him how to ride a bike, kick a ball about with him in the park and teach him how to stick up for himself. All of this running around my head and he wasn't even born yet... and besides it could have turned out to be a lass in a pink dress for all I knew at the time!

Towards the end of 1989, I realised that it would soon be time for me to depart the good old dependable homely den of no.10 Warren Avenue. Taking a look around at the four well-lived in walls of my Mum's living room, remnants of 1970's brass still visible on the mantle-piece and the wood panelling still earning its rightful place above it... I cast my twenty-something mind through the back pages so far. Listening carefully, I could hear my long-since departed Dad moaning at my Mum for burning the toast and her kidding him on that the cheap margarine he had spread on it was real best butter. They argued like cat and dog my Mum and dad, but never a truly cruel word was ever said. I could see our Paul winking at me with his cocky cheating confidence, knowing that he had a card up his sleeve for the communal Christmas night card games. Peering down at the carpet, I could see and hear a mini James Hunt whizz around the Scalextric track determined to win, but unfortunately crashing at the last minute and piling straight into our old ginger cat who sat in the middle ready to swipe the cars off the track... and making us all laugh. And laugh we did within those four solid walls... in-between family rows and the bread cake wars, insecurities, poverty and loss... scraping together to pay the milkman and saving up for a few days at the seaside... Mum and Dad, brothers, mates, girlfriends, granddads and grandmas, Uncles, Aunties, nephews, punk rockers, mods and dogs and cats... we all laughed and lived some of the best times of our lives there.

As I made my way to sneak out for a crafty pint with our Paul round at the club on that dark winter night of 1989, I cast away those memories for the time being: soon I would be making new ones with a little family of my own. Turning for the door, I heard a swoosh sound and the traditional flying dishcloth came whizzing straight past me, landing on the kitchen sink. "Tony," Mum gave me a departing laughing gesture... "When this kid of yours comes along, I hope you get one just like you, you crafty conning stubborn bugger!"

The years following saw many changes, and as is always the case... nothing stays the same and so it shouldn't: our Paul even saw his retirement dream come true after counting down the years, days and hours for over a decade and I finally faced my 9-5 job nightmare head on. I rarely saw many of my old pals as time went on: Terry Sutton continued to be a musician and did stay in touch, whilst John never picked up a bass guitar again. Barney also turned up one day in 1994 to see me before disappearing yet again for another decade. As for the Gregory's Girls... I lost touch with most of them too.

Sadly much of the cast of my story slowly faded away, one way or another. Friends moved on and relatives passed away (including my favourite much-loved Aunty Amy). My Mum's coal fire kept a burning bright right through to her sad passing away in 2000 following a brave battle against cancer, which left a hole in my life as huge as when I lost my Dad all those years ago. Tommy the serial killer punk cat made his final journey with a one way ticket to see the vet in 1994. Amazingly he went without a fight or a single lift of his notorious fighting paw, as though he knew his time was up. My father-in-law (and friend), Don sadly left this world in 2010 and my mate, John almost died twice losing a leg in recent times and his life will never be the same again, yet he has found a new far stronger optimism that he so desperately needed. We all changed and our expectations of each other changed along the way, sometimes resulting in some of us having to break free of our past and move ahead for pastures anew, such is life!

Still... back in 1989, a new world of responsibility was now knocking at my door and life's many challenges would be not far behind, maybe even including the dreaded mortgage. As impending fatherhood approached, much of my old insecurities, frustrations and feelings of loss subsided. Throughout the years, as memories fade and the world around us constantly evolves, I have kept a strong hold of my beliefs and my inner determination to question the system of things and the whole rotten corrupt establishment. I still say 'NO' from time to time when the man in charge comes along with his rules and regulations and I still remain a rebel and an outsider. I will never fit into any institutions or gatherings of respectability and authority (at least not without subverting from within) and, though, I may not stand physically manning the barricades of discontent, or wear a tired old uniform of youth's forgotten fashions.... throughout it all, the punk kid within me never truly died!

I never did become a Rock Star, a poet, an artist or a spokesman for a half-filled pub or anything even close. My musical career never reached any further than that life-defining Mod Rally of 1985 in Scarborough and my songs never reached much further. But most important of all I tried and I gave it my very best shot!

I eventually came to realise that, throughout all of those years, the true thing I had been sub-consciously searching for was creative self-expression: through school, punk, Art, Soul, poetry, performing and writing.... that was my elusive yearning for identity and self-worth! Little did I know that it had been right there within me all through the journey; no wonder I had been confused!

The kid on a red chopper bike, the frustrated punk with an attitude, the angry young Mod in a 3-buttoned suit with a guitar pushed into your face says his farewell. Thank you for joining me.... Maybe it's now time for a new generation to be chronicled: kid on an X-Box 360 or lad in a hoodie anyone. OK.... Maybe not!!

The first instalment to the book you have just read is 'Kid on a Red Chopper Bike: a ride through the 1970's'

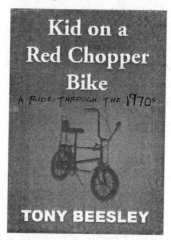

Other books by the same author

Available from all good book shops and at
www.ourgenerationpunkandmod.co.uk

Acknowledgments

Many thanks to

Paul Jesperson for proofing
Dave Spencer – for yet another quality cover
Pete Skidmore and Neil Kitson for The Jam photos
David Mushcroft for kind use of 1977 Paul Weller photo
Mods at Scarborough photos –Steve Peoples and Andy Bull

Punk drawings created at Rawmarsh Comprehensive 1978-1980 by the author

Rotherham Stuff facebook group, Sally Burton (South Yorkshire Times), Neil Anderson and ACM Retro, Rotherham Advertiser (photos and news features), Jonny Parkinson, John Harrison, Ian Deakin, Steve 'Zal' Downing, Carl and Margaret Egleston (Sound of Music photos), Terry Sutton (The Way photos), John Quinn, Nigel Lockwood, Captain Bob Taylor and Shaun Angell (for the miner's strike info and input), Stuart Sutherland (For kind use of Big Country photo), Jamie Evans, Marsha Armitage, Claire Alan, Gail Scothern, Sylvia (for a decade of 80's haircuts and patience with my demands), Lynne Haythorne, Louise Mckinnley, Kevin Mundy, Gary Penkith, Simon Cardie, Kevin Wells, Gary Stables, Nigel Noble, Angela Adams, Debbie Ogden (Sheffield Star), Andy Coles (1980's Rotherham photos), Mark Bothamley, Karen Warburton (For that unexpected inspiration), Jan Deakin (R.I.P) for the fantastic 1985 'The Way' photo session

Marples punk photos courtesy of Kristan James Melik), Joe Strummer at Top Rank photo thanks to Nick Hawksworth

My two lads, Dean and Sean

But most of all – thanks to my fiancée Vanessa for the support and patience throughout all the months of doubt